Hyper-Productive Knowledge Work Performance

The TameFlow Approach and Its Application to Scrum and Kanban

Steve Tendon
Wolfram Müller

J.ROSS PUBLISHING

Copyright © 2015 Steve Tendon and Wolfram Müller

ISBN-13: 978-1-60427-106-5

Printed and bound in the U.S.A. Printed on acid-free paper.

10 9 8 7 6 5 4 3 2 1

Library of Congress Cataloging-in-Publication Data

Tendon, Steve.
  Hyper-productive knowledge work performance : the tameflow approach and
its application to Scrum and Kanban/by Steve Tendon and Wolfram Müller.
     pages cm
  Includes bibliographical references and index.
  ISBN 978-1-60427-106-5 (hardcover : alk. paper) 1. Knowledge
workers. 2.
  Knowledge management. 3. Leadership. I. Müller, Wolfram, 1969- II. Title.
  HD8039.K59T46 2014
  658.4'038—dc23
                                  2014037479

Phone: (954) 727-9333
Fax: (561) 892-0700
Web: www.jrosspub.com

CONTENTS

FOREWORD

By Robert K. Wysocki, PhD, CEO EII Publications, LLC

Steve Tendon and Wolfram Müller have written a remarkable treatise: ***Hyper-Productive Knowledge Work Performance: The TameFlow Approach and Its Application to Scrum and Kanban***. This book opens a door that leads to improved productivity and better management practices. Successful application of the *TameFlow* approach brings about what is referred to as a state of *"hyper-productivity"* where an organization acquires a delivery capacity that is comparable to that of competitors several times larger. A key success factor for a hyper-productive organization is the ability to adopt empirical and experimental practices, with short-term planning, incremental budgeting, rapid execution, and short feedback loops. Practical examples of the *TameFlow* management approach are given in, but not limited to, the field of software development. This book focuses on creating business value through knowledge-work in contemporary information-based organizations.

The first part of the book focuses on management concepts. Lead author, Steve Tendon, examines and deconstructs the conceptual foundations of a hyper-productive organization. While at Borland International, he first encountered and experienced organizational hyper-productivity. Later an independent study by AT&T Bell Laboratories revealed astounding levels of performance by one of the company's software development teams. To this day it remains the most productive project ever documented in the field of software engineering. Reflecting on the insights gained from his experience and on the findings of the case study, Steve was inspired to devise the *TameFlow* management approach.

TameFlow is not a methodology in itself, but rather an approach that can be superimposed onto any preexisting value-creating management practice. As one of the key aspects of *TameFlow*, this idea of superimposability is very powerful. *TameFlow* centers around *Pattern Theory*, which Steve uses to analyze and deconstruct both popular and lesser-known approaches. He then remixes and combines the observed productivity patterns with his own concepts to create the conditions that generate hyper-productive levels of performance. Despite the superficial appearance, this recombination of patterns is not a mash-up of different methodologies; rather it is a more powerful configuration, due to the generative nature of patterns. This results in a cross-pollination of elements from different methodologies which enable performance improvement by several orders of magnitude.

Attaining and sustaining a hyper-productive state within an organization is a complex undertaking. Achieving hyper-productivity comes from both top-down support and bottom-up effort, but most importantly, it depends completely on the understanding and support of the leadership team. The culture of a hyper-productive organization must embrace and support an empowered worker in a creative and open environment. Any business process that constrains creativity acts to the detriment of achieving hyper-productivity. Hyper-productivity can only flow from the organization not just upon having created the conditions that support autonomy and creativity, but also staying actively committed throughout the process, with the confidence that you can make it happen.

The experience of reading this book is also an epiphany into the inner workings of complex project management. Steve dives deep into that realm, providing a well-documented research history and firmly established empirical conclusions. You will benefit most by adopting a willingness to let go of preconceived notions. By staying open and receptive to the material, the approaches and concepts presented offer better ways of working. We owe a debt to these authors for having enough insight and conviction to clearly communicate the exceptional advantages that hyper-productive organizations enjoy.

In the second part of this book, we get an in-depth understanding of how Lean, Kanban, Scrum, Theory of Constraints, and Throughput Accounting define an interdependent model at the project execution level. However the successful implementation of this model is not guaranteed unless you are willing to go the distance. As the authors point out, few companies have reached a state of hyper-productivity in even one of their lines of business, let alone across the entire organization. Hyper-productivity is a fleeting state; one that requires constant cultivation of the right conditions. Despite one's eagerness, hyper-productivity won't happen by next Tuesday. To create the conditions of success, continuous effort must be made to tweak and refine them as the project development unfolds.

The conversion of assumptions into knowledge is the hallmark of *TameFlow*. As long as a process generates knowledge or business value, it should be supported even if it contradicts conventional theories and practices. Discovery-driven planning systematically converts these assumptions into knowledge as the venture evolves. When new data are uncovered, they are incorporated into the emerging plan. Discovery-driven planning is the mantra of *TameFlow*.

Traditional financial management is a major impediment to a knowledge-based organization attempting to achieve hyper-productivity. Conventional budgeting processes are not only dysfunctional, but also a real barrier to business growth and value creation. One alternative is that of a short-term financing process aligned with a lightweight planning process. This is the idea behind the Incremental Funding method, a financial model that maximizes return on investment (ROI) in a knowledge-based organization. The Incremental Funding method, Beyond Budgeting, Cost of Delay, and Throughput Octane are some of the alternative financial models that can successfully be used with the *TameFlow* approach successfully.

The whole concept of incrementally funding a knowledge-based project needs to be extended to program and portfolio management. In order to maximize ROI, funding must be aligned with the most promising efforts. Through iteration, a complex project follows an unpredictable journey whose expected business value can change, both positively or negatively. Therefore incrementally reallocating funds across the projects and programs within a portfolio is necessary in order to reduce risk.

While reading this book I also encountered for the first time the concept of the *Buffer Burn Rate* and the charts used to visualize it. In terms of project status and performance reporting, the Buffer Burn Rate is a great tool for communication with stakeholders. It is robust and incorporates other derivative reports like Buffer Fever Charts and Buffer Control Charts which can be used to track trends and provide early and leading signals of future problems. My ideal report is an intuitive, graphic report and those featured in this book exceed that expectation.

Understanding the nature of knowledge-work from a business and organizational perspective is critical for the success of any project. Emphasizing adherence to defined procedures over adaptability of approach is not conducive to hyper-productivity. Hyper-productive organizations favor a product focus over procedural compliance; the former supports commitment to customer satisfaction, while the latter is self-absorbed and dispersive. In a hyper-productive organization executives must let go of "command and control" habits and practice engaged participation, just as if they were a team member themselves. Creating a "Unity of Purpose" and a "Community of Trust" are the main responsibilities of the executive, as they are the major elements for generating hyper-productivity. For this reason hyper-productivity occurs more frequently when organizational units are led by enlightened leaders who become a role model for all team members.

TameFlow introduces concepts and principles that promote the continual transformation of an organization from one that is productive to one that is hyper-productive. Steve and Wolfram correctly point out that the project management landscape is dominated by so-called "wicked problems." Those are problems for which causes can't readily be identified. Such problems cannot be managed through deterministic processes. The only approaches that work are empirical ones. A hyper-productive organization is a *double-loop learning* organization (product loop, process loop) heavily invested in continuous refinement of both process and product. Continuous refinement is critical for every journey towards hyper-productivity.

After reading this book, my final reflection is that it could have been titled: *"The Best Infrastructure for Delivering Business Value from Complex Projects."* The combination of Steve's empirical work, which is solid enough to stand on it's own, and the unique innovations of his co-author Wolfram Müller, a thought-leader in Critical Chain Project Management, is a phenomenal contribution to management theory. The authors have done an exemplary job in communicating these principles and, as a result, they have truly earned my support and respect for what they have accomplished.

Robert K. Wysocki, PhD

Robert K. Wysocki has over 45 years combined experience as a project manager, business analyst, information systems manager, business process expert, consultant, and training developer and provider. This thought-leader and best-selling author has written 24 books on project management and information systems management. His books have been widely adopted by executives, practicing program and project managers, business analysts and consultants, as well as by more than 350 colleges and universities worldwide. Dr. Wysocki has trained more than 10,000 senior project managers and he is a sought-after speaker.

In 1990 he founded Enterprise Information Insights, Inc. (EII), a project management consulting and training practice specializing in the design and integration of advanced project management methodologies, business processes, PSO establishment and training. His client list includes AT&T, Aetna, BMW, Eli Lilly, IBM, Novartis, Ohio State University, Sapient Corporation, The Limited, The State of Ohio, Wal-Mart, Wells Fargo, ZTE, and several others.

ABOUT THE AUTHORS

Steve Tendon, creator of the *TameFlow* management approach, is a senior, multilingual, executive management consultant, experienced at leading and directing multi-national and distributed knowledge-work organizations. He is an expert in organizational performance transformation programs. Mr. Tendon is a sought-after adviser, coach, mentor and consultant, as well as an author and speaker, and was just named a Fellow of the Lean Systems Society. Steve helps businesses create high-performance organizations and teams and holds a MSc. in Software Project Management from the University of Aberdeen.

Mr. Tendon has published numerous articles and is a contributing author to *Agility Across Time and Space: Implementing Agile Methods in Global Software Projects*. Steve is currently a Director at TameFlow Consulting Ltd, where he helps clients achieve outstanding organizational performance by applying the theories and practices described in this book. Mr. Tendon has held senior Software Engineering Management roles at various firms over the course of his career, including the role of Technical Director for the Italian branch of Borland International, the birthplace of hyper-productivity in software development. Borland's development of *Quattro Pro for Windows* remains the most productive software project ever documented. This case was Mr. Tendon's source of inspiration that led to his development of the *TameFlow* perspective and management approach.

Wolfram Müller, thought-leader and expert in Critical Chain and Advanced Agile Project Management, is CEO of Speed-4Projects, and Director of Sales and Senior Consultant for VISTEM GmbH & Co. KG. Wolfram's formal education is in Mechatronics and Mechanical Engineering, which he gained from Karlsruhe Institute of Technology (KIT) and Hochschule Karlsruhe-Technik und Wirtschaft in Germany. Early in his career, Wolfram was developer and project manager for BARD/angiomed, and gained first-hand experience in the development and manufacturing of medical devices. At this time, he learned how the tools of the traditional project management work and about their drawbacks. From 2000 to 2010 he worked for 1&1 Internet AG. He began as a developer and later was made Head of their Project Office, and was responsible for more than 500 projects. He used ideas from the Lean, Critical Chain, Theory of Constraints (TOC), and Agile realms to achieve success. Based on this, he developed add-ons to Agile methods to make them compatible with Critical Chain, an approach to project management based on TOC concepts. His focus is always on speed, throughput, reliability and agility. Mr. Müller has published numerous articles, is co-author of the book *The CIOs Guide to Breakthrough Project Portfolio Performance*, and a professional speaker.

ACKNOWLEDGMENTS

Thanks to Rudi Burkhard for connecting Steve and Wolfram. Thanks to all reviewers for excellent comments, insights, suggestions, critique, and even encouragement. In particular: Mike Burrows, Dimitar Bakardzhiev, Adail Muniz Retamal, Paul Merino, Pascal Van Cauwenberghe, Simon Harris, Andy Carmichael, Rüdiger Wolf, Niranjana Koodavalli, Stefan van Aalst, Kirk Bryde, Zsolt Fabok, and Dmitri Koleno.

The authors are grateful to Drew Gierman, Stephen Buda, and the staff of J. Ross Publishing for all their support and effort put into the production of this book.

Web
Added
Value™

This book has free material available for download from the
Web Added Value™ resource center at *www.jrosspub.com*

At J. Ross Publishing we are committed to providing today's professional with practical, hands-on tools that enhance the learning experience and give readers an opportunity to apply what they have learned. That is why we offer free ancillary materials available for download on this book and all participating Web Added Value™ publications. These on-line resources may include interactive versions of material that appears in the book or supplemental templates, worksheets, models, plans, case studies, proposals, spreadsheets and assessment tools, among other things. Whenever you see the WAV™ symbol in any of our publications, it means bonus materials accompany the book and available from the Web Added Value Download Resource Center at www.jrosspub.com.

Downloads for *Hyper-Productive Knowledge Work Performance: The TameFlow Approach and Its Application to Scrum and Kanban* include spreadsheets to support all necessary functions for TameFlow-Scrum, including determining a reasonable due date, execution monitoring for a release, and portfolio overview.

Part I

TameFlow Principles of Hyper-Productive Knowledge Work Performance

---

1

A CASE OF SOFTWARE
HYPER-PRODUCTIVITY

It has become almost an urban legend, but a well-grounded legend, that there is a *software crisis*. This belief originated in the late 1960s and more than 40 years later, the software industry still seems to be stuck in this crisis. Projects run late, cost too much, don't deliver what is really needed, and so on. Software development seems like the realm of inefficiencies and underperformance.

It is also debatable whether the performance of individual programmers can vary by as much as an order of magnitude or not. Both anecdotal evidence and objective studies show this to be true. You don't need to get acquainted with many programmers and see them at work to draw that conclusion yourself. It is a wise conclusion that über-programmers really do exist, and that they can outperform their peers by a factor of 10 or more.

From the early starts in mainframe rooms, the activity of programming has evolved from being the lonesome intellectual exercise of isolated individuals, to a concerted team effort requiring more and more collaboration between several individuals. There are many reasons for this. On the one hand is the emergence of software technology stacks—technologies that require specialized skills, from the back-ends to the front-ends, traversing all the middleware in between—and the always deeper knowledge needed for domain specific application programming. More people are required to master all of these skills—no one individual (with a few exceptions of legendary programmers), can truly know all of these technologies in depth.

On the other hand, the sheer size and scope of modern projects have grown to the extent that they can barely fit in the mind-space of a single, isolated programmer. To all this, we have to add the ever changing business environment and business competition that put even more pressure on being able to change more quickly. In short, any significant piece of software needs a team effort in order to be successful.

A legitimate question is whether or not a team can possibly reach levels of stellar performance similar to those of the individual über-programmers. Just bringing together a number of skilled individuals does not seem to cause this hyper-productivity to happen (though having good raw material to start with is obviously a prerequisite).

There have been countless efforts at taking average teams (a.k.a. *immature* teams) and improving them (making them more *mature*) through *process improvement* initiatives. The archetypal approach is represented by Capability Maturity Model Integration. However, even if teams undertaking such initiatives do indeed improve in a number of so-called *process areas*, they often are still only marginally better. It is rare that such initiatives make a real, substantial difference that can be counted in orders of magnitude of improved performance. Yet, there have been examples of teams that did this—software organizations that outperformed all of their competitors and software teams that reached hyper-productivity. One such instance is that of Borland International.[1]

THE CASE OF BORLAND QUATTRO PRO FOR WINDOWS

When I (Steve Tendon) was at Borland, I didn't know that it was a hyper-productive organization. I just noticed after leaving Borland that the other places I worked at were ... let's just say, *slower*. It wasn't until I read Jim Coplien's papers (Coplien, 1994) that I realized there was a reason for this.

Actually, in that paper the term *hyper-productivity* was not even used—the most exciting wording referred to *phenomenal productivity*. In a later paper, Coplien (1996) coined the term *hyper-programming*, and only later did the term *hyper-productivity* appear in Jeff Sutherland's many papers about Scrum.

Coplien's work highlights how software development is a highly social activity, wherein the patterns of communication and interaction that happen between individuals are important factors. Traditionally, software development has been examined in terms of process rather than in terms of this social dimension. The study thus focused on roles that could be found in software development organizations. It is through the combination of roles and the communication and interaction patterns that happen in between them that a highly productive software development organization can emerge.

Most Productive Ever and Precursor to Scrum and XP

Software hyper-productivity is the capability of building production grade software at a speed that is greater by orders of magnitude than the industry standard. Coplien (2007) reported about the *Borland Quattro Pro for Windows* (QPW) project, at Borland International, describing it as *most remarkable by any measure*, and as setting the standard for Agile development in the early 1990s. Coplien also recounted how his earlier article from 1994 was influential on the formation of Scrum. In fact, Coplien's study was highly influential on the shaping of both Scrum and XP and, notably, Jeff Sutherland, the creator of Scrum (Sutherland, 2012), writes:

> We were prodded into setting up the first Scrum meeting after reading Coplien's paper on Borland's development of QPW. The Quattro team delivered one million lines of C++ code in 31 months with a 4-person staff that later grew to 8. This was about 1,000 lines of deliverable code per person, per week, the most productive software project ever documented. The team attained this level of productivity by intensive interaction in daily meetings

with project management, product management, developers, documenters, and quality assurance staff. [...]

Each developer on this project generated 1000 lines of production C++ code every week for three years. In comparison, productivity on the recent Microsoft Vista project was 1000 lines of code per developer per year. The Borland Quattro Project was 52 times as productive as the Microsoft Vista project measured by lines of code.

To reiterate: A team of 8 people delivered 1 million C++ lines of production code in 31 months. As of today, this is still the most productive software project ever documented. But the performance feat was even more amazing! Coplien (2007) tells how the team actually made two prototypes before delivering the final product, and while the time was reported for those prototypes too, the corresponding code metrics were not included in the final count. So the actual productivity was much higher than the already amazing figures that were reported.

Barbarians, Not Burrocrats!

These events took place during the last years of Borland International's legendary period (1982–1994), when the company was still led by the original founder (Philippe Kahn) and was fighting with Microsoft and Lotus for the top spots as a software superpower.

Borland International was extremely successful. For instance, it was the first company ever to make Microsoft withdraw from an entire market (the Pascal compiler market). Yet, in that fight, Borland International was the underdog, in terms of size and resources. The company had to do things differently.

Philippe Kahn had very clear ideas about what was needed (Weber, 1992): Microsoft was five times bigger than Borland, so Borland had no other choice but to become better, leaner, and faster than Microsoft. *Better? Leaner? Faster?* This sounds a lot like what is promised by current Agile methods such as Scrum and XP, and Lean methods (e.g., the Kanban Method). How did it work out at that time, when these methods were unknown? Philippe Kahn was inspired by the history of Central Asia, and how the nomadic tribes were able to expand into "civilized" Europe. In an interview, he described them like this (Weber, 1992):

> They were austere and ambitious, eager for victory but not given to celebrating it. They were organized around small, collaborative groups that were far more flexible and fast-moving than the entrenched societies of the time. They were outsiders and proud of it. They were barbarians.

That idea of being organized around small, collaborative, flexible, fast-moving, outsider, and proud groups, was the key. The whole company saw themselves as Barbarians—*Barbarians, Not Burrocrats!* became the company's unofficial slogan. It can be seen in Figure 1.1 as it appeared on a T-shirt that circulated in the company at that time.

Now, aren't small, flexible, fast-moving, collaborative groups what Agile/Scrum/XP and Lean/Kanban are all about? Why then did not these methods lead to that software hyper-productivity that was seen at Borland?

Figure 1.1   The Borland Barbarians, as illustrated on a T-shirt of that period

Organizational Culture

The key to achieving software hyper-productivity is in the company's organizational culture. Excellent technical skills are necessary, as are illuminated managers, technology, and infrastructure, along with software processes and methods—all of these are necessary, yet insufficient. The key lies in the organizational culture, and organizational culture starts at the top.

Philippe Kahn was known as an executive who had an understanding of software (Weber, 1992). In fact he was a computer scientist himself and certainly understood computers and software. However, he also understood the nature of software from a business and organizational perspective. It does not mean getting into the technicalities of programming and coding—it means understanding the nature of human creativity, and the individual and social processes that foster it, in an organizational setting. (We will explore this topic in greater detail in later chapters.)

Communication is another key ingredient. Even the most junior developer could e-mail Philippe Kahn and get a reply. Fisher (1992) wrote:

> Borland insiders credit their "high bandwidth" communications with increasing the company's efficiency. "If a programmer has an idea, he can raise it with

everybody who matters in an hour, and have a decision made in two hours," said Hamid Mirza, Borland's vice president for database development.

What most people will reflect upon when reading the above quote is the *flatness* of the organization, but that is not the key point either. The key point lies in the frequency and patterns of communication. The *flat* organization is just a consequence of such communication and interaction patterns, not its cause.

Coplien came to the most important insight: his study of the QPW case and Borland International's internal communication practices led him to appreciate and, above all, document the organizational patterns that can benefit software companies (Coplien, 1995, 1996, and 2004). It is within those patterns (and others) that you can find numerous, real elements that lead to hyper-productivity, as we will examine shortly.

LOSING HYPER-PRODUCTIVITY

The best evidence that software hyper-productivity stems indeed from the company leaders, and the culture they can instill in the organization, comes from Borland International itself. In 1995, after considerable growth, professional management (yes, the Barbarians are still laughing today) took over, and replaced Philippe Kahn. After a series of management blunders and numerous changes in strategic direction, the company declined and eventually settled on making *software test and quality tools* with a focus on application life-cycle management solutions.

Most stunning, in the meantime the company had lost all of its original hyper-productivity. This became ironically evident in 2008 when Peter Morowski, then Borland International's Senior Vice President of Products, wrote an article for the *Agile Journal* (Morowski, 2008) telling how between 2006 and 2008 he had lead an Agile enterprise transformation program. Go figure!? The company that held the unmatched software productivity record, had inspired Scrum and XP, and had given Coplien the raw material to develop his software organizational patterns—that same company—now had to *learn* how to become Agile. What had happened?

In that article, Peter Morowski presented the company as a traditional software delivery organization (sic!) that became sold on Agile and then adopted Agile consistently. Naturally, this produced some good—the article listed a number of benefits of the Agile transformation—but the original hyper-productivity and the results thereof were never regained.

This sad case evidently demonstrates that while it might be of value if single development teams learn to become Agile, it is way more beneficial and important if the company's leadership understands the nature of software (or, more extensively, the nature of knowledge-work), and the drivers that can truly lead to hyper-productivity. It is about leading the entire organization to hyper-productivity. Just as leaders can lead a company to conquer the hyper-productive state, they can also make the company lose it entirely.

Software Hyper-Productivity Is Transferable

If you can lose hyper-productivity, is it possible to gain it, or are hyper-productive software teams true outliers that just happen to be "born" with a unique capability? If hyper-productivity is to be viable, then learning how to be hyper-productive must be a transferable skill. Scrum is not delivering that with the exception of those few projects documented by Jeff Sutherland himself. So the question remains: Is software hyper-productivity something that can be taken from one organization to another? Can it be learned? Or can it even be created so that an ordinary, average team becomes hyper-productive?

To reply to that question, I relate my own experience: I was with Borland during the period when Coplien made the QPW study, so I have firsthand experience of how it was to be in that company during that period.[2] Naturally, I am proud to have been with Borland International at that time—that experience shaped my entire professional career thereafter. I have since continued in Borland's tradition, and I have personal productivity records that are comparable to those cited. While I was there, I took up the methods and processes—especially the mindset and attitude—that characterized Borland International at that time. I have since continued to learn more about and develop my own approaches as to what makes hyper-productive software organizations really tick and perform.

My own personal productivity record was established in 1995–97 while leading the core team of a company developing a commercial banking application. The core team of four software engineers delivered 600,000 lines of Delphi[3] production code in two years. How does this compare? It is certainly in the same league as the famous QPW team—but I have too much respect for the QPW team to even dare to compare my team to theirs. Granted, our application was much simpler to develop than QPW, and a lot of productivity gains were made by using a Rapid Application Development environment like Delphi, rather than a pure C++ compiler, as in the case of QPW. On the other hand, I have no difficulty believing my team was several times more productive than the industry average—even discounting the fact that I had worked at Borland, that I had a deep knowledge of Delphi, and that the application was an uninspiring *Create-Read-Update-Delete* (CRUD)[4] application, with lots of screens and data.

Yet, this was a case of real software hyper-productivity. Besides, all this happened 3–5 years before the Agile Manifesto (Beck, 2001) was published, and long before Agile, Scrum, XP, etc., was popular. My early experience at Borland International allowed me to repeatedly achieve hyper-productivity well beyond industry averages, on a number of diverse projects, with different teams, technologies, countries, and problem domains. So, to answer the question, at least according to my experience: Yes, hyper-productivity is a skill that is transferable, learnable, and even derivable.

So, hyper-productivity seems to be transferable, provided there is a common thread between one team and the next. It is akin to the transmission of cultural values from one generation to the next. This is even more evident if we consider what happened inside Borland.

THE BORLAND PORTFOLIO

While Coplien's study considered only the QPW product, the mode of operation that characterized that team was not unique to it. In fact Quattro Pro was being built in C++. What is stunning is that the spreadsheet software was being built with Borland's own C++ compiler, *while that very same compiler was under development!* Coplien (1994) recognized this extraordinary feat. This was possible because of the tight coupling between the QPW team and the Borland C++ team. The spreadsheet program was one of the largest projects handled by the C++ compiler. Each of the two projects was contributing to the quality and performance of the other.

Clearly, software hyper-productivity was spread throughout Borland. It had become a distinctive part of the company's corporate culture. I can testify that the same approach was used with all other products too, such as: Paradox (a database), Object Vision (a visual programming environment), Sprint (a word processor), and the famous Turbo/Borland Pascal compiler (programming language).

So the Borland *method* actually managed a portfolio of very complex products, often interdependent one on the other, with intertwined timelines and milestones, and shared resources (especially in the QA and Documentation departments). And in all cases, productivity was extraordinarily high, and the products were of extremely high quality and performance.

This answers another recurring question: whether Agile/Lean processes can scale or not. Obviously they can, and it is possible to scale *while* maintaining hyper-productivity. It is definitely possible to use a Scrum-like, Agile approach to manage a portfolio of projects. Not only that, but it is possible to do so and achieve unprecedented software productivity records, deliver exceptional products, and make it into a repeatable process. Repeatable, that is, for and within that single organization.

However, the question is not if it is possible to use Scrum (or Scrum-like methods) to manage projects and portfolios in a hyper-productive manner, because the Borland case shows it is possible. The key question is if such methods are duplicable, if they can become a sort of defined process (shrug!) or template that other organizations can pick up to manage their own projects and portfolios. This is precisely what many methods are striving to institutionalize—to give a cookbook wherein you can find the recipe to hyper-productivity or, at least, to improved productivity.

Instead of trying to establish a *defined process* (a blueprint that could be used like a cookie cutter), Coplien resorted to a patterns approach. Patterns are very different from cookie cutters because they are generative. They will not duplicate or replicate the features and structures of other organizations or teams; but they will allow you to generate similar features and structures that help in moving towards hyper-productivity. Patterns leave the necessary wiggle room to pick, combine, and apply them to one's own context—they are not prescriptive like defined processes.

Despite having *been there!* and *seen it!* (at Borland) and *done that!* (leading hyper-productive teams) myself, I have a decisive negative stance on the possibility of replicating hyper-productivity from one organization to another through process and methods. The patterns approach, which we will discover soon, is better suited because it allows you to generate the social structures that *may* be conducive to hyper-productivity.

There is also evidence in the repeated failures of Scrum at achieving hyper-productivity (with just a few exceptions). Jeff Sutherland (2007) notes only a minority of Scrum teams reach a hyper-productive state, notwithstanding that Scrum was conceived of for the very purpose of achieving five to ten times *normal* performance. While the intent of Scrum is good, it does not always lead to the desired results. Something else is needed.

Possible and Transferable, but Not Duplicable

Coplien tried to examine the Borland case like a social anthropologist, not like a software process methodologist. He used social network theories, social network analysis, sociometric modeling, socio-grams and socio-matrices, interaction grids, and eventually came to patterns and pattern languages for software development (Coplien, 2004).

Pattern languages have been used in architecture, mathematics, and natural sciences. Often in the context of software, there are references to the works of Christopher Alexander that used patterns in architecture; but in the case of Coplien the source of inspiration comes more from the usage of patterns in social anthropology (Kroeber, 1948). Such patterns tend to capture the real social organizational structure, and model the relationships and communication paths between roles (Coplien, 2004). Coplien (1996) considered software development as a *social activity*. The insight is to consider the individuals in the organization according to their roles, and then model the social network of communication that is established between the roles. That social network represents a number of significant performance attributes of the organization, and it can be subject to both quantitative and visual analysis. The analysis performed on those diagrams allowed Coplien to discover patterns of organization and process that were typical of high-performance teams.

What stands out is that there is a strong sociological dimension identified by Coplien. Curiously, Coplien used an object-oriented analysis technique to model the social dimension of the teams. He resorted to CRC (classes, responsibilities and collaborators) card modeling—not to model an object-oriented system, but to model the teams and the internal relationships between the team members. He modeled roles and responsibilities, and represented the collaboration between roles as a graph. The nodes of the graph were the roles and the edges were the collaborations between the roles. The edges were also weighted according to the intensity of the coupling between the two roles. Coplien devised many visualization techniques to represent such graphs. They could be drawn as force-based networks; as topologically sorted hierarchies; as directed graphs; as interaction grids; and others. In particular, the adjacency diagram and the interaction grid give incredible evidence and insight about how the inner workings of the organization actually functioned; and explained why Borland was so different from any other organization.

By examining the social organizational structure of high performance software organizations (such as Borland), it becomes self-evident that such methods are not duplicable: they are too dependent on the *specific social structure* of the organization at hand. They are further dependent on the organization's individuals, their skills, and personalities, with illuminated leaders (like Philippe Kahn), coding wizards (like Anders Hejlsberg), project managers (like Gary Whizin), product managers (like Zack Urlocker), R&D leads (like Bob Warfield), and so on. (I mentioned just a few of the legendary people who worked at Borland at that time.)

When examining the adjacency diagrams and interaction diagrams describing the Borland Quattro Pro team, and comparing them with similar diagrams of other organizations (Coplien, 1996), it becomes evident that organizations are *structurally different*. This means that the methods of an organization like Borland are *not* transferable to another because the underlying social structure is different. The difference is so marked that it becomes clearly discernible in these diagrams.

This does not mean that the collection of such diagrams does not present *commonalities*. In fact it was by studying such commonalities that Coplien was able to identify the organizational patterns for software development, as we will see in the next chapter. If such methods cannot be transferred at the team/project level, they will be even less so at the organization/portfolio level. However, by studying Coplien's work on patterns, you can be inspired by the patterns that have worked in other organizations and then generate your own productive organizational structures through pattern application. This does not mean to replicate the organizational structures of others. You generate some similar structure that enables productive patterns of interaction and communication.

WHY CARE?

It is beyond any doubt that software development capabilities have improved immensely over the last 15–20 years, especially with the advent of Agile/Lean approaches. On the other hand, this is not that big of an achievement, since the productivity levels of traditional approaches dwarf in comparison. So, should one be happy and get complacent? Isn't software hyper-productivity just a Chimera—a monstrous fantasy that exists only as a dream?

The QPW case was used by Sutherland (2003) to present hyper-productivity as an alternative to scaling. It was an example of how 40 developers could perform as 500, and deliver the project in half the time. The case of Borland and a few implementations of Scrum by Jeff Sutherland demonstrate that software hyper-productivity is indeed possible.

Since the most successful Lean/Agile approaches, while dwarfing the traditional ones, would be dwarfed themselves compared to hyper-productive approaches, hyper-productivity is worth pursuing. Even if the state of hyper-productivity is not reached, the mere effort of striving to reach it will increase performance well beyond your current levels. That is why it is worth pursuing. Even if you don't get there, you will still have improved so much more from where you were.

In his original paper, Coplien (1994) commented that the "phenomenal" productivity he had seen at Borland was thought-provoking, and encouraged organizations to look at Borland's case to find inspiration for their own improvement ambitions. This is even more relevant today than what it was in the early 1990s. Nowadays every other software team does, or claims it does, or thinks it does *Agile* or *Lean*. The point is, if everybody is doing it, what advantage does Agile/Lean bring to you? It is just a leveled playing field. It is a *best practice* that is there—equal for everybody.

The question is: will you be waiting for the *next practice* to come along before you move? Or will you make an effort to learn how to improve continuously? Because that is what this is all about. Hyper-productivity is achieved by never standing still, but by continuously evolving and improving. Even if you were not to approximate the levels of productivity of the teams and organizations examined in the literature, the effort of getting there will prepare your organization for entering, staying, and winning the game.

If you don't move, your competitor for sure will. For instance, consider that it was a drive to compete that motivated the creation of the Toyota Production System when Taiichi Ōhno (1988) himself explained that he was surprised to discover that nine Japanese workers were needed to do the work of one American worker. This is what spurred him to strive to deliver the work done by 100 workers with only 10. He had to improve one order of magnitude just to get equal to the American automotive industry. We know he managed to do that, and then got even better. Granted, this example is from the world of automotive manufacturing, but if Toyota first caught up to, and then outperformed the

American competitors, it shows that aiming for hyper-productivity has its rewards. Toyota had to improve 10 times *at least* just to get equal.

So How Do You Get There?

If these methods cannot be transferred, a legitimate question is: How do you get there? First we need to know what *there* looks like. In the next chapter we will take a deeper look at what the social structure of a hyper-productive organization looks like.

REFERENCES

1. In this and in the following chapters, I (Steve Tendon) refer extensively to Borland International and the study that Jim Coplien made of Borland in the early 1990s which he described in many of his subsequent writings. Disclaimer: Steve was part of Borland International during that period—so be forewarned: He might express a biased opinion.
2. Steve Tendon worked with Borland International for over seven years: first as a contractor (1987–1989), then as their Technical Director at their Italian branch (1989–1991), and then as a contractor again (1991–1994). As their Technical Director in Italy, he was responsible for: development methodology; scheduling; testing; quality assurance; budgeting; media distribution; developer relationships; sales engineering; technical support; technical personnel selection and technical leadership. Steve brought to the Italian market the following shrink-wrapped products: Paradox 3.0, Turbo C++ 1.0, Turbo C++ Professional 1.0, Paradox 3.5, Quattro Pro 2.0, Turbo Pascal 6.0, Borland C++ 2.0, ObjectVision 1.0, Quattro Pro 3.0, and Paradox 4.0 for DOS. Furthermore, he worked with the International team at Borland's headquarters, implementing and testing software localization and internationalization tools that were then used to make the national editions of all software packages.
3. *Delphi* refers to the Object Pascal Integrated Development Environment developed by Borland, and currently a product of Embarcadero; this *Delphi* has nothing to do with the *Delphi* estimation technique, nor with the Oracle of Delphi!
4. CRUD stands for *Create-Read-Update-Delete* and refers to the fundamental operations that are done with a database.

2

SHAPES AND PATTERNS
OF HYPER-PRODUCTIVITY

When Coplien conducted his study during the period from 1990–1993, one of the main challenges was that of comparing different organizations in a meaningful way. He and his colleagues examined over 40 very different software development organizations. Eventually they came up with a visual way of representing the essential traits of software organizations, wherein the hyper-productive ones stood out from all other ones. One of the most important insights was that of viewing software development teams and organizations as *social bodies.*

The difficulty of maturing this view was described in Cain (1996b), and related to the stereotype of computer programmers being solitary and antisocial individuals, with little attention for social concerns. With the maturing of the view that software engineering teams and organizations are really about human nature and interactions, it becomes more and more important, even for computer people, to consider their organizational behavior as a manifestation of organizational psychology and social anthropology rather than an application of management policies or processes norms.

Notwithstanding the difficulties, the research of Coplien and his colleagues took a sociological view of software processes, using the tools used by sociologists. In particular, he was able to represent his findings with two kinds of graphical or visual representations: the natural force-based social network diagram and the interaction grid.

NATURAL FORCE-BASED SOCIAL NETWORKS (ADJACENCY DIAGRAMS)

A peculiar visualization technique is the social network diagram, also known as the adjacency diagram. An example is shown in Figure 2.1. The diagram derives the sociograms used to display social networks by Moreno (1934). The innovation of the adjacency diagram is that it renders the forces of the links through spatial placement—it not only shows the links, but also the forces that keep them together. Cain (1996b) gives the key insight that this visualization technique (through placement based on forces) amplified the

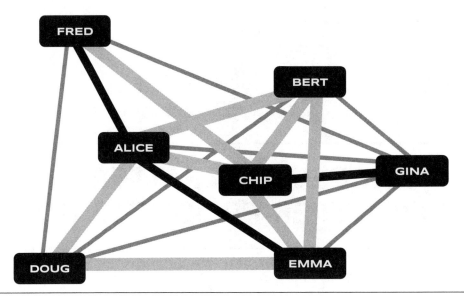

Figure 2.1   Example of an adjacency diagram

sociogram data. Not only did such data become more visible, but it also became easier to spot the formation of particular configurations or patterns.

The diagram renders graphically the forces that keep together a group of individuals, or roles, as was the case. It is an attempt at depicting the social glue that makes a group what it is. Coplien (1995) describes such diagrams as a network of roles and the communication paths between them. The diagram is able to depict the coupling between the roles, simply by representing it through the distance between the nodes of the network. The rendering of such diagrams will put the roles with the most communication at the center, and the "quiet" roles at the periphery. Cain (1996b) described how the rendering algorithm actually worked. Initially all nodes were placed randomly on a plane; inverse square law repelling forces were set up between all pairs of nodes; then the edge between any two nodes represented an attracting force, proportional to the intensity of the interaction between those two nodes. When all forces reach a balance, the graph is visualized in a stable state.

The outcome is a two-dimensional representation of the organization's interactions. Furthermore, color is used in an expressive way. The nodes are color-coded to render the intensity of interaction with neighboring nodes. In Cain (1996a) we find a more detailed description of the color coding. Not only did shades of red represent the intensity of collaboration, but additional differently colored lines could be overlaid, giving a visual representation of communication paths between the roles. So such visualization rendered both collaborations as well as communication paths between all roles.

The resulting visual representation gives an intuitive visualization of the organization's social structure. The arcs are not directed, as focus is on the coupling between the roles, rather than the flow of information. Information flow is almost always bidirectional, and takes the form of conversations or meetings.

Another powerful description is provided in Coplien (1996), where the idea that a collaboration is rendered through an attracting force between the nodes; a force that is proportional to the intensity of the collaboration. When these forces interact, they will arrive at a stable state. Not only are the most active roles centered in the middle, but you can also spot clusters of roles, which represent groups with a strong affinity. In this way the visualization makes it easy to discern the key roles in an organization, and also any effective suborganization.

The Adjacency Diagrams of Quattro Pro for Windows

When Coplien and his colleagues examined the adjacency diagram for the Quattro Pro for Windows (QPW) team, they noticed how that graph was highly connected. The interpretation they provided was that information was spread to everybody. Every role was in some way connected to every other role, and there were no *black holes* (that is, roles that would not be communicating a lot).

The diagram highlighted the centrality of the four roles of the Architect, the Project Manager, the Product Manager, and Quality Assurance (QA). Borland's products were acclaimed for their quality, and unsurprisingly the QA role is in the center. The Architect was important, and ensures conceptual integrity to the software that was being built. Also Phillipe stood out as being active in the communication—naturally, that was Philippe Kahn, the Chief Executive Officer (CEO) of the company.

The Project Manager and the Product Manager had a central role—one of their primary duties was to convey the communications of the Vice President and the CEO to the developers. (As we will elaborate on later, these two roles are very similar to the Scrum Master and Product Owner role in Scrum.) These kinds of diagrams are representative of how immediately different one organization might be (visually and structurally) from another. Such diagrams have no resemblance to the classical organizational charts which are most often used to depict how an organization is structured. These diagrams give a better rendering of what really happens in between the *white spaces* in an organizational chart.

The study by Coplien collected evidence that hyper-productive software organizations were structurally different from other less-productive ones; and within their structures, information and collaboration between roles flowed differently. This is even more apparent when examining the organization's interaction grids.

INTERACTION GRIDS

While the social network diagram emphasizes the coupling between roles, interaction grids try to represent the structure of directed interactions. In a square matrix, columns represent the roles that initiate an interaction, while the rows represent the roles that are on the receiving end of the interaction. The axes are sorted by communication intensity, and the most active roles are put closer to the origin of the graph; in other words, the axes are ordered according to the roles' coupling to the organization as a whole. The roles that are at the center of the social network diagram will be close to the origin of the interaction grid; while the roles that are in the periphery of the social network diagram will be the furthest from the origin of the interaction grid. An example can be seen in Figure 2.2.

Each point in the plane represents an interaction; and because the points capture the direction of the communication, the graph is not necessarily symmetrical. Different levels of color shading represent the number or levels of interactions. Coplien (1996) explains

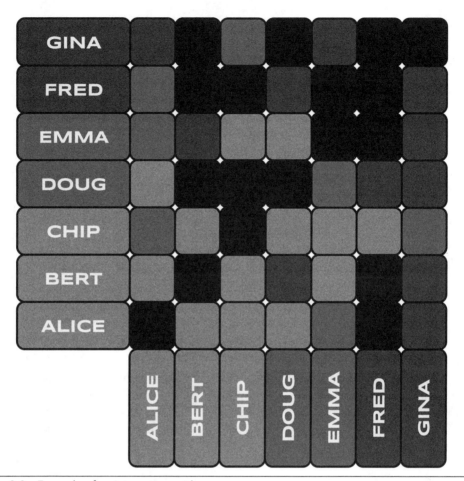

Figure 2.2   Example of an interaction grid

that rows and columns are ordered according to the amount of collaboration, so that the most active roles will be placed near the origin of the grid. Even in this case, expressive color coding is used. Each square in the grid shows the degree of collaboration between two roles—the more intense the collaboration, the darker the shading.

These diagrams can be thought of as organizational portraits. The position of key roles in the diagrams can contribute positively or negatively to the organization's overall functionality and performance. Naturally, only the organization itself will be able to see (through introspective analysis) any problems that might be reflected through such portraits, but which would escape the observation of outsiders.

The interaction grid is like a *heat map* of the collaboration that happens within an organization. The darker the shade, the more intense is the communication. Most organizations are characterized by interaction grids where the predominant color is black, with only a few squares of even darker shading.

The Interaction Grid of Quattro Pro for Windows

When Coplien and his colleagues examined the interaction grid for the QPW, they reported that all communication was evenly spread between roles, and how the reach was very broad. Nobody was left out of the loop. The diagram showed a lot of darker shades indicating how intensely the team used to communicate. Cain (1996b) compares a good organization's interaction grid—where communication is even and strong—to the appearance of a quality woven fabric.

In the case of the QPW team, there was a limited number of roles. By having few roles, Borland did not have to optimize communication flow. For larger organizations to be effective, work must flow inward in order to ensure high communication saturation. The fewer the roles, the more effective the communication. Notably, Philippe was directly involved in the project.

Borland's interaction grid was different from what was found in other companies. The bottom line of all the above is undoubtedly this: the QPW project was an outlier with respect to most other projects/organizations researched by Coplien. For this reason, the kind of productivity that was typical of Borland is not easily duplicable in other places.

OTHER METRICS

While the adjacency diagram and the interaction grid are the two most significant tools for visually rendering organizational structures and properties that relate to hyper-productivity, Coplien also used some other significant metrics and graphs. They will be described here briefly, just to reiterate once again how the case of QPW was of a unique kind.

Connectedness

In Coplien (2007), the measurement of *connectedness* was introduced as the number of roles that each role communicates with. Even when plotting the connectedness of several cases, QPW was placed as an extreme in terms of having the highest level of connectedness.

Communication Saturation

Coplien and his colleagues also analyzed data across projects, considering the roles, collaborations, and the organization size (intended as the number of unique roles, not headcount). The obvious finding, in Coplien (1996), was that only a subset of all potential collaborations actually materializes. In simple terms, any single individual will entertain collaborations only with a subset of all employees in the organization. The not-so-obvious finding came out of examining the exposure surface of roles with respect to others. An organization with n roles will theoretically have $n(n-1)/2$ possible communication paths. The ratio of the actual collaborations to the possible collaborations is known as *communication saturation*.

A diagram in Coplien (2007) is illustrative of how, in terms of communication saturation, the data point for the QPW case was unusual—highlighting a relatively high level of communication saturation (greater than 89%). The interpretation was that almost everyone in the team communicated with everyone else, so that everyone was constantly aware of what was happening in the project.

A high level of communication saturation is characteristic of hyper-productive organizations; and it is one explanation why such organizations have fewer roles. Communication is key for arriving at higher levels of productivity. However, because communication bears a cost, it is too expensive for large organizations to have high communication saturation. In other words, large organizations cannot afford to be hyper-productive.

In the earlier paper (Coplien, 1996), the conclusion was that large organizations can become more productive by reducing the number of roles. Jeff Sutherland, when presenting Scrum has often stated that if "Performance = Communication Saturation," then "Daily meeting with few roles = Performance." The conclusion appears to be that small, tightly-knit teams that communicate *frequently* about *all* their work will perform better than larger ones that communicate less about subsets of their work.

Communication Intensity Ratio

Another revealing measurement is the *communication intensity ratio:* the ratio between communication activity of the most active roles to the average communication activity of the organization. This gives an indication of how much communication is focused on a single role. Highly productive organizations often have low communication intensity ratio. The significance is that communication is more evenly spread throughout the many roles of the organization (Coplien, 1996).

This metric is not as strongly correlated with high productivity as the other ones mentioned earlier, but it is useful as a confirmation. A diagram in Coplien (2007) presented the communication intensity ratio of the organizations studied by Coplien and his team. The data point for the QPW case was amongst the lowest.

FROM SHAPES TO PATTERNS

Once all these graphs and diagrams were collected, profiles of successful projects could be drawn. Coplien (1996) characterized such projects by the following attributes:

- Organizations were simple
- Work flowed inwards
- Work was distributed evenly
- The process was iterative
- Success was compensated

Actually these conclusions were only the summary of a much broader work that resulted in the identification and classification of organizational patterns, later exposed in great detail in Coplien (2004).

In this context the term *Pattern* is used as a very technical term meaning an *Alexandrian Pattern*. An Alexandrian Pattern is basically a solution to a problem in a context.

Patterns of Communication and Organization

By collecting and categorizing typical recurring patterns from a number of organizations, Coplien's study effectively mapped out a social anthropology of software development organizations. The whole approach was inspired by the *Pattern Languages* in architecture, as pioneered by Christopher Alexander (1977 and 1979).

The intent was to identify models of software development as it happens in reality, in contrast to models built from principles. A number of patterns were recurring in many organizations. They can be thought of as fingerprints of certain kinds of organizational structures. Some examples are shown in Figure 2.3.

For example, organizations that developed applications in well-understood domains often exhibited a hub-spoke-rim structure. Cain (1996b) explained such structures in greater detail, drawing the conclusion that from a sociological viewpoint, they represent high-context cultures exhibiting shared models, knowledge, and vocabulary. In other words, the structure is a manifestation of a shared vision. When there is a shared vision, there is less need for strong coordination between the roles.

Eventually many more patterns were documented. Once the catalog of patterns was compiled, the research focused on finding those patterns that characterized highly productive organizations, to find out if any particular organizational shapes correlated to productivity.

Hyper-Productive Patterns

Some patterns were unique to the hyper-productive organizations. The unique shapes of their adjacency diagrams and interaction grids gave away their presence. Coplien and his

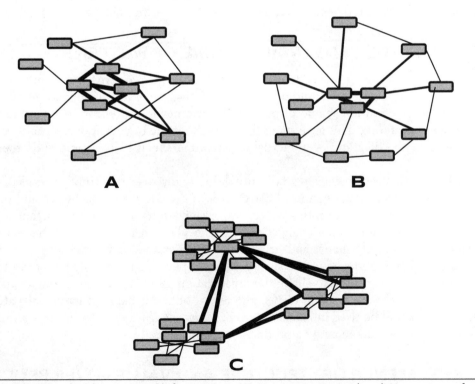

Figure 2.3 Sample adjacency graph fingerprints. (A) An organization with a distinct *center of action*. (B) A *hub-spoke-rim* configuration. (C) An organization with *cliques*.

colleagues had just to identify what those patterns were like. For example, two of such patterns were:

- **Distribute work evenly:** Both workload as well as communication is evenly distributed among roles; the organization has a "low centrality."
- **Work flows inward:** The software developer is often at or near the core of software organizations. Highly productive organizations have collaboration flows toward the developer at the center, who directly adds value to the product. Less productive organizations often have managers at the center, and collaboration flows from the manager to the other roles.

Many more patterns were identified and eventually documented in Coplien (2004). Those two cited above are the easier ones to spot on the graphs and diagrams, as they are associated with peculiar and recognizable shapes in the adjacency diagrams or configurations in the interaction grids. Further hyper-productive patterns can be found by deeper organizational analysis, as described by Coplien and his colleagues.

We will see later, that from the perspective of hyper-productivity, we will identify two foundational or *Noble Patterns:* the *Unity of Purpose* and the *Community of Trust*. One might wonder why only two patterns are taken as the key to hyper-productivity. Naturally these two patterns alone will not create a hyper-productive organization, but they are foundational. They set the stage—the preconditions that enable further organizational patterns to be developed and applied. Without the two foundational Nobel Patterns, hyper-productivity will not develop, even in the presence of other patterns.

THE POWERFUL GENERATIVE NATURE OF PATTERNS

Coplien and his colleagues started to become aware of arriving at some very significant conclusions—that these patterns could be used in an active, generative manner. Cain (1996b) reveals that they became capable of predicting sociometric values for new organizations they were encountering. This gave them the hunch that the organizational structures they were seeing in the diagrams were actually generating specific observable and emergent behavior.

This finding was very promising: not only did they discover recurring patterns of such structures; but those patterns showed correlation to the organization's health and performance. The idea started to form that by making organizations adopt positive organizational structures, positive and lasting changes would take place in the organization's behavior, too. These were not only shapes and structures, but generative patterns.

In other words, the idea is to use such generative patterns to literally give form to the organizational structure, and to shape the organization in a way that is conducive to high performance. They were starting to become aware of the generative nature of patterns. Such patterns could be used in an *act of organizational design* to create the structure of an organization that would generate a productive organization.

THE PREVALENCE OF STRUCTURE AND VALUES OVER PROCESS

Why would one want to actively give form and shape to an organization? A synthesis of Coplien's findings was presented in Coplien (2004). Coplien observed that despite following software processes, organizations doing so keep on failing. Conventional wisdom would conclude that either the process was not adhered to, or the process was missing something. The insight that emerged from the research was that the very concept of following a process was not the appropriate paradigm to start with. The key insight is that an organization's structure is more stable, and it is a reflection of the values and principles that drive it.

The difficulty with any process is that in the majority of cases it is foreign to the organizational culture. This is why it is so difficult to bring in a process from the outside. The successful processes are those that emerge from the patterns of interaction and the paths of communication that are at work in the organization. Those patterns and paths determine the social structure of the organization—structure that is founded on the organization's values. Therefore, the values of the organization have a double foundational valence; they determine both what is done and also how it is done (Coplien, 2004).

Also, there is an important difference on the focus of highly productive organizations compared to less productive ones. While the less productive focus on compliance to process, the more productive focus on the product, because they exhibit a strong commitment to satisfaction to customers. This is worth underlining: attention to the delivery of the product is in no way a weakening of the objective of giving attention to the needs of the customer. On the contrary, hyper-productive organizations satisfy customer needs by always being able to quickly and accurately incorporate, and even anticipate, the needs of the customers.

Patterns of productive software development typically have a stronger focus on their *product* than on anything else, because the product embodies strong structural elements which are a reflection of the structure of the organization. An organization that focuses on its products is in reality reflecting on its own structure; therefore, *by improving the product, they are improving their structures* (Coplien, 2004). The patterns not only focus on the product for its own sake, but do so from the viewpoint of facilitating communication, learning, and improving. Communication is the cornerstone of the whole edifice. The patterns are there primarily to create the conditions for effective communication, and that changes the values of the organization itself.

Using patterns in a generative way to evolve organizational structure is an approach that brings huge benefits. However, it is a process that requires a lot of time. Typically some catalyst is needed to make it all happen, like a crisis or some external event (Coplien, 2004). Given most business settings, there simply is not enough time or willpower to undertake such a route deliberately. Fortunately, there is a shortcut: *Scrum*. Scrum offers a foundation for quickly setting up the conditions that *may* lead to more effective structures.

EARLY SIGNS OF SCRUM

The case of Borland QPW had a deep influence on the creation of Scrum. The roles of Project Manager and Product Manager are vital. They stand out very clearly in the QPW team's natural force-based social network diagram. From the diagram, it is *visually* evident how the Project Manager and the Product Manager roles, with their centrality, can be seen as the direct ancestors of the Scrum Master and Product Owner roles of Scrum. If the same diagram is drawn for a Scrum team, the Scrum Master and the Product Owner would be placed in similar positions. In fact, in a later interview,[1] James Coplien stated:

[Jeff Sutherland] in '92 had his first Scrum sprint, and then Jeff came across my article, and after reading the article he introduced daily stand-ups and Scrum Masters into Scrum. Before that there were no daily stand-ups and there were no Scrum Masters.

Coplien himself learned about this through Prof. Ikujiro Nonaka who delivered a keynote talk in 2013, and presented a slide[2] with a timeline of Scrum showing the definitive influence of Coplien's paper on the daily stand-ups and Scrum Masters.

In Scrum there is this dysfunctional notion that the Scrum Master role (in particular) has the purpose to protect[3] the team from interference by management. The Borland Project Manager and Product Manager were more like a delegate or an ambassador representing the viewpoints of leadership in the daily operations of the team. This is very far from the idea, so typical of Scrum, where the Scrum Masters are there to protect the team from management. (We will see later that this idea of Scrum is really antithetic to hyper-productivity; see the section entitled A Counterproductive Role: the Scrum Master starting on page 70 in Chapter 9.)

Another key aspect is the direct involvement of Philippe Kahn, the CEO of the organization. This happened very often in informal ways. Frequently you could see Philippe Kahn having lunch with various team members at the famous Borland Cafeteria. It was famous not only because of its open air space and excellent food,[4] but also because the cafeteria was a key component in the development process.

Certainly for visitors, it must have looked strange to see the CEO of this company (that retained well over one thousand employees) constantly mingle with one team after the other. The Project Manager and Product Manager were the people who had to *represent* the CEO in his absence—their role was definitely not to protect the team from his interference.

Those informal lunches that Philippe Kahn held with the development teams (and all other meetings that happened frequently) were, in fact, the progenitor of Scrum's stand-up meetings. Jeff Sutherland (2007b) states that these daily meetings of Scrum were inspired directly by the case of Borland.

At Borland, the frequency and intensity of meetings was astounding. These meetings could go on for several hours and the majority of the team members' time was spent in such meetings.

The meetings were far from being ineffective; instead, they productively led to better communication and built a shared vision (Coplien, 2004). During those meetings the team kept on improving the architecture and the code, but they also kept improving the process itself. Gabriel (1996) described his surprise in finding that the QPW team had such meetings almost every day, and that they could last several hours. They were not light meetings; they were not about planning and good intentions, but about highly technical issues like architecture, interfaces, algorithms, data structures, and other technical topics. Unlike most meetings in other companies, these meetings were not counterproductive, and absolutely not about protecting turf and seeking credits for results. The more important effect of these frequent and long meetings was to give *everyone* an understanding of *all* changes that were happening or being contemplated.

After the meeting, all engineers could go off and quickly take care of their part of implementation to support the decisions that had been made, which in turn led to quick validation or rejection of any new idea. Furthermore, this open process made architecture a first-class artifact of the whole development effort—effectively leading to its continuous improvement and extension.

The interactions between all members ensued that everyone was aware of what all others were doing, and in particular anybody could understand how their own efforts were contributing to the larger picture. The intensity and depth of conversation gave rise to rich communication patterns between all components of the team. Code reviews, code reading, or code walk-throughs were *rarely* used, if at all, because of this widespread and deep understanding of what was going on. Every member had deep faith in, and respect of, the abilities of their peers, effectively demonstrating how the Community of Trust pattern can have a direct impact on the coding practices of an engineering team. As a consequence of all open discussions, Gabriel (1996) highlights:

> After a year, the team was filled out with technically savvy individuals, even in management and marketing positions.

It is no wonder that Scrum teams, with their attempt at structuring, compressing, and reducing that level of communication and interaction to a few repetitive, ceremonious, and scheduled meetings, have not been able to reproduce the performance level of Borland International.

SCRUM AS PREPACKAGED PATTERNS

Scrum was deeply influenced by Coplien's study of the QPW team. At that time, organizational patterns were still in an embryonic state and being developed by Coplien and his colleagues. Sutherland took the parts from the QPW case, combined it with his own experience in the military and the *New New Development Game* ideas of Takeuchi and Nonaka (Takeuchi, 1986). The result was Scrum.

One of Scrum's major success factors is the simplicity of its constituent components. Explaining the whole of Scrum takes no more than 10-15 minutes. This simplicity is often illustrated with diagrams similar to the one shown in Figure 2.4. It is not coincidental that two of the major elements in this kind of diagram are *Roles* and *Meetings*.[5] Naturally the intent is to facilitate the emergence of productive communication within the development team.

The third element, *Artifacts*, gives the roles the *things* about which conversations can be engaged during the communication. It is evident how all of this relates to Coplien's study, and to the conclusion that the intensity and paths of communication between roles are the secret ingredient to creating productive teams. In a nutshell: *Scrum is successful because it empowers effective and focused communication between few roles.*

Scrum's Rediscovery of Patterns

A few years after its start, after Coplien had started to formalize organizational patterns, and after the first instances of the organizational pattern language were published (Coplien, 1995), Scrum started crossing paths with the pattern movement again.

The patterns that were underlying Scrum's simplicity were identified more explicitly. In Chapter 28 of Harrison (2000), Mike Beedle presented a paper entitled *Scrum: A Pattern*

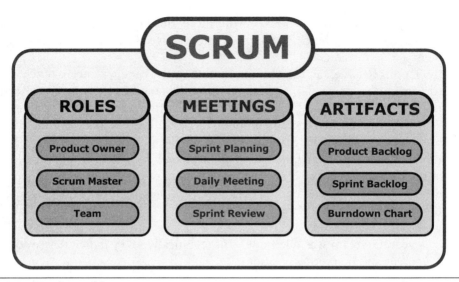

Figure 2.4   Simplicity of Scrum

Language for Hyperproductive Software Development, co-authored also by Ken Schwaber and Jeff Sutherland (and others), where he explained how Scrum could really be considered as a collection of patterns. A revised edition of the paper (Beedle, 2000), presented the same concept, but as an extension to Coplien's organizational patterns. In the summary of that paper, Beedle describes how Scrum can be thought of as an *extension pattern language* which is added to existing organizational pattern languages. The idea is that by *combining* the Scrum patterns with other organizational patterns, you can arrive at high performing software development organizations. Furthermore, the decomposition of Scrum into constituent patterns is also seen as helpful for those organizations that need to adopt only those parts of Scrum that make sense in their particular context.

Maybe the most significant aspect here is the open-ended mindset where Scrum is seen as a collection of patterns which can be selectively applied to a specific situation, and that can be combined with other patterns.

These patterns are now known as *First Level Scrum Patterns*, and were illustrated by Beedle (shown in Figure 2.5), where the light gray boxes are Coplien's organizational patterns and the dark gray boxes are the Scrum patterns.

Later, in 2008, Jeff Sutherland and James Coplien met again, with the intention of better mapping out the organizational patterns with respect to how they appear and actually become constituent elements of Scrum (Coplien, 2008). They identified many more patterns, and represented all of them in a directed graph, where the direction of the arrows indicated which pattern provided the context for another. When comparing the Scrum patterns with those that Coplien (2004) had identified in the Quattro Pro for Windows team, Coplien found a substantial overlap, but also that some patterns were peculiar to Scrum.

Scrumbuts, Blue Pills, and Red Pills

Scrum has enjoyed an overwhelming commercial success. Recently, a respectable business analysis firm reported that well over 80% of all software shops were employing Scrum.

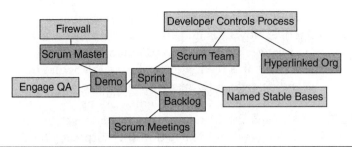

Figure 2.5   First level Scrum patterns

During the last decade many recognized thought-leaders of the Agile movement have adopted Scrum, such as: James Coplien, himself, Alistair Cockburn (founder of the Crystal process), Ron Jeffries (one of the fathers of XP), and many others. Many have proclaimed that *Scrum won the Agile war!* (if there ever was one).

This overwhelming commercial success is partly due to the simplicity of Scrum. It is easy to understand Scrum at least superficially. It is much more difficult to truly apply all principles and (hidden) patterns that underlie those simple rules. For this reason, the term *Scrumbut* has been coined: to capture the situation where a team employs Scrum, but then fails to do some part of it, or replaces some rules and practices with others of their own finding. Quite unsurprisingly, these *Scrumbuts* do not deliver the promises of Scrum.

Coplien and Sutherland acknowledge the problem, and talk about *Blue Pill Scrum* and *Red Pill Scrum*. Blue Pill Scrum is the adoption of the superficial aspects of Scrum, the ceremonies, the roles, etc., without really understanding why they are there and what is supposed to happen in terms of communication dynamics. Red Pill Scrum is when the deep effects of the underlying patterns are entirely internalized by the team. Sutherland (2009b) expresses the difference in terms of potential productivity gains, in terms of Blue Pill being in the range of 10–100% improvement, while Red Pill is in the range of 500–1500% improvement. Blue Pill Scrum involves minimal organizational change, and is often a *Scrumbut* (*Scrum* without all of the practices, *but* with tweaks and modifications). Red Pill Scrum has a deeper organizational impact, often with full involvement of management which becomes proactive. It is quite obvious that Red Pill Scrum is positioned as the gateway to hyper-productivity. Nonetheless, hyper-productivity seems like a difficult target to reach.

Scrum Does Not Lead to Hyper-Productivity

Borland International's methods, as documented by Coplien's study, contributed to the shaping of Scrum. They not only prodded Sutherland into inventing Scrum, but gave rise to two of the landmark practices of Scrum, the stand-up meeting and the key roles of Product Owner and Scrum Master (see the section *Early Signs of Scrum*). In fact, in Sutherland (2011) (and in many other earlier papers by Sutherland), Coplien's paper about the Borland QPW case is acknowledged as triggering the daily stand-up meetings and the Sprint cycle.

With such premises and the huge number of patterns shared with the QPW team, it seems likely that Scrum would easily duplicate the productivity of the QPW team and consistently deliver hyper-productivity, but that is far from being the case.

Scrum has built a great deal of its success on the promise that it will make software organizations more productive. Now, it is undeniably easy to make any traditional software organization improve and deliver an increase in productivity. Scrum can boast about many such cases. That's not a *big deal*. It is the majority of Blue Pill Scrum implementations. The point is, that notwithstanding such improvements, they are all a far cry from achieving hyper-productivity—even with the Red Pill implementations.

Sutherland (2006, 2007, and 2008) made real efforts to get to the hyper-productive state. Yet very few Scrum projects have reached it. It is surprising how small this number is compared to the widespread and popular adoption of Scrum by many software development organizations. Schwaber (2011) explains this by stating that the majority of Scrum teams do not *play it as its rules state*, that is, they employ Blue Pill Scrum rather than Red Pill Scrum. Sutherland himself has acknowledged that hyper-productivity is an outlier, and that the results achieved by Borland International are unlikely to be replicated. In Sutherland (2010a), he uses the *Putnam Productivity Index* to show the results achieved by some of his projects as compared to industry averages *and* to the QPW team. It was clear that Borland's performance is still quite unattainable.

Sutherland (2005) has categorized Scrum in various types (Types 1, 2, and 3) to represent increasing capability levels which correspond to increasing levels of organizational agility. Therefore, it seems important to bring Scrum to the whole organization as such, and not limit its field of action to the development team alone. This is an important insight because it is one of my key tenets for successfully reaching hyper-productivity. Yet very few organizations adopting Scrum are capable of getting anywhere close to hyper-productivity. All the while Borland consistently achieved hyper-productivity across a wide portfolio of products and for a period of several years.

REFERENCES

1. The video of the interview with James Coplien in July 2013 is available at http://scrumology.wistia.com/medias/rvf5po3qfb and the corresponding transcript is available at http://scrumology.com/how-a-bell-labs-researcher-impacted-the-Scrum-framework/
2. The slide referenced by Coplien can be seen on the Scrumology.com website at http://scrumology.com/wp-content/uploads/2013/07/20130827FooCaf%C3%A9.key_.pdf
3. James Coplien informed me in a private e-mail that: *The roles [of Scrum Master and Product Owner] were inspired by the Toyota Chief Engineer, which was split into a product part and a process part. The original goal had nothing to do with protection. That came in the 'governancization' of Scrum by Schwaber in 1995.* However, there is enough evidence in the voluminous Scrum literature that the roles, especially the Scrum Master role, evolved to protect the team from management interference.
4. The Borland Cafeteria introduced to the world the *Turbo Burrito* (in line with all of its *Turbo* ... branded products) which probably can be qualified as a programmer's best type of nutrition, considering the outstanding results that ensued. If Borland's productivity records cannot be reproduced, then maybe that is the real missing secret ingredient.
5. Scrum *Meetings* are also known as Scrum *Events*.

3

THE NATURE OF KNOWLEDGE WORK

Before we can examine the question about how executives and managers might gain a deep understanding of the *nature of knowledge work*, we need to gain that understanding ourselves, no matter what role we have in our own organization. This chapter will focus on the nature of knowledge work, and in particular, how it is represented by software development.

FROM RATIONALISM TO EMPIRICISM

The field of software development is relatively young, but it has progressed quickly. In just a few decades it has undergone maturing processes that have taken much longer in other fields. During the last decade Agile methodologies have gained widespread acceptance, and are becoming mainstream. Transitioning to Agile is undertaken by well-established traditional software development organizations, as well as by more rudimentary cowboy-style development shops. It is interesting to reflect upon why this transitioning is taking place, and what consequences it bears.

Peter Wegner (1997) examines the evolution of computer technology. He is concerned about computational complexity, and about giving proof that interaction cannot be expressed by algorithms, explaining the evolution from *Turing Machines* to *Interaction Machines*, broadening the realm of computability to include interactive computations. His observations provide an interesting perspective and help interpret the reasons behind the transition towards Agile methodologies.

Wegner discusses the evolution from philosophy to the natural sciences—noting how it took 2000 years to go from Plato's ideal world to empiricism, through Descartes, Hume, Hobbes, Hegel, Kant, Marx, Russels, Boole, Hilbert, and Gödel. Wegner states:

> Modern empirical science rejects Plato's belief that incomplete knowledge is worthless.

Managing incompleteness is a key distinguishing mechanism between philosophical rationalism and scientific empiricism. The fact that knowledge work, and software in particular, deals with uncertainty is well established. In this sense, uncertainty can be considered as a lighter form of incompleteness. More importantly, it can even be thought of as a concrete manifestation of incompleteness, and in particular, a form of incompleteness that can be experienced by human intellect and psychology. Uncertainty is part of everyone's everyday experience. Uncertainty is more concrete and tangible than rational ideas.

Uncertainty, Incompleteness, and Wegner's Lemma

Uncertainty is inherent in software development, as noted by many scholars. Watts Humphrey exposed the *Requirements Uncertainty Principle* (Humphrey, 1995):

> For a new software system, the requirements will not be completely known until after the users have used it.

Hadar Ziv expressed the *Maxim of Uncertainty in Software Engineering* (a.k.a. *Ziv's MUSE*) in 1996:

> Uncertainty is inherent and inevitable in software development processes and products.

Earlier, Harlan Mills came to the conclusion in 1972:

> There is no such thing as an absolute proof of logical correctness. There are only degrees of rigor [...] which are each informal descriptions of mechanisms for creating agreement and belief in a process of reasoning.

A notable consequence of Mill's statement is that uncertainty is implied by the need of reaching *agreement* and *belief*. These two words naturally carry the significance that social and psychological aspects are relevant; and therein lies one of the natural success factors of Agile approaches, as we shall see shortly.
   Wegner (1997) remarked that:

> Before Gödel, the conventional wisdom of computer scientists assumed that proving correctness was possible (in principle) and simply needed greater effort and better theorem provers.

Then Wegner articulates the most powerful statement, later formalized mathematically and known as **Wegner's Lemma** in 1999:

> Incompleteness implies that proving correctness of interactive models is not merely difficult, but impossible.

Naturally, having a mathematical proof that it is impossible to prove the correctness of computer programs has paramount consequences for computability—but there's more. Wegner's studies about the consequences of combining interaction with computational incompleteness also bear monumental consequences on the approach to problem solving. Wegner (2006) compares approaches, and notices that traditional ones restrict problem solving to thinking and question-answering, but one should recognize that:

> [There are] interactive forms of problem solving that depend on the behavior of the world rather than on *a priori* human beliefs.

Problem solving proceeds through interactive forms that are affected by the behavior of the world. Like the statement of Mills, Wegner's statement (when considering humans in addition to computers proper) bears the implications that bring in the dimension of sociology (interactive forms) and psychology (behavior).

It follows that software development and knowledge work are an inherent social and psychological human activity, and therefore they must be managed with approaches that not only take into account, but also actually take advantage of the social and psychological dimensions.

RATIONALE FOR EMPIRICISM IN KNOWLEDGE WORK

Agile methods acknowledge the role of interactivity, both between humans participating in the process, and between humans and the systems under development. Notably, one of the principles of the *Agile Manifesto* (Beck, 2001) is about "valuing individuals and interactions [over processes and tools]." This principle implies the broadening of the scope of concern of any agile methodology to include psychology (individuals) and sociology (interactions), and therefore such an approach becomes more comprehensive than conventional—a purely technical approach.

Agile, by taking into account psychology and sociology, covers incomplete (pun unintended!) areas of traditional approaches.

Interactions Demand Empiricism

Jeff Sutherland, the founder of the Scrum methodology, often cites Humphrey's Requirements Uncertainty Principle, Ziv's MUSE, and Wegner's Lemma as theoretical foundations for Scrum. Sutherland exposes a powerful conclusion, referring to Wegner's Lemma, and states (Sutherland, 2001):

> Here was mathematical proof that any process that assumed known inputs [...] was doomed to failure.

In the same vein, Schwaber (2001) describes how Scrum was conceived as an empirical process contrasting simpler *defined* processes, and refers to a process expert (Babatunde, 1994):

> It is typical to adopt the defined (theoretical) modeling approach when the underlying mechanisms by which a process operates are reasonably well understood. When the process is too complicated for the defined approach, the empirical approach is the appropriate choice.

On such basis, Schwaber suggests that an empirical approach is more appropriate.

EMPIRICISM IN STRATEGIC MANAGEMENT AND ARCHITECTURE

Just as incompleteness caused the evolution from rationalism to modern empirical science, one could interpret that incompleteness is playing a similar role in propelling the transition from traditional methods to Agile ones. While invoking the transitioning from rationalism to empiricism as an explanation of the transitioning from traditional to Agile methodologies might seem far-fetched, there are other more recent, contemporary precedents to support this as a general trend.

In Goldin (2006), Andrea Omcini observes that interaction is a critical aspect in understanding complex systems, and it has emerged as a key approach in fields such as biology, physics, social, and organizational sciences. In Nerur (2007), Sridar Nerur observes how the conceptual shift from traditional to Agile has been experienced in other fields, like architecture and strategic management. In architecture, design problems were originally treated as a well-defined sequence of steps that had to be spelled out and followed. However, Nerur observed that iterative design approaches, with cycles of analysis and synthesis generating continuous feedback and communication between all phases, were used as early as 1963.

More significantly, with regards to strategic management, Nerur noticed a shift from a mechanistic viewpoint to one that reckons uncertainty and complexity. Contemporary approaches to strategic management have abandoned the notion that the world is unchanging and foreseeable, and replaced analysis and reasoning with incremental learning, participatory decision making, and feedback—effectively transforming strategy formulation into an emergent process. This was a dynamic process of problem solving, with iterative cycles and stakeholder involvement; the same kind of process that can also be seen in software development.

We will come back to the significance of empirical approaches in strategic management in the next chapters of this part of the book because they are the key to bridging the daily work of top executives to the management of a software development or knowledge-work organization. For the moment, it becomes crucially important to fully understand and internalize the conclusion of Wegner (1997), that the key is in recognizing incompleteness as inescapable, and hence the necessity of moving from rationalism to empiricism.

As explained by Nerur (2007), contemporary management theories already incorporate concepts and approaches that are typically inspired by empiricism. So it is promising to realize that those in charge of strategic management should be able to understand and relate to these conclusions and then act accordingly.

It stands to reason that because knowledge work demands empiricism, any management approach that intends to deal with knowledge work must be compatible with an empirical approach. Most contemporary management approaches are inherently deterministic rather than empirical. For instance, the widespread use of budgets and budgeting is an example of deterministic, *a priori* thinking about future outcomes. Notwithstanding that strategy making is within the realm of empiricism, looking beyond strategic management, all the rest of operational management is *not* attuned to empiricism. The conclusion is: management has to embrace empiricism.

4

MANAGEMENT'S PROFOUND UNDERSTANDING OF KNOWLEDGE WORK

The evolution of Scrum, arguably the most successful Agile method, has developed to the point where its proponents (and in particular Scrum's original founder, Jeff Sutherland) are actively trying to extend the use of Scrum to the organization as a whole, and not limit it to the development team alone. This is important, as it highlights a significant deficiency in Scrum: the lack of complete support for it by the entire organization and its leader.

A hyper-productive team can only exist within an organization that supports the team's effort *entirely*. The kind of organizational support that is required can only be found if the two noble patterns of *Unity of Purpose* and *Community of Trust* are pervasively present throughout the entire organization. For this to happen, it is necessary that the Chief Executive Officer (CEO) (or business owner) step up to a role of truly enlightened leadership, and that the organization as a whole stands behind the initiative.

We will say more about the importance of leadership later. We will also examine what is required for the organization and the team. For now, though, we want to focus on another dimension that is a precondition to enlightened leadership—that of *profound knowledge*.

PROFOUND UNDERSTANDING OF THE FUNDAMENTAL PROCESS

Deming, one of the most important thinkers about business and management, is known for sustaining the need for developing a profound understanding (Deming, 1993) about your business. It is of essence to possess a theory of knowledge about the *entire system* that constitutes your business.

It follows that anyone who owns, or is in charge of, a knowledge producing business, should have a *profound knowledge* about such knowledge development. In the case of software businesses, this is seldom the case. Except for those companies that were founded, grown, and led by individuals with a software development background, the majority of companies where software development is a critical part of business are led by people who do *not* have a software development background.

Unsurprisingly, in these cases, the obvious reaction to the claim that managers should have a profound knowledge about *software* is a total dismissal of the concept. The idea is deemed to be too technical, unrealistic, or unworkable and this is entirely justified because the impression is that managers need to know about all the technicalities and intricacies of that huge body of knowledge which is collected under the term of computer science and software engineering.

This impression, though, is a fallacy and in itself a misunderstanding. The assumption that a profound understanding about software development (or other knowledge-based work) requires deep technical knowledge is without any foundation.

The CEO and all of senior management can develop a profound knowledge about the nature of the knowledge-based process, without possessing any technical notion at all. In fact, those in charge of business management already possess the required skills and abilities to do so; but they lack the awareness about it.

The intent of what we are trying to achieve here is to make business managers aware of the fact that they are already *capable* of stepping up to the leadership role that is required of them to transform a knowledge-based organization into a hyper-productive one. People in upper management simply need to develop the awareness about themselves already possessing such capability and knowledge, and then consistently apply that insight to the management of the knowledge-producing organization. These are two distinct challenges, because creating awareness alone is not enough—managers must also develop the willingness to deliberately apply these capabilities to the daily management of the organization. Unfortunately, ingrained practices are working against this.

THE WICKED PROBLEM OF STRATEGY MAKING

The first step is to establish a frame of reference which can be recognized by management as something they already know and have deep familiarity with. We will look into *strategy making*. Surprisingly, strategy making has many things in common with knowledge-work processes.

In a Harvard Business Review article, Camillus (2008) presents a convincing interpretation of the nature of strategy making. Strategy making is seen as a *wicked problem*. The distinguishing trait of wicked problems is that they cannot be solved; yet it is possible to deal with them. Strategists handle such problems in practice.

Wicked problems were first described by Rittel (1973) and later by Conklin (2005). Wicked problems can be recognized because they are characterized by 10 properties which were described by Camillus (2008) as follows:

1. **There is no definitive formulation.** Unlike ordinary problems, wicked problems cannot be described by a precise *problem statement*.
2. **There is no stopping rule.** Unlike ordinary problems, which cease to exist once a solution has been found, wicked problems are ongoing, and the search for a solution never stops.
3. **There are no clear-cut solutions.** Unlike ordinary problems, wicked problems do not have solutions that can be impartially considered right or wrong. There might be multiple solutions, and the choice is ultimately a judgment call.

4. **Solutions cannot be tested.** Unlike ordinary problems, where the correctness of a solution can be proven immediately, the ways in which wicked problems are addressed have different consequences over time. It is difficult to evaluate their effectiveness.

5. **Solutions are "one-shot" operations.** Unlike ordinary problems, where solutions can be tried and dropped and it is possible to progress through trial and error, with wicked problems every attempted solution will bring about irreversible consequences.

6. **Solutions are not enumerable.** Unlike ordinary problems, which can be described through an exhaustive list of potential solutions, wicked problems can have an undefined number of potential solutions.

7. **A wicked problem is incomparable.** Unlike ordinary problems, which can be classified together with other similar ones for which there are similar solutions, a wicked problem is *one-of-a-kind*. Experience does not help resolving wicked problems, as there are no precedents.

8. **Wicked problems imply other problems.** Unlike ordinary problems, which are self-contained, wicked problems coexist with other problems; and there is no one single root cause that can be identified.

9. **Wicked problems have multiple representations.** Unlike ordinary problems, which can be described by a single uncontroversial statement, wicked problems can have multiple representations. Different stakeholders will have different perceptions and ideas of the problem and its causes.

10. **There is no right to be wrong.** Planners confronting wicked problems cannot afford failure because the impact of decisions will be so large and actions will be so costly that the problem solver will be held liable.

Camillus provides the caveat that these 10 properties should not be taken as criteria testing for wickedness; they should be considered as guidelines to allow one to judge if a problem is wicked. What is most striking is that there invariably is a social dimension that contributes to the wickedness. Camillus observes that wicked problems are more likely to appear when companies are exposed to major changes or extraordinary challenges. Notably, this all happens in a social context. The *degree of disagreement* among stakeholders is a sign of the wickedness of the problem. Hence, wicked problems are difficult to deal with not only because of the technical difficulties, but also because of all social complexity they cause. Camillus sees confusion, discord, and lack of progress as signs that an issue could be wicked.

Unsurprisingly, *social context, disagreement among stakeholders,* and *social complexity* are all traits that characterize all knowledge work and software development projects in particular as soon as we look beyond the technical field proper. In the field of software development, wicked problems have been recognized by Degrace (1990), and are ordinarily dealt with by practitioners in a number of ways. These are the key features that will allow executive management to recognize that they do indeed have not only familiarity, but also a deep understanding of the fundamental processes involved in knowledge work and software development because strategy making is typically a wicked problem.

Coping with Wicked Problems

With regards to strategy-related issues, Camillus identifies five characteristics that reveal the presence of a wicked problem:

1. There are many stakeholders with different values and priorities.
2. Causes are complex and tangled.
3. The problem is difficult to comprehend and changes with every attempt to address it.
4. The challenge has no precedent.
5. There's nothing to indicate the right answer to the problem.

Camillus advises coping with wicked problems in an illuminating and simple way. It is necessary to involve stakeholders, to make sure that all opinions are listened to, and to facilitate communications. Rather than becoming more systematic, companies can use social-planning processes and aim at generating a shared understanding of the issue and promoting a joint commitment about potential resolutions to try. Disagreement will be inevitable—the objective is to let stakeholders appreciate one another's positions. They should be able to reason about the different interpretations, and work collaboratively toward resolution. It is not only a matter of obtaining the ideas and opinions of all stakeholders; it is also a matter of involving them to find the solutions. Giving space to everybody to air their ideas helps to generate new perspectives, develops collective intelligence, and counters group-thinking and cognitive biases. The group as a whole will be better at confronting the problem than the individuals alone. Stakeholder involvement complicates coordination and planning, yet it increases the potential for creative solutions. The result is also buy-in and support from all involved parties.

Camillus further stresses the importance of actually documenting stakeholder's assumptions, ideas, and concerns as a means of communicating about the plans; and the planning process is seen as a vehicle for communication.

Empiricism at the Heart of Strategy Making

Since the world is complex, it is impossible to know which strategies will work and which won't, let alone what consequences might come out of them. Effective strategy making is less deterministic, and more empirical. Camillus explains that companies should experiment with a number of feasible strategies, even when the outcomes are very uncertain.

There is a risk that all strategists run, because the outcome might be counterproductive and lead to analysis-paralysis. This is exacerbated by the nature of a wicked problem, because every attempt at addressing it will alter it, and hence require yet another change in strategy. The risk is to keep analyzing forever, rather than doing something.

Therefore the best approach is empirical. It is better to test some strategy, and consider it as a starting point. The outcomes will reveal more information about the problem at hand. In other words, smart companies deal with wicked problems by running experiments and then learning from the mistakes they will inevitably make. Companies should encourage risk taking, even in the face of business failures. Unexpected, unsatisfactory outcomes contribute to the necessary organizational learning. As we will see, this kind of advice is what is practiced when strategy making takes the concrete form of an emergent, iterative process.

Such a process has a profound social learning dimension at its heart. Organizational learning processes are at the heart of strategy making; likewise, they are at the heart of knowledge work. Recognizing this is the essence of executive management's gaining awareness of themselves already possessing the capabilities needed to manage a knowledge-based organization. What they need to understand and acknowledge is that knowledge work is really about organizational learning (and not only about technical and intricate topics). Let's see how we can gain that insight, with the help of two different approaches: one stems from economic theories and another from the parallel with collaborative performance arts.

CAPITAL GOODS AND SOCIAL LEARNING PROCESSES

The majority of business managers have a background in economics. Many will have earned MBAs, and have familiarity with economic theories. There are many economic theories, and most seem unrelated to knowledge work or software development. Luckily, there are some that have profound significance with respect to what happens (or should happen) in a healthy knowledge-work organization. Let's examine one economic theory's view of a software development organization, which we consider as representative of any knowledge-work organization.

In Baetjer (1998) we find the viewpoint of a capital theorist of the Austrian School—the viewpoint that software products are considered as capital goods. According to this school of thinking, any capital goods are an embodiment of knowledge. Specifically it is knowledge about how to execute some kind of production.

Because goods are seen as embodied knowledge, there is an important social dimension involved in their development; a social dimension that centers around organizational learning. The reason is that such knowledge is spread among many individuals, and mostly it is tacit, incomplete, and continuously in a state of change. New capital goods are necessarily developed through a process that is a social learning process, which brings the accumulated knowledge to fruition.

The need to capture this dispersed knowledge through a social learning process and embed that knowledge into a product or service is, in essence, the high-level process that governs the development of any knowledge-based product or service. Management executives need to internalize this insight, and thereby become aware of the fact that the process they use for strategy making (the social learning process), is really the same process they should use for managing any knowledge-based organization.

Knowledge about Product and about Process

Baetjer (1998) further extends the connection with capital-goods theory by examining the structure of capital goods and the relationships between capital goods. The relationships between capital goods can be considered as:

- A relationship of **complementarity**: when different capital goods are used together.
- A relationship of **dependency**: when one capital good is used to produce another.

The categories of capital goods mentioned are two: fixed capital and working capital. In the early days of computing, things were simple. The programming language (and its compiler) was the only fixed capital to care about. There were no intermediary artifacts to work with. Programmers literally started with a blank screen.

However, that has changed today with an increasing variety of programming tools and software technologies. Now even working capital can be recognized in the form of class libraries, design patterns, components, services, and many other artifacts which can be used directly or adapted for the programmer's intent.

Recognizing a distinction between fixed capital and working capital in the software development process suggests this important viewpoint: all software infrastructures (such as operating systems, database management systems, networking software, etc.) chosen to support your business can be classified as working capital that is used for producing your business software solution. A similar consideration can be made with respect to all digital tools and digital representations that are commonly used in knowledge-work.

In addition to complementarity and dependency, a third significant relationship is identified as the relationship between the items of capital goods and the knowledge about the process needed to produce them.

This last point is very significant as it highlights the importance of knowledge in the capital goods theory. The knowledge is not only that which is embedded into the products being made, but it is also that knowledge that is about the process used to make the products. The entire infrastructure (your technology stack) is ordinarily considered as an asset that you acquire; but in this economic theory it is considered as working capital.

It is like the raw material that you transform by developing your own work (code, in the case of software) on top of it, adding economic value. The technology stack can be considered as the input to your transformation process, while the product or service delivered is the result of the labor of your organization (whereby with organization we mean anybody involved in the transformation process, and not only the engineering or hands-on teams proper).

The labor that realizes this transformation process is effectively the transformation of dispersed knowledge represented by the collective mind of your organization into embodied knowledge that is encoded by the product or service being delivered. The transformation process itself results from the application of the collective knowledge about the production process.

Capturing all of this collective knowledge from the individual intellects involved implies a social learning process, whereby the knowledge is transferred, elaborated, and enhanced between individuals before it finally becomes a tangible product or a service that can be experienced by customers. At the same time, the collective mind of the organization will develop knowledge about the process it employs.

STRATEGY MAKING, ARTFUL MAKING, AND SOFTWARE DEVELOPMENT

The insight to be gained is that management needs to recognize that the fundamental process involved is the one of social learning. It is refreshing that a capital theorist states that producing software is essentially a social learning process. It is also notable that this happened three years before the Agile Manifesto (Beck, 2001) was published.

The social learning dimension in software development has been highlighted by many proponents of Agile methodologies. Most notably, Cockburn (2001) sustains:

> [Software development is] a cooperative game of invention and communication.

This aspect, the cooperative game of invention and communication, is what allows us to bridge software development not only to the theoretical economic model of capital goods theory which might be familiar to some managers, but also and more important for the practical consequences to the actual daily experience that managers have. In fact, senior management is very familiar with social learning processes and cooperative games of invention and communication because this is exactly what they engage in when formulating, executing, and validating their business strategies. Managers proceed through an emergent and iterative process, which can be thought of as shown in Figure 4.1.

An informal corporate model for strategy development often follows these four steps. The model is informal, because it is not explicitly exposed, manifest, or defined. The four steps often materialize with activities along these lines:

1. Mid-managers research the subject.
2. Mid-managers present their ideas to senior managers.
3. The proposals are discussed with senior managers; new ideas might emerge and get incorporated in the proposed strategy.
4. The process repeats.

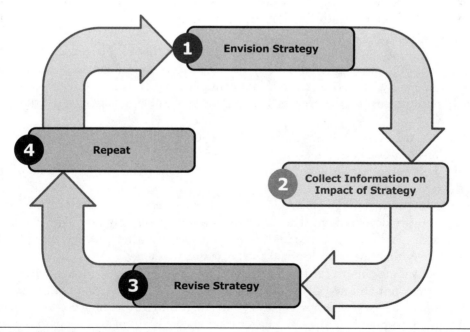

Figure 4.1 Strategy making

What is striking here, is that this management process is in essence very agile—though the resulting strategies might not always be as agile as the process itself. This strategy-making process can be compared to how the collaborative performance arts develop their plays:

1. Actors prepare for their roles.
2. Actors meet frequently to rehearse the emerging play.
3. The director and actors discuss each piece of the work as just experienced.
4. The process repeats.

While being developed through an apparently chaotic process, which involves frequent social interactions, all these collaborative performance arts are nonetheless extremely reliable, and deliver what is expected. The show that is not ready by the opening night will not be long-lived.

The connection with collaborative performance arts is significant. The processes employed are not master planned, but are iterative and emergent. Naturally the similarity connects to how agile software development processes typically unroll:

1. Developers discuss with customers concerning what the software should do, and then write some code.
2. Developers regularly build the system into an executable program that can be run, demoed, tested, and used.
3. Developers and customers discuss the episode of the last run, presenting any new ideas about change.
4. The process repeats.

The same kind of iterative and emergent process can be found in all knowledge work. The essence of all of these iterative and emergent processes is a loop that looks like the one shown in Figure 4.2.

It is in the third step, reconception and adaptation, that all plans and actions are *re-thought* by taking into consideration any new information, changes, or learning that has happened in reality. The process of rethinking implies exploring new directions, and trying again, basically repeating the process. It also implies learning, acceptance of criticism, and reflexivity.

In essence, this is a high-level feedback loop whereby the process adapts to reality, and a final working solution emerges, eventually. In the unrolling iterations of this loop, the social learning process that produces the capital goods (the knowledge-based product or service, in our case) takes place.

We see here that strategy making is very similar to collaborative performance arts, and to Agile software development. Therefore, it should be natural for company executives to embrace agility as an obvious mode of operations because they practice an agile process each and every time they develop, and then execute, a strategy.

Notwithstanding the preexisting profound understanding of the fundamental process, management is not able to put it into practice. It is unfortunate that despite appreciating the utility of feedback loops in strategy making, they get lost once the strategies are actually put into practice by line managers and staff. Often, management promotes the

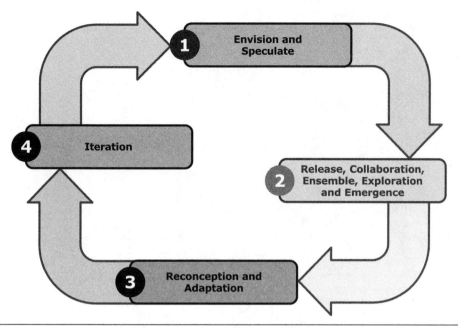

Figure 4.2   Iterative emergent process

operational use of more stringently defined processes which fundamentally hinder any learning to happen in the first place, even though learning is essential.

Senior executives who are successful at strategy making possess the essence of what is needed to successfully manage a knowledge-based organization. They know how to create strategies; they know that constant communication is imperative; they know that all of this is achieved through a social process of organizational learning. Now they need to acknowledge, internalize, and put into practice the concept that managing a knowledge-based organization is essentially the same as strategy making.

There are two powerful forces that prevent management from effectively leading a knowledge-based organization—their own (negative) attitude towards fostering a learning organization, and the conventional ways of exercising financial responsibility. In the next chapters we will see the implications of this and possible ways to overcome the impasse.

5

MANAGEMENT'S RESPONSIBILITY AND LEARNING ORGANIZATION

The outcome of the social learning process is not only the collective knowledge about the problem and solution domain (and obviously about the resulting product or service), but also the collective knowledge about the process by which the product is made.

The two levels of knowledge—one about the product being made, and one about the way the product is made—find a parallel in Chris Argyris' *Double-Loop Organizational Learning Theory*. Most organizations are skilled at improving and/or innovating their products and services, but few organizations truly exercise reflective introspection to improve or innovate their own processes. The former apply single-loop learning, while the latter apply double-loop learning.

PROCESS INNOVATION AND DOUBLE-LOOP LEARNING

One of the most spectacular cases of double-loop learning comes from Toyota, with their Toyota Production System, where innovation happened first and foremost in the processes employed. Toyota came late to the automotive industry (compared to incumbents like Ford and GM). Lateness notwithstanding, Toyota became the industry leader mainly through process innovation, rather than product innovation. Another company that has achieved spectacular results through process innovation is Zara, the Spanish clothing retailer. These two companies demonstrate the power of innovation in the processes involved.

To be able to exercise process innovation, an organization must not only be able to think about the problems they need to solve, but they must be able to *think about how they think* about those problems. According to Argyris (1991), in a landmark article aptly entitled *Teaching Smart People How to Learn*, it is very easy to confuse learning with problem solving. While problem solving is certainly essential, it is putting attention on finding and fixing errors in the external environment. True learning happens when the focus is inward. Managers must reflect on themselves and how they behave; and especially how they might inadvertently be the cause of the problems. Only with such insight will they find motivation to change. They must mature the wisdom that their way of looking at and addressing problems might be a problem in its own right.

In order to become hyper-productive, an organization must learn how to exercise double-loop learning, and not only improve their products, but also the processes that they employ. Argyris (1978) sustains that double-loop learning is even more necessary in rapidly changing and uncertain conditions like today's typical markets, in order to make informed decisions. Decisions must not only be informed, but they must be taken with the right knowledge, and the right knowledge can only be acquired through learning. In Argyris (1977), we find a revealing statement about how organizational learning takes place. Basically, it is about detecting and correcting errors. An error is defined as any part of knowledge or knowing that inhibits learning. Thus, the real errors are not in the problems, but in the knowledge that one has about them.

A double-loop learning organization is, therefore, one that corrects any dysfunction that impedes further and deeper learning; any dysfunction that impedes the full development of Deming's *profound understanding* of what the organization is (deliberately and knowingly) doing. One such major dysfunction is often found at the top of the organization.

THE EXECUTIVE'S ACHILLES' HEEL

In the previous chapter we discovered how company management has the ability to lead knowledge-based organizations because that ability is what they ordinarily exercise in strategy making. While management might be made aware of their possessing such ability (used in strategy making), one real obstacle is their deeply rooted unwillingness to deliberately exercise those abilities in the different context of managing the knowledge-based organization.

Dealing with Failure

A learning organization becomes such only if top management is willing to learn. More specifically in our case, is the willingness to learn to apply their ability in a different context. Unfortunately, most top managers are *not* willing to undertake this learning. A major impediment is deeply rooted in their view of themselves, and in the very fact that they are (usually) successful professionals. Argyris (1991) explains that professionals excel at single-loop learning. Most of their academic and professional life is spent acquiring mastery of some knowledge-based discipline, and then applying it to the real world. Professionals become very successful in their disciplines; and this also means that they rarely experience failure. By rarely failing, professionals have not learned how to deal with failure, let alone learn from failure. When their single-loop learning habits fail, professionals tend to become defensive. Criticism is not accepted, and others except themselves are found to blame. The learning ability becomes inactive, exactly when it is needed most.

The inability to reckon, deal with, and learn from failure is a major impediment; it is the executive's *Achilles' heel*. It impedes reflective improvement. The power of double-loop learning happens only if it becomes the true reflective, reconceiving practice; otherwise there will be no real improvement. Martin (2012) observes that when failure happens, managers will rarely consider how they, themselves, might have contributed to the problem. Instead, they seek the causes outside themselves, and tend to blame others (employees, customers, lack of time, and resources) and convince themselves that any such causes are beyond their control. So, instead of accepting and learning from failures, they set themselves up to repeat them again and again.

Defensive Reasoning

In the case of executive management, and in the quest of reaching hyper-productivity, managers will often gain the insight that the way they ordinarily manage a knowledge-based organization is the foremost *cause* of that organization's poor performance. This insight might be too much to muster. Rather than humbly admitting fault, and learning how to manage appropriately, managers will fall into defensiveness. One common reason for defensiveness is related to feelings of embarrassment and guilt. According to Argyris (1991) managers are uncomfortable with the idea of examining their own role critically. Often the idea of being inadequate while being well paid creates this sense of guiltiness.

However, it is not only about feeling guilty; usually this is combined with fear of failure. Top managers set very high standards—even and especially for themselves. They have had successful careers, and hence seldom experienced and dealt with failure. In other words, they have never had the opportunity to develop a tolerance for failure and the feelings thereof, let alone the skills to deal with such feelings. This makes managers not only fear failure, but also *fear the fear* itself on an emotional level because they are very aware that they cannot cope with it as they cope with all other challenges in their professional lives.

Change Has to Start at the Top

The defensive behavior of top executives will contaminate the whole organization; defensiveness becomes a reflexive routine and spreads to all subordinates, effectively institutionalizing defensive routines. In such an environment, learning is impeded because nobody is capable of admitting the need to learn anything at all. It is therefore management's highest responsibility to become capable of learning. Argyris (1991) exhorts about starting the change at the top. If that does not happen, then top managers will not develop ownership for any change that might originate from below. The transforming of reasoning patterns coming from below will appear strange, and even perilous or threatening to the top executives. The situation deteriorates; the senior managers will be stuck in believing they care by ignoring or overruling the challenges (according to the incumbent reasoning patterns). Yet the subordinates will perceive that as defensive behavior.

The enlightened leader will not only be open to learn, but will also encourage subordinates to confront him and expose leadership mistakes and failures. Without an open dialog, learning will not take place. Argyris (1991) warns that unless top managers develop an awareness of their own defensive reasoning and counterproductive behavior, there will be no effective improvement. Any change initiative will be just a short-lived fantasy.

PROMOTING OPENNESS AND DIALOGUE

Naturally, for any change to be effective it has to be connected to real business problems and results. However, before any such results can be seen, the change in culture, mentality, and attitude has to percolate down through the entire organization. Managers must not only (re)learn how to learn, but must also foster a work environment that encourages learning. They should encourage their subordinates to talk about any issues that have never been addressed before because it was perceived as being not politically correct. It might take time for this to happen, but the results are within reach, and worth pursuing. Argyris insists that managers must have the determination to persevere. In the long run, the organization will become more open, and will be able to create more choices for flexibility and adaptation. It becomes the norm to question anyone's reasoning; and anyone would accept that the questioning is not an expression of mistrust, but a means to promote collective learning.

In a commentary in Argyris (1991), Harmidous Tsoukas refers to this kind of organization as a post-modern organization. In such an organizational environment, individuals are more fully engaged and freely present their ideas and show their feelings. The daily decisions of all employees create an environment that is rich in information which develops with doubts and challenges. Decision making is more frequent, and further spread throughout the entire organization. There are more places, times, and opportunities for employees to make decisions. This kind of "informated" workspace is the fertile ground for the organization to develop into a reflexive organization. There are more moments to feed back, and reflect on, the information about how the organization is performing its business, and about the results that it achieves. For all this to happen, employees must feel free to question and express doubt about any aspect of the organization. This kind of organization does not need to defend the archetype of *macho* management, which is foreign to doubting and uncertainty. In this new kind of organization, doubt, disputes, and reflexivity are essential aspects that foster collective learning. A knowledge-based organization must obviously advocate the discovery and exchange of ideas. Yet, for ideas to develop, criticism and debate are necessary. That is why it is so important to create space for criticism and reflexivity; it is at the heart of healthy organizational learning.

Tsoukas goes even further and invites knowledge workers to undertake a moral task. Yes, they all need to accept criticism, validate ideas against evidence, and gain the insight that often they, themselves, are part of the problems they have to resolve. Yet, at the end, all this is a matter of everyone's individual responsibility to develop such an acceptance. Thus, it is a moral issue.

6

DISCOVERY DRIVEN PLANNING

We concluded the previous chapter with Tsoukas' exhortation about management's *moral* task of being open to criticism. Argyris called attention to how successful managers are challenged when they need to learn; and in particular when they are exposed to criticism that might highlight failures in their actions or thinking. This brings us to the crux of the matter with respect to management's critical role in guiding a knowledge-based organization in general, and leading it to hyper-productivity. While senior executives do possess the ability to manage a knowledge-based organization (as we saw when looking into their ways of handling strategy making), they do not exercise that ability in practice, and hence are a prime cause in their organization's poor performance. Executives need to be open to learning about this insight; and then learn how to overcome their own, self-imposed limitation. Executives need to learn how to reason productively upon their own role and the consequences of their thinking and acting.

They have to face and resolve an inherent conflict related to their actual management practices in use, compared to the insight and the gaining of awareness about their actual ability to master the fundamental processes governing a knowledge-based organization. These are instances of Argyris' conflict between the espoused and the in-use Theory of Action.

A LATENT CONFLICT

The insight that the overall process governing knowledge-based methodology is *emergent* and *iterative*, and driven by social learning through communication and interaction between all parties involved, leads naturally to a more empirical style of management, wherein even financial responsibility needs to be exercised differently; it also needs to become emergent and iterative.

Buy or Create Knowledge

The conventional perspective of standard capital investment, where you buy equipment or assets, is no longer useful, as it does not match the emergent and iterative process.

Investments in knowledge-work are more similar to the funding of new ventures, where you invest in order to buy or create knowledge.

The empirical, emergent, and iterative process has to be applied to the investment process as well, because full qualification of costs and benefits at the start cannot be expected, for the obvious reason that all knowledge is not available at that time. That knowledge will be acquired in due course, through all communication, interaction, and discovery that happens during the social-learning process by means of which a knowledge-based product or service is created.

The insight must be gained whereby it becomes understood and acceptable that funding must become iterative and incremental. It is only by this way that financial investments can be exercised in a responsible manner with respect to the need to reconceive and adapt in the emergent, iterative process that is the essence of a knowledge process.

Management's Conflict: Plan or Experiment?

While management might indeed attain the understanding that it makes sense for funding to become iterative and incremental, and might even recognize the parallel with how they perform strategy making, conventional financial management assumes a definitively more deterministic stance: usually by proceeding through conventional budgeting practices and up-front qualification of full costs for the development of the entire project. (This happens even in the majority of those shops that have adopted Agile approaches.)

A better approach to exercising financial responsibility is one that is more empirical, hence making it compatible with the nature of knowledge-work. The knowledge that eventually emerges through this kind of process is the knowledge that will allow a knowledge-based business to step up to hyper-productivity. McGrath (2010) observes that in traditional strategic planning, success is measured by how close forecasts come to actuals, and concludes that this is *nonsensical* when there is a high level of uncertainty. An astute insight is that if anyone could precisely predict outcomes despite uncertainty, then most likely even the competition would be able to do so and there would be no tangible benefit in the prediction.

In McGrath (1995) the concept was presented in even more incisive terms. When there is uncertainty and complexity, traditional planning and control can become counterproductive. In a low uncertainty environment, future outcomes can be projected from the past; scope of effort can be sized, investment levels can be determined, timelines can be established. In such a static world, holding managers accountable for meeting the numbers is sound logic. However, when uncertainty starts to increase, you face the risk of people favorably distorting the estimates. In fact that is what ordinarily happens; so the numbers that had little or no foundation to begin with, get even more insignificant. Yet they will be hit and managers will appear to be performing their duties well.

Because knowledge-work is an empirical process, exploration and risk taking must be favored rather than avoided; it is in the failing of the experiments that learning happens and value is created. Conventional risk aversion is counterproductive. McGrath (1995) elaborates on the idea that you want to avoid causing people to fear taking even small risks because of their inability of predicting outcomes. It is important to prevent people from feeling as if they failed, especially when their work actually created knowledge and deeper understanding that could have greater potential than the missed forecast. This is underlying the rationale supporting a planning approach that concedes that uncertainty is a fact of life and accepts that outcomes can be different from what was planned. More importantly, it supports a disciplined management approach that works notwithstanding high degrees of uncertainty.

Failure must be considered as an inescapable part of the process, and not an exception to it. The approach must nurture learning. Therefore, rather than insisting that managers hit the numbers, discipline should be exercised with respect to expenditure levels, bringing out the assumptions that support the decisions taken, and promoting awareness about exhausting all ways to gain relevant knowledge before taking commitments that might be irreversible.

An empirical approach will allow the organization to learn as much as possible, at the lowest possible cost. Experimentation promotes hyper-productivity and competitiveness; and experimentation feeds back into the process itself, promoting continuous improvement. In this sense, experimentation is not only critical in terms of knowledge discovery, it becomes an effective source of competitive differentiation. Those organizations that become better at conducting experiments and gaining a better conceptual model (specifically, knowledge) about their competitive domain will be able to move more quickly than their competitors.

It is unfortunate that the majority of managers are not experienced in managing under high uncertainty (as when starting new companies). They are well versed in running established and stable companies, but the methods that work for established companies do not work for managing knowledge-based companies. The best way to run a knowledge-based organization is as though it is in a perennial start-up mode.

THE DISCOVERY DRIVEN PLANNING APPROACH

When senior executives gain the insight about the validity of an empirical approach to management, and the time comes to put it into practice, this is when deep internal conflicts arise. Because the business has been driven successfully to its current state through its current management practices, it is assumed that those practices are appropriate. In most cases, any suggestion to change them will be welcomed by fierce defensive reaction, despite any espoused, reckoned understanding.

Management will face the internal conflict of not wanting to appear as the cause of the current bad performance. If *their* approaches need to change, then *their* methods must have been wrong; and as we have seen in the previous chapter, successful managers who have rarely failed, do not want to, and do not even know how to deal with failure. Rather than confronting these feelings, they will continue with conventional practices which are counterproductive to the achievement of hyper-productivity; thus perpetuating the current unsatisfactory organizational performance level.

Organizational hyper-productivity must translate into financial hyper-performance. It is therefore essential that the methods used for the financial management of the organization become compatible with, supportive of, and conducive to organizational hyper-productivity. Traditional financial management, based on cost accounting and budgeting exercises, are one of the major causes that impede achieving organizational hyper-productivity. Unfortunately, suggesting that management can exercise financial responsibility in a way that is compatible with the emergent, iterative process that is knowledge-work, runs counter to their intuition; and is dismissed as unattainable.

Fortunately there are alternatives to cost accounting and budgeting that better support the purpose, and that can give management the peace of mind that they do exercise financial responsibility in an accountable way, yet in a manner that is entirely compatible and not counterproductive to the knowledge-work process.

The first approach we will examine here is *Discovery Driven Planning*. In the landmark article, McGrath (1995) suggested adopting Discovery Driven Planning as a practical approach that recognizes there is a difference when planning for a new venture, and when planning for an established enterprise in an established line of business. In the conventional setting, future outcomes can be extrapolated from past experience because they are founded on dependable knowledge rather than on hypothesis. In the conventional context, deviations from plans are bad.

The past experience based planning that is valid for an established business is foolish with the high degree of uncertainty that is typical of new ventures. New ventures are based on creating future visions about entities and effects that are unknown and uncertain; and especially that are not obvious to the competition. The predictability based on the reliability of established lines of business does not exist in such a setting. Instead of using predictable knowledge, managers must make assumptions about possible futures in which the business wants to prosper. The assumptions-to-knowledge ratio quickly rises. What is more: it will be discovered that most of such assumptions (about unknowns) are wrong. So large deviations from originally planned objectives will be common with new ventures; to the point where they might need fundamental redirection. (This need is the basis of *pivoting* in the recent *Lean Startup* approach.)

The presence of unknowns and uncertainty and the need for fundamental redirection are characteristics of knowledge-work. Therefore, while McGrath focuses on the differences between established and new businesses, the ideas of Discovery Driven Planning are fruitful even when examining a typical knowledge-based organization (whether established or new). The key factor is the acknowledgment that the whole process is about discovery. In fact, when a start-up is formed, almost nothing is known, while almost all is assumed. In traditional planning, the assumptions are past facts derived from historical data; they are not guesses or estimates that need to be validated with a reality check.

In Discovery Driven Planning the intent is to systematically transform assumptions into knowledge as the business develops. Whenever new information is found, it is fed back into the evolving plan. The potential of the business is discovered as it develops (hence the term *discovery*). While the approach is a dynamic one, it still imposes disciplines; though they are different than those expected in conventional planning.

A process that *systematically transforms assumptions into knowledge* is exactly the kind of process that managers use in strategy making; so familiarity has to be assumed.

A Disciplined Approach

By adopting the Discovery Driven Planning approach, the conversion of assumptions into knowledge, while starting off with many unknowns and uncertainty, happens in a disciplined manner. McGrath (1995) explains that the discipline is represented in four areas represented by four documents (a reverse income statement, a proforma operations specification, a key assumptions checklist, and a milestone planning chart), which are continuously updated as the business activity develops and as new information is discovered. In a later paper (McGrath, 1999), the disciplines become five, with a more generic and formal connotation:

1. Framing
2. Benchmarking
3. Strategic translation of operations
4. Assumption testing
5. Managing to milestones

The noteworthy part is that the approach is built on assumptions that have to be checked and tested. The need to reconceive and adapt is inherent in the rolling update of the documents, as new data are uncovered—in other words, when discoveries bring about new learning.

Counting the Beans Backward

What is most disconcerting for the conventional manager is that the whole approach works backward. In McGrath (1995) this is highlighted by explaining how to use the reverse income statement. This income statement runs from the bottom line up, starting with the desired profits, and working backward (or up the statement) to establish what revenues are necessary to deliver such profits, and what costs can be sustained. In other words, profitability is what drives the planning by imposing the corresponding revenue and cost discipline. The precise indication of a target profit (from which one works backward) gives the exercise a clearly defined goal. (This is interesting as we can make a connection with the Theory of Constraints: having a clearly defined goal is a very important aspect of general management.)

This reverse income statement is simply a statement of how much revenue is necessary to generate enough profit to make the initiative worth pursuing. The next step is the articulation of operations envisioned to make the business operational, with pro forma operations specs: a list of necessary activities, and a worksheet to see if those activities can be realized within the allowable costs. Even this document is a rolling, work-in-process document that will change in due course.

Tolerance for Failure

Recognition of the iterative and emergent nature of knowledge discovery and creation permeates the entire approach. Therefore, there is space for tolerance for failure.

If an idea is valid, the supporting assumptions can be identified and the underlying conceptual model can be continuously updated as new information is uncovered. By constantly accumulating new knowledge, any major shortcomings in the business model will become apparent soon. Any inadequate idea can be discarded before major investments are undertaken.

In most conventional planning methods it is highly unlikely that *inadequate ideas* get discarded. Tolerance for failure is one of the virtues that needs to be learned, internalized, and nurtured by the manager who wants to lead a hyper-productive knowledge-based organization. Failure is not perceived as a deficiency, but as an integral part of the learning process. It is through learning-by-failing that the process can refine, reconceive, and adapt the underlying assumptions.

Assumptions Are Constantly Checked and Rechecked

A key discipline is about the active management of assumptions. A checklist of assumptions is used to make sure each one of them is considered, discussed, and rechecked as the business develops. New discoveries are brought back into the (revised) reverse income statement, which will highlight whether or not the business is still sustainable. If it is not, then the refinement of the assumptions must be repeated until the expected performance can be met; or the business proposition should be discarded.

Through failure and iteration more information becomes available. Tolerance to failure can go to the extreme case, where the whole business is scrapped.

The assumptions are checked often to ensure that decisions can be taken appropriately. The milestone planning discipline has the precise purpose of giving a formal instance for assumption testing.

Instead of holding managers accountable for meeting the plan, they are held accountable for formally planning to learn by using milestone events to test their assumptions. Any major resource commitment is postponed until evidence is gained that the next step is sustainable.

Conventional plan-driven approaches prevent learning; learning comes out of the systematic testing of the assumptions. Funding and commitments are based on signals emerging from the discovery process, and not from a best-guess, wishful-thinking plan which deviates from reality the more it is followed. By incorporating the ability to learn and to reconceive, the business can benefit from a real advantage. McGrath (2010) concludes that entrenched businesses often miss opportunities (or threats from competitors) because their traditional management systems do not encourage knowledge discovery. In such environments, it is difficult to *give license* to plan to experiment and learn; it is an idea contrary to the expectation that plans should simply be worked out. For such a transformation to succeed, it is necessary to have a strong internal champion; or a series of severe failures of traditional methods that expose the need to use a different planning logic. However, when that happens, the outcomes of the transformation bear deep positive consequences.

Discovery Driven Planning was conceived of for the purpose of managing new ventures, or more generally, situations of high uncertainty and high complexity. Any significant knowledge-based project invariably faces high uncertainty and high complexity; therefore the ideas of Discovery Driven Planning are relevant, and should be kept in mind.

7

BUDGETS CONSIDERED HARMFUL

In most companies, one of the most entrenched business practices is budgeting. The intent of budgeting is agreeable: conceiving future plans in terms of expenses and revenues, controlling the allocation of resources, defining targets, motivating managers and personnel, and showcasing the organization's performance. However, as early as 1952, Chris Argyris (1952) highlighted the negative effects of budgets. Some dysfunctions might be expected, like mere reactions when employees are protesting about or resisting the constraints imposed by the budgets. Other, more severe dysfunctions might be caused by the budgeting process itself, such as: exploitation of employees, perceiving accountants in an adversarial manner, fending off criticism toward management, or transforming the budgeting process into a sheer ceremony.

Budgets have even deeper negative consequences; especially when, as is often the case, performance evaluation is centered around budget achievement. Again, the intent is agreeable: budgets are used to review managers' performance, with the idea that the closer the actual figures are to the budgeted one, the better the manager has obliged to commitments. Often though, those same managers are asked to express the estimates (of expenses and revenues) that shape the budgets. As Becker (2010) puts it:

> You will never get a realistic and honest forecast if the bonuses and performance evaluation of those carrying out the forecast depend on it.

Oestergren (2008) highlights several other aspects. Budgets discourage honesty because managers will try to lower their targets (in order to achieve them more easily); all the while they try to get more money (to create autonomy and safety). Budgets give managers a false sense of being in control, making them believe that the future is manageable. The whole budgeting process is effectively an expression of absence of trust and confidence between top managers and the rest of the organization.

BEYOND BUDGETING

A management approach known as *Beyond Budgeting* proposes to abandon budgets altogether. Despite the name, the Beyond Budgeting approach is not only a financial alternative to the conventional use of budgets and the practice of budgeting; it is effectively a management philosophy, supported by 12 principles. The first six principles are leadership principles, while the last six are process principles.

The principles have evolved through time, and the latest formulation can be found at the Beyond Budgeting Roundtable website.[1] At the time of this writing they were:

1. **Values**: Bind people to a common cause; not a central plan.
2. **Governance:** Govern through shared values and sound judgment; not detailed rules and regulations.
3. **Transparency:** Make information open and transparent; don't restrict and control it.
4. **Teams:** Organize around a seamless network of accountable teams; not centralized functions.
5. **Trust:** Trust teams to regulate their performance; don't micro-manage them.
6. **Accountability:** Base accountability on holistic criteria and peer reviews; not on hierarchical relationships.
7. **Goals:** Set ambitious medium-term goals; not short-term fixed targets.
8. **Rewards:** Base rewards on relative performance; not on meeting fixed targets.
9. **Planning:** Make planning a continuous and inclusive process; not a top-down annual event.
10. **Coordination:** Coordinate interactions dynamically; not through annual budgets.
11. **Resources:** Make resources available just-in-time; not just-in-case.
12. **Controls:** Base controls on fast, frequent feedback; not budget variances.

BEYOND BUDGETING IS ATTUNED TO THE EMPIRICAL APPROACH

Because ordinary budgeting requires forecasting, typically one year in advance, along with commitment to those forecasts, it becomes impossible to exercise the kind of empirical management which is necessary to successfully manage a knowledge-work organization.

Svenska Handelsbanken, a Swedish bank, is one of the largest organizations that have adopted this approach. Lennart Francke, interviewed in Daum (2003), described the reasoning process of the bank's early Chief Executive Officer, Jan Wallander. Mr. Wallander was convinced that forecasting in a complex business setting was impossible, and that it was wiser to manage according to reality instead of referring to a stale, dated, and fictitious budget. The mere presence of a budget draws attention away from facts and events that happen in reality; and impedes adaptability as all effort goes into following the detailed plan. Mr. Wallander thought of the budgeting process as a futile bargaining practice between the involved parties.

By being focused on what really happens, an empirical approach is nurtured. Therefore, besides all other purported advantages, what is of highest worth with respect to the nature of knowledge-work is that the Beyond Budgeting method is better attuned to the empirical, emergent, and iterative nature of knowledge-work.

According to Hope (2003), rolling forecasts should be used to capture the flow of information that comes from reality. Such rolling forecasts are updated every quarter. The very fact that they are revised periodically, support the *reconceiving* of the strategies according to the evolving situation in the marketplace. Rolling forecasts are therefore a tool that supports continuous adaptation.

Rolling forecasts are different from ordinary budgets primarily because there is not a finish line (at the end of the fiscal period). Also they do not determine target numbers against which actuals have to be compared. Instead of conformance to budget, all performance is measured through key performance indicators (KPIs). The fixed annual budget targets can be replaced by long-term goals based on benchmarks. For example, the KPIs can relate to target profits, cash flow, cost ratios, customer satisfaction, quality, and others. Performance is benchmarked with respect to internal or external groups, or the corresponding numbers in preceding periods. The indicators will have a financial nature towards the top of the organization; and an operational nature towards the front lines.

Significantly, the KPIs are seen as the basis for testing assumptions and reconceiving. They are typically not represented by point figures, but with ranges to better manage risks and test the assumptions underlying any strategy that requires investments. The horizon of the rolling forecasts can cover five to eight quarters into the future, to support long-term planning. Yet the forecasts are regenerated each quarter, in order to continuously reevaluate the current plans with respect to changing market conditions.

Continuous reassessment of assumptions as conditions change is paramount to supporting an effective knowledge-work organization; the need to reconceive and to test assumptions is inherent in the process. Empirical control is exercised by taking into consideration feedback information from the market, as managers and workers are encouraged to communicate. An eye is kept on catching unexpected patterns or trends while they happen, so that the business can quickly change direction if necessary. Strategy is not enforced from above, but emerges from below.

Because rolling forecasts are constantly refreshed, they are more accurate than yearly budgets. The approach refrains from being large-scale, up-front, and plan-driven. Managers and even workers are encouraged to take action when conditions require it. Unlike the ordinary budgeting process, where targets, resources, and rewards are negotiated on an annual basis, with the Beyond Budgeting method, trust is given in the manager's ability to allocate resources as necessary to capture the opportunities that emerge from the ever-changing market conditions. The noble pattern of a *Community of Trust* lies at the heart of the approach. Managers are trusted to behave appropriately, according to current market conditions—not to blindly follow a plan. The reward is not in hitting the numbers, but in beating the competition.

BEYOND BUDGETING SUPPORTS THE NOBLE PATTERNS

Budgeting is, in any case, a huge drain of resources. Running the process can consume a great deal of effort and take an unwarranted amount of time—as all interested parties engage in endless negotiations to make the budget favorable for them. The process encourages gaming the system and several dysfunctional behaviors. According to Bartram (2006), typically there are five games that managers engage in when they are confronted with budgets:

- **The Sky is the Limit**: this happens when managers strive to get as large a budget as possible instead of realistically asking for what they need.

- **Mine is Bigger than Yours**: managers measure each other's status inside the company according to the size of their budget.
- **Cooking the Books**: this happens, for example, when revenue declaration is delayed after targets have been met, so that the excess revenue can be used for future targets instead.
- **Hey Big Spender (a.k.a., "use it or lose it")**: managers feel compelled to spend the whole of their budget, otherwise they will see it cut the following year.
- **Bonus or Bust**: when managers pay more attention to the metrics that determine their own salaries or bonuses, rather than focusing on targets that actually benefit the business.

All these games generate conflicts of interest, and a culture of mistrust and adversarial confrontation, which is in stark contradiction with one of the key tenets of this book: hyper-productivity can only be attained when the organization exhibits the *Unity of Purpose* and the Community of Trust patterns. Naturally, when departments and managers fight each other to control their share of the budget, then Unity of Purpose does not exist, nor does a Community of Trust.

This is the main reason why a company engaging in conventional budgeting practices will never achieve hyper-productivity. The consequential conclusion is that any company pursuing hyper-productivity must forgo using budgets entirely; otherwise the Unity of Purpose and Community of Trust patterns will be undermined at their roots.

Hope (2003) explains one important characteristic of Beyond Budgeting: there is no incentive to cook the numbers since there are no set targets or penalties for missing them. With rolling forecasts, all information is constantly visible to everyone in the company; it is the transparency that provides the necessary control, with peer pressure, to ensure the correct management decisions.

Furthermore what is most noteworthy about Beyond Budgeting is that the first six principles completely support the two founding patterns of hyper-productive organizations—the Unity of Purpose and the Community of Trust patterns—while the last six principles completely support an empirical approach that is compatible with the nature of knowledge-work. This is why the Beyond Budgeting approach should be seriously considered when aiming at becoming a hyper-productive knowledge-work organization.

A NOTE ON THE LEAN STARTUP PERSPECTIVE

Both *Discovery Driven Planning* as well as *Beyond Budgeting* show that in uncertain, fast-moving, and competitive environments, rapid experimentation and evolutionary learning are vital. Any strategy that executive management might conceive of, should embrace experimentation and prototyping, along with the key idea that a job is really never quite finished. The main lesson from Discovery Driven Planning is that business model assumptions should be explicitly articulated and tested. In McGrath (2010) it is suggested that any business idea needs to be validated in reality. Progress is assessed through explicit checkpoints, where assumptions are tested. If necessary, plans are changed. Even the decision to stop is acceptable, or to redirect the effort and try something different.

A recent school of thought that takes the decision to stop or redirect to the extreme consequences is the *Lean Startup* movement, first described by Eric Reis (2011). While the

Lean Startup movement is not directly related to knowledge-work, it goes without saying that it is entirely in line with the empirical approach described in this book.

REFERENCES

1. http://www.bbrt.org/beyond-budgeting/bb-principles.html

8

CREATING A SHARED VISION AT THE TEAM LEVEL

A hyper-productive organization builds on hyper-productive teams. Therefore, you must gain *Unity of Purpose* and build a *Community of Trust* not only at the organizational level, but also at the team level. Chapter 15 describes how you can align partial interests that develop within an organization, with the business's interest. In this chapter we will see how it is likewise important to align the personal interests of individuals with the direction of their teams and with the overall interest of the business.

The frequent, direct, and intense interactions that happen in a hyper-productive team have their functional foundation in the patterns of Unity of Purpose and Community of Trust. How to achieve this at the team level is different than how you can do so at the organizational level. Naturally, a universal common metric (like financial throughput) should still be the guiding driver; but at the team level more specific practices are needed.

THE PROBLEM: TRUE TEAMWORK IS DIFFICULT TO ACHIEVE IN A BUSINESS SETTING

The Unity of Purpose and Community of Trust patterns can be embraced at the organizational level. Various departments and individuals will collaborate during daily business operations. The patterns help in making such daily collaborations and interactions more meaningful and directed towards a well-defined, common goal.

However, when it comes to the actual team, or teams, engaging in immaterial work, the intensity and frequency of collaborations and interactions need to be taken to higher levels. It is not a coincidence that we use the word *team* in this context. Teamwork is always supported by any organization, just like—when inquired—support is given to a Unity of Purpose and Community of Trust—at least in principle. Unfortunately, in most organizations this remains only a nice declaration of principle. In practice, lip service is paid to the actual realization.

Teamwork can be seen in its fullest meaning in sports teams or in military organizations. True teamwork is seldom found in business organizations, let alone in knowledge-based organizations, where, whether it is an ingrained stereotype or a fact, there are many individuals with strong personalities, who often prefer to work as loners rather than together with peers.

The problem is that for a knowledge-based organization to become hyper-productive, true teamwork is absolutely necessary. It is therefore of prominent importance to have actionable practices that really make a team spirit emerge from inside the group(s) of individuals that work together in their creating of knowledge.

A DARING SOLUTION: JIM MCCARTHY'S CORE PROTOCOLS

Jim McCarthy has identified what he calls the *Core Protocols* for constituting healthy teams. These protocols prescribe specific behaviors and modes of interaction that facilitate the emergence of those structures and patterns of communication which characterize hyper-productive teams. These practices are primarily related to how individuals feel and behave with respect to their peers. Feelings and personal interests play a prominent role, because it is by aligning those personal interests with the team's purpose that team spirit can grow.

The Unity of Purpose pattern is realized in terms of a *shared vision*; the behaviors induced by the Core Protocols will help any team that decides to act accordingly to get to a state of shared vision conducive to hyper-productivity.

The Core Protocols are truly actionable and, above all, personal. Each individual of the team must be personally engaged in applying the Core Protocols.

THE COMMITMENTS AND PROTOCOLS

The whole of the Core Protocols are listed online at Jim McCarthy's website.[1] There are eleven Core Protocols that build on top of a set of eleven *Core Commitments* that all team members should accept and adhere to. Naturally, first and foremost, all team members must also understand and believe in these protocols and commitments.

The commitments are personal and can be considered as a constitution upon which the whole team and the interpersonal relationships between team members are built. The Core Protocols and the Core Commitments are listed in their entirety in Appendix A.

In particular, there are eleven Core Protocols that cover four specific areas, or steps, that are needed to develop a shared vision and that need to be executed in sequence:

1. **Checking In**: the significance and implications of personal presence, increased disclosure, and true engagement
2. **Deciding**: how the team can exercise unanimous decision making to aggregate collective value and manage accountability
3. **Aligning**: motivating and setting common goals
4. **Envisioning**: when the shared vision becomes tangible

While we will not look at all protocols in detail, we will examine those that are most significant for the purpose of building hyper-productive teams, in relation to the noble patterns of Unity of Purpose and Community of Trust.

CHECKING IN

While co-location is often cited as an indispensable ingredient for effective teamwork, there have been examples of distributed hyper-productive teams (Sutherland, 2008). The distinguishing element is not distance versus co-location, but presence and engagement versus absence, disengagement, disconnection, and even hostility.

Here presence and absence are to be interpreted not only in a physical sense, but more importantly as an attitude, a state of mindfulness towards what is happening and what one wants to happen with and within the team.

The Check In Protocol

The *check in* protocol is both an enlistment procedure and an interpersonal connectivity process. The enlistment procedure affirms (and reaffirms) the individual's commitment to be part of the team. The interpersonal connectivity process allows individuals to show their moods and feelings, since reciprocal understanding of moods and feelings are an essential component of true team work.

The check in protocol is more than a roll call. McCarthy (2012) explains that while an ordinary roll call simply asks, "Who is present?", the check in protocol also asks: "What's going on with you?"

Every person concludes the individual check in with a clear statement: "I'm in!" The intent is to reaffirm the person's commitment to seek energy, awareness, and mindfulness; and basically to participate in the team work by playing by the rules.

To play by the rules is all about the promise to engage, whether the presence is physical (in person), or virtual (such as through a chat or video conference). Many Agile stand-up meetings become rituals and ceremonious—people are present but not engaged. When a team member does not feel engaged, he shouldn't be there in the first place, wasting the rest of the team's attention and intellectual bandwidth. It is an act of personal integrity, responsibility, and accountability to be engaged when interacting with the team. Just physical presence and a ritual declamation of standard sentences in a predefined format are not enough. Engagement has to be intellectual, emotional, and deliberate.

The emotional part is of extreme importance. It is only when team members are aware of their peers' feelings and don't fear exposing their own that they will be able to effectively aggregate their IQs. This is why there is an explicit phase of statement of feeling, where the speaker says:

> *"I feel [one or more of MAD, SAD, GLAD, or AFRAID]"*

These are the four fundamental emotions indicated by developmental psychologist Jean Piaget as conducive to cognitive development in children. It is the same work that inspired Seymour Papert to develop the Logo programming language, and later Alan Kay to conceive of the Dynabook. Since they are deep and primordial emotions, the fact of stating them explicitly has a powerful effect on group development, and on the interpersonal interactions that can take place thereafter.

The Check Out Protocol

There are times when individuals just need to take a rest, or cannot be at the top of their performance. Team-oriented individuals will acknowledge their state and inform the team that they cannot exercise the presence and mindfulness that is ordinarily required. This commitment makes it mandatory for the individual team member to literally leave the team once he/she is aware of being unable to live up to the Core Commitments.

Conversely, the rest of the team will have understanding for this situation; and will continue in the daily routines without that person who is pulling out. In fact, they are required to let the person go and not to talk about that person, or try to chase him or her.

Sheer peer pressure and the building of the team spirit will ensure that this protocol is not abused.

The Pass Protocol

Similar to the *check out* protocol, the *pass* protocol allows an individual to skip participating in the process, again with full understanding and no questions asked by the rest of the team. McCarthy (2012) explains that any individual can pass on any activity of the Core Protocols, at any moment, and for any reason, with no further questions asked.

The pass protocol allows a team member to decline participating in any activity, except the *decider* protocol for voting on a decision. Unlike the check out protocol, the pass protocol doesn't require the participant to materially leave the group.

DECIDING

Any business or project is full of unending decisions. In other chapters, we highlight that taking on a decision is one of the most important moments of any organization; a moment where the various souls and interests might emerge and turn into covert (or even overt) conflicts. At the organizational level, the selection of an appropriate metric like that of financial throughput can be critical for determining Unity of Purpose and a Community of Trust. The whole idea is to avoid partial interests and compromises. This happens to be a key tenet of the Theory of Constraints: compromises are always indicative of some kind of dysfunction, disharmony, or conflict that is not explicitly addressed.

The decider protocol is equally uncompromising; the key tenet is that all team decisions must be taken unanimously. Any team member has the right to propose new ideas; and their acceptance or rejection by the rest of the team is resolved immediately. Likewise, any team member has the right to veto any proposal. A single veto will irremediably dismiss any proposal. Unanimity is an absolute requirement, a precondition before any action is taken.

Not only do team members have the right to make proposals, but they are actually bound by the Core Commitments to present any valuable idea they might get as a proposal to the team. Likewise, they are all required to support the ideas that have been chosen. McCarthy (2012) expresses clearly: to get the greatest leverage the team needs to invest itself in progressing with explicit commitments from all individuals towards achieving the team's purpose. How the team makes decisions has a major impact towards this end.

Resolution Protocol

The decider protocol and the *resolution* protocol are tightly related. The point is that proposals have to be either accepted or rejected; and the acceptance or rejection should be arrived at quickly. The objective of the decider protocol is to arrive at either an adopted plan or a rejected proposal. A proposal might be supported by a majority of team members, but that is not enough for approval.

That is when the resolution protocol comes into play; to escalate support to the whole team or to definitively reject the proposal. The protocol expects the proposer to formulate the question: "What will it take to get you in?" and quickly arrive at either the extension of the proposal (by adopting the outlier's changes) for its final acceptance, or the definitive rejection through withdrawal by the proposer.

The important aspect is to keep moving forward, and to produce new ideas as quickly as possible with unanimity. (Note that this decision-making process is similar to that of a jury in a legal case that requires a unanimous decision—in other words, this approach is well-founded and proven in judicial systems.)

Decision Making as the Key Team-Building Process

The decider and resolution protocols constitute one of the most important phases in building and maintaining a healthy team environment. In fact, it is required that all members remain present until a decision is resolved (either taken or rejected); also the decider protocol is the only exception where it is not allowed for those who are present to pass.

The members have to be mindful about how their participation either moves the group forward or slows it down. They are required to give their full attention to the decider protocol over any other activity. Because unanimity is required, the effect of the decider protocol is not only that of actually taking on decisions, but is also that of bonding the team. During the execution of the decider protocol, focus has to be razor sharp. Members may speak only if they are the proposer, or when addressed by the proposer. Full attention is given to all words spoken.

Once a decision has been taken this way, each member must feel personally responsible and accountable for achieving the result of the decision even if the decision was taken in their absence. This obviously makes it compelling for team members to actually be present and participate in the decision process. All members are obliged to keep themselves informed about any decisions taken in their absence.

Decisions are taken or rejected quickly. Those that are rejected must quickly be replaced by new ideas—anyone who rejects a proposal must also be ready to propose a better idea immediately. Argumentation with someone who rejects an idea is forbidden; instead it is expected that the objector immediately presents a better idea.

The point is to be able to generate as many useful ideas, as quickly as possible. Knowledge-work development is a highly intellectual activity; anything that prevents the generation of ideas, or that might slow down the rate of generation of ideas must actively be countered. Furthermore, the ideas generated by the aggregation of intellects, through unanimity, will be much more considerate of the infinite factors that might be at play; and that might escape the single individual's attention. Ideas are the currency of the knowledge-work team.

Ecology of Ideas

The *Ecology of Ideas* pattern relates the health of a team to the rate at which new ideas can be generated. The higher the rate of production (the flow) of ideas, the healthier and more connected the team. It is a direct measurement of the intensity of communication within the team. A high rate of idea generation is a sure sign that the team is ready to consider anybody's idea. The more ideas—the more choices—the more likely that good ideas will find their way over bad ones. Acceptance of new ideas needs to be sustained solely by the qualities of the ideas themselves. Ideas should be so powerful as to have a vitality of their own, not only in the intellects that generate them, but also in the collective memories they create and in the team artifacts in which they become embodied. The allure and the lucidness of an idea will determine its acceptance by the individual psyches and the collective mind of the team.

This way of taking decisions naturally weeds out weak ideas—those ideas that don't approach unanimity at first vote will typically be withdrawn by the proposer as soon as the situation is evident, and those ideas that almost gain unanimity will be subject to the *resolver* protocol and equally be approved or rejected as quickly as possible. Likewise, anyone voting *No* must be prepared to come up with something better for unanimous approval.

Protocol Check and Intention Check

Sticking to the spirit of the Core Protocols can be challenging. There are two protocols specifically designed to keep the team on track.

The *protocol check* is invoked whenever anybody believes that any other protocol is used incorrectly, or when a Core Commitment is being broken. The protocol check can be invoked during any other activity. When protocol check is being invoked, the person calling for it must either state the correct use of the protocol, or ask for help in clarifying it.

The *intention check* helps in bringing forth the purpose of a team member's behavior. It can be invoked when a negative outcome is being sensed. The purpose is to assess the integrity of a member's intentions. The protocol means to bring out any potential conflicts, before they become irreparable. Naturally, whoever raises the intention check must also be prepared to resolve any conflict that might arise by the check. Those being asked about their intentions are also expected not to react defensively, and also to state what responses or behaviors they might expect from others as a result of their own.

The intention check is a powerful protocol that enables the continuous progress towards a common team alignment.

ALIGNING

Alignment is the cornerstone for achieving Unity of Purpose within the team level. All team members must develop a common sense and feeling. They must all pull in the same direction.

The power of McCarthy's approach stems from recognizing the motives that drive individuals at a personal level. The key is to transform this personal interest into a driving force. The individual's diverse interests are brought into one beneficial direction. Alignment happens when every single team member has a clear understanding not only of what he desires for himself, but also of what he expects from the team, and what the team demands from itself and from him. The alignment protocol induces individuals to explicitly answer the questions:

- What specifically do I want?
- What is blocking me from having what I want?

These questions are repeated in a recursive manner, not unlike the *Five Whys* root cause analysis technique, in order to truly expose what are the individual's personal drivers. Not only does the protocol expose these drivers, but it makes it compelling to exhibit a clear behavior (signal) to allow any team member to indicate to their peers that they are engaging in pursuing their personal goals. Conversely, the team members, when they sense this signal, can give the single individual full support in his engagement. Furthermore, each individual is allowed to ask the other members for help.

McCarthy (2012) highlights that personal goals will always matter more than company goals, and they give the ultimate explanation as to why individuals are involved in the company life. The reasoning is that if a team is made aware of what its members aspire to, then everyone can aid other teammates to attain their personal goals. A powerful consequence of team members being clearly committed to supporting each other in achieving their personal explicitly stated goals is that individual responsibilities are transformed. Individual team members become accountable for behaving congruently to their personal goals. If individuals consistently act to undermine reaching their own personal goals, then it is fair to expect them to (explicitly) change their goals or their own behavior. By exposing and acknowledging personal goals, productivity can increase dramatically, because then it becomes legitimate to ask for help.

What is being recognized here is the "What is in it for me?" factor that is always present in most people's minds with very few exceptions. Recognizing that individual interests are key drivers which override any company interest is the critical insight; by aligning all those individual interests, one creates a culture of alignment.

In general, most corporate environments are ignorant about alignment. What is worse is that there is no standard way by which alignment can be realized, let alone acknowledged that it has been attained, or monitored over time. Most management methods mightily ignore interpersonal communication standards, as those exemplified by the Core Protocols, and thereby reduce the collective energy. Most companies will ignore their employees' personal goals and interpersonal communication about them; consequently there will be chaos driven by the variety of divergent interests. Divergent interest will make the organization settle on mediocrity, as if it were a standard that cannot be improved on.

A hyper-productive organization has zero tolerance for mediocrity; implying that every single individual's feelings and goals must be taken into account and aligned to the company objectives.

ENVISIONING

The Unity of Purpose pattern is an overall, organization-wide driver. That purpose must be supported by each team's vision of what they're trying to achieve. This means that all individuals on a team must develop a shared vision giving meaning to their efforts and work.

A shared vision happens when all members have a similar manner of interpreting reality and a deep sense of affiliation with one another. The team sees and feels as one; they are all sharing the same reference models of thinking, and the same dimensions and scales of discernment and judgment. Note that this is not to be confused with the dysfunction of groupthink, since any tendency to complacency or group appeasement is kept out by the team's ability to think critically even through the collective experience.

The value of the experiential component of developing a shared vision cannot be understated. It is more than sharing a vision as such; it is about developing a sense of belonging and trust, in direct support of the noble pattern of a Community of Trust. It is important that the shared vision be of such height that any team component would consider it impossible to achieve alone. There must be an element of challenge that requires a concerted effort of all team members to be met. The daily endeavor towards that shared vision object will give the members an ongoing validation about their own personal efforts and their peers' support. The shared vision becomes the team's highest purpose, and nothing will be more important in their mind. All team members will understand and decipher important facts and events in a similar manner, as a consequence of sharing the same belief and values about their purpose, their products, and their processes and practices.

There is an important difference between the organization's Unity of Purpose and the team's shared vision. While the Unity of Purpose must be the same for the entire organization, the shared vision applies only to a given team, division, or unit.

For example, in the case of Borland, the Quattro Pro for Windows team and the Borland C++ Compiler team shared the Unity of Purpose in making Borland a successful company; but one team had the shared vision of creating the most innovative spreadsheet, while the other one had the shared vision of making the fastest C++ compiler. The shared vision aligns a team of people working on the same project, product, or service. The Unity of Purpose applies to the higher level of giving one inspiring objective for the organization as a whole.

VALIDITY AND CAVEATS

McCarthy's Core Protocols are undoubtedly a most powerful means for creating a shared vision and a strong team spirit. The limitation lies in the direction of the shared vision, with respect to the Unity of Purpose of the organization as a whole. Creating a shared vision is not enough; that vision must be aligned with the rest of the company's goal. Provided that you develop a goal-aligned vision, using McCarthy's Core Protocols is one of the most powerful and effective ways to build a healthy, focused, and productive team.

REFERENCES

1. The Core Protocols can be found at: http://www.mccarthyshow.com/online/

9

CRITICAL ROLES, LEADERSHIP, AND MORE

[A] mine exploded [...] the Grand Master himself, now seventy years old, grabbed a helmet and sword and rushed out to meet the assault. The knights and the towns-people, encouraged by his example, picked up any weapon they could find and flung themselves into the breach with him. (Maltaculture, 2014)

One extraordinary example of hyper-productivity is *The Great Siege of Malta*, one of the bloodiest episodes of war. Between May and September 1565, the island of Malta in the middle of the Mediterranean Sea was the stage of one of the most amazing feats of warfare: 700 soldiers[1] of the Knights of Malta, fought off the attacks of an invading Turkish fleet forty thousand men strong. One reason for this success was the leader of the Knights of Malta: Grand Master Jean Parisot de la Valette.

The above quote exposes the essence of leadership: to be an example that others want to follow. In a hyper-productive organization, some roles rise to prominence for the impact they have on the organization as a whole to be able to consistently reach and maintain a state of hyper-productivity.

THE PATRON ROLE

The highest commander-in-chief, the effective *leader* of a hyper-productive organization is typically the Chief Executive Officer (CEO) of a business; though in larger companies it could be the director of a division or the head of a business unit, or the like. This effective leader role is undoubtedly the most important. It is the leader who will instill the culture, energy, and motivation necessary for getting to hyper-productivity.

Grand Master de la Valette set an example for others to follow. Likewise, hyper-productive teams will exhibit some instance of the *Patron Role* pattern suggested by Coplien (2004).

Coplien also makes significant observations about the etymology of the word *patron*, which derives from the Latin *pater*, the French *patern*, and the English *pattern* (making the full connection to the ideas of organizational patterns). Naturally, the meaning is something that is to be considered for imitation; an archetype to be copied; an example or model deserving imitation; or an example or model of particular excellence.

In other words, the leader has to set the example. Coplien characterized Borland International's CEO, Philippe Kahn, as tightly coupled to the development team (of Quattro Pro for Windows). The CEO was constantly close to the team (they even played jazz together). This closeness is also one explanation why that team had a strong communication coupling.

Play by the Rules of the Game

Setting the example often means entirely relinquishing the command-and-control mentality that is so ingrained in general management. In order to reach hyper-productivity, the effective leader (the CEO) must basically be part of the team, and participate with the same rights, obligations, and commitments established for the team.

For instance, if the team uses the *Core Protocols* and the *Core Commitments* (described in the previous chapter), then the leader, in person, needs to embrace the protocols and commitments, and conform to the team's internal mode of interaction. The idea that there is an individual bossing around is unacceptable and entirely incompatible with a state of hyper-productivity. By being part of the team and accepting the commitments and protocols, it is understood that the CEO has no intention of imposing any decision unilaterally, despite formally having the power to do so. If the CEO wants a decision to be accepted, he must subject himself to the rules of the *decider* protocol, and be ready to see his proposals rejected. Even the latest hire, for instance, a junior trainee who just joined the team has the right to veto the decision.

Naturally, this is an enormous step for most CEOs; so counterintuitive that most will not be able to make it. This is obviously a huge redefinition of the very role of the CEO (or whatever the title of the effective leader happens to be). In most business organizations, the CEO will not be ready to relinquish authority and subject to something like the Core Commitments and Core Protocols. But this is what distinguishes the leader of a hyper-productive team (and, even more so, a hyper-productive organization), from the manager of just another average business.

A business leader who is not prepared to do this is not caring enough; and naturally he will get the results thereof. Many will object that these suggestions are incompatible with organizations beyond a certain size, where divide-and-conquer and delegation are inevitable. However, let's not forget that one of the main motivations for pursuing hyper-productivity in the first place is to avoid gigantic organizations. Borland International's eight programmers on the Quattro Pro for Windows team were as productive as 400 Microsoft programmers. It is certainly easier to develop a close relationship with eight people, rather than 400.

Hyper-productivity is not hyper-activity. It is about doing more, with less; and doing it faster. It is a consequence of speed (among many other things)—speed in generating ideas and options, speed in decision making, and speed in execution. Speed comes when there is balance in all parts and features of the organization; which in turn, means balance between centralized control and anarchy.

There must be such a balance between centralized control and anarchy. Often a patron role, or even benevolent dictator, is the one who can take the decision most quickly;

especially when the organization as a whole is at a standstill and does not really know what to do or where to go. Quick decisions by illuminated leaders who are trusted by their organization can be vital to the organization's survival in times of instability. Quick decisions by a leader can prevent unnecessary and maybe even deadly drag in the decision processes. Once such quick decisions are taken, in virtue of the leader being a trusted member of the team, the leader's decision will be trusted; and the decision will be followed by speedy and quick execution by the whole organization. Speed of execution is a consequence of trust in the leader's decisions.

During exceptions, crisis, or critical moments, even hyper-productive teams might come to a standstill because of unknown facts and unforeseen events. This is when leadership can make a difference. Trusted leaders can take quick decisions and have them executed rapidly. That's why leaders need to be part of the team, so that reciprocal trust develops. Teams must trust their leaders to take this responsibility of making critical decisions in critical moments. Leaders must trust their teams to execute. Then, once the crisis is solved, things go back to a normal state of a peer-driven organization, guided more by fellowship and covalence, than by authority and command.[2]

LESSONS FROM OPEN SOURCE PROJECTS

While the leader can step up to make decisions unilaterally in virtue of his position of authority, he should refrain from doing so. His position is not something that should be abused; instead it should be resorted to only in cases of extreme necessity. Nonetheless, in a healthy organization, the team will readily subject themselves to the leader being the final arbiter for decisions that cannot be set through other means. It is in these cases that the leader actually becomes the agent who removes insurmountable barriers that hinder progress—though there are dangers in doing so. One might be tempted to resort to voting, but that might be even worse.

One important lesson comes out of open source projects, especially those that grow into big ones. These projects seem to be driven by chaos and appear to be unmanageable by any orthodox management approach. There are far-reaching consequences that derive from the nature of open source licenses, and that impact the role of leadership.

It is well known that in open source software there is often a benevolent dictator role; a supreme authority that can take decisions unilaterally, very much like a CEO in a company. But is it really so? Paradoxically, open source projects show us the way when there effectively can be no supreme authority at all.

The Power and Consequences of Forkability

People participating in open source projects can be assured to have certain rights, which primarily regard the source code, but also usually cover the collaterals, like documentation. These rights are summarized by Bruce Perens in Dibona (1999) as:

- The right to make copies of the program, and distribute those copies
- The right to have access to the software's source code, a necessary preliminary before you can change it
- The right to make improvements to the program

The rights given by the open source license change the very nature of the interactions that are allowed and acceptable in the community. Not only does it weed out corporate style managers and other bullies, but it is also essential to keep the community cohesive. The significance of this is highlighted by Fogel (2005): the very element that keeps developers together is the code's forkability. Anyone can walk off with a copy of the code and start a new, alternative project. Ironically, the cohesive force derives from the *potential* of forks. In fact, forks seldom happen, because they are bad for all. Usually, when a project is in danger of forking, huge efforts are made to avert the possibility.

The ability to fork explains why there cannot be true dictators in open source projects. Although it is held in common belief that there are (benevolent) dictators determining the fate of an open source project; such a dictatorship is very limited in its powers. They would be like monarchs whose kingdom could be copied away by any subject, at any time. Naturally, such rulers would necessarily behave very differently from those that held real absolute powers.

So the realization is about the powerlessness of the dictator—the dictator has no power at all over the project. This is the inevitable consequence of all open source licenses: no one is given more authority than anyone else in determining how the source code can be used. If just anybody can simply walk away and take all the code and the entire project with him or herself, then the interesting question becomes: how can you manage if there are no binding ties? The answer is you cannot; your only choice is to step up and in front as a leader. If that works in an open source setting, it becomes even more powerful in a team built on the Core Commitments.

The Power and Consequences of Community

Business managers have a hard time understanding the open source culture; but that culture is very much conducive to hyper-productivity, if and when it is combined with the other elements described in this work. Understanding this culture is a learning experience which can be very valuable for the hyper-productive organizational leader. This kind of learning experience was described prominently by Goldman (2005). The open source movement might seem ruled by gangs, yet they are founded on communities. These communities share culture, lexicon, rituals, praxis, values, principles, and philosophies. To join such a community implies understanding all these aspects sufficiently to be able to interact with the community on equal terms. It becomes a matter of cultural understanding. Managers accustomed to the corporate environment might be surprised to discover that participation in open source communities is more like a social activity than an engineering undertaking. They have to discover that it is all about community building, gaining credibility within the community, dealing with the politics, being good citizens, internalizing the principles and the governance rules. The artifacts of the source code and documentations are only one part of it; another part is the people. People who bond, communicate, interact, build their own folklore, and relate in friendships and affiliations. People who constitute a community with their own conventions might be as diverse and challenging to accept as a foreign culture.

This description of an open source community is fitting even for a tightly-knit team functioning under the Core Commitments and the Core Protocols. In such a team you have the forming of a community that interacts, develops customs and traditions, and builds friendships—a team that creates a community wherein a culture is created. Hence the relevance of the open source governance approaches.

The Open Source Governance Model

What does it mean to exercise leadership in a community of culture? Insight can be gained in the open source projects that grow large and develop governance structures. When projects grow, the original founder (the benevolent dictator) will simply not be able to handle all decisions. Delegation becomes a necessity, and with that governance and management. Given the nature of open source, Fogel (2005) suggests establishing a constitution, working by consensus, and using voting systems; in other words, finding an alternative non-dictatorial governance system. The common threads of these alternatives is that they are based on consensus supported by voting (as a fall back when consensus is not found). Consensus though, is less than optimal; it is a state that everyone is willing to accept, but not necessarily what they really want. On the positive side, consensus is a well-defined state and it is easy to identify. Consensus is reached (on any topic) when someone declares it has been found, and there is nobody raising objections. If objections and debates are still raised, and the situation deadlocks, the resolution is found in voting.

The interesting and more relevant observation comes later in Fogel's analysis, considering the drawbacks of voting. Voting is usually considered a good and fair way to resolve issues. In reality it is not, especially in the quest of hyper-productivity in knowledge-work. Voting is not good because it abruptly ends the discussion and consequently stops the creative thinking about the issue being debated. Stopping creative thinking prevents finding new solutions, even such new solutions that could be truly accepted by everybody in a unanimous way. Unanimity is definitely a sign of a team reaching a hyper-productive state; consensus and voting are not. It is not uncommon that fierce debates generate new ways of thinking that will find a broader acceptance than the original adversarial positions. Even if such a solution is not found, lively discussion can serve to negotiate a compromise that is accepted by consensus, which is still better than the short-circuiting of voting. Compromising makes everybody a little bit unhappy; while voting will make some people unhappy and others happy. With a compromise there is a common *fair* price to pay—everyone will be a little unhappy. The short-circuiting of voting has the immediate benefit of settling the issue, so that progress can continue; however the settling is reached by counting votes, not by rational conversations through which a common viewpoint can be developed.

To summarize, there are two relevant aspects to consider:

- Voting *ends the creative thinking* about the problem; hence voting should be avoided in hyper-productive teams. This is one of the reasons why the *decider* protocol requires unanimity. Unanimity is a goal with a double purpose—to force thinking in creative ways, and to get the complete buy-in of all members to fully support the energetic execution of any decision taken. Without unanimity, there is simply not enough thrust to reach the state of hyper-productivity.
- With compromise *everyone is a little bit unhappy*. Again, the value of unanimity is evident when everybody is happy with a decision, they will support it with utmost energy, and half-hearted efforts will be avoided. Half-hearted efforts obviously cannot lead to hyper-productivity.

THE THINKING PROCESSES OF THE THEORY OF CONSTRAINTS FOSTER UNANIMITY

There are moments in a community's development when conflicts arise. During these moments, the leader of the organization might be tempted to exercise authority and arbiter a decision. This is exactly what happens in the majority of organizations; unsurprisingly those are the ones that are not hyper-productive.

An arbitrated decision will create a situation similar to voting; it finally settles a question, but some people will be unhappy. *Unity of Purpose* and *shared vision* start to crack and crumble.

The illuminated leader will take the radical position that compromises, voting and authoritarian decisions (even and especially those that he/she could take by him/herself) should be avoided in all cases and at any cost. Hyper-productivity is attainable exclusively when there is undisputed unanimity between all people involved.

Then what should one do when conflicts cannot be resolved through the decider protocol; when someone does not agree with a proposal and is not able or willing to propose an alternative, better idea; or when the counterproposal is met with a veto by the original proposer? Resorting to authoritative arbitration should be the extreme exception.

The leader should strive to build an environment where such fundamental disagreements will not arise in the first place. Landy (2010) stresses that a leader helps team members to relate to one another. The leader supports the team members to participate in cooperative rather than independent effort. The leader should make the team aware of the social nature of their work. Ultimately, the leader creates a healthy climate in which leadership emerges from, and is carried out by, the group. This is entirely consistent with the fourth value of the Kanban Method: encourage acts of leadership, at all levels.

There are many theories about leadership, which can be used to frame the actions of a leader like the Leader-Member Exchange theory, the Servant-Leader Model, and so on. However, none of these offer truly actionable advice. In particular, none focus on how to create unanimity.

In other chapters we show how the Thinking Processes of the Theory of Constraints can be used to conduct root cause analysis, and how decisions can be taken and executed inside one's own Span of Control or just suggested and prompted in one's Sphere of Influence.

When a team is in a deadlock situation and unable to decide on any given issue, instead of arbitrating a decision, the hyper-productive leader might consider the option of resorting to the Thinking Processes, all the while renouncing his/her own authority. In other words, the leader will renounce the span of control and consider all team members as belonging to the sphere of influence. In this way, the leader will force him or herself to resort to convincing logical reasoning by applying the persuasion techniques and the conflict resolution techniques of the Theory of Constraints. In this manner, unanimity might be regained even in the most adversarial situations.

A COUNTERPRODUCTIVE ROLE: THE SCRUM MASTER

The current widespread adoption of Scrum has effectively made a series of hyper-productive *anti-patterns* become the norm, rather than the exception. There is no doubt that the adoption of Scrum will increase the productivity of just about any organization. It is easy to double or triple productivity when the starting point is abysmally low on the productivity scale. Scrum will undoubtedly achieve that. But then it stalls, and will not be able to achieve *hyper-productivity*. The fact that Jeff Sutherland has been able to document only five or six projects that have reached the hyper-productive state is revealing. Equally revealing are the many statements by Sutherland, Schwaber, and other Scrum experts, about the majority (up to 90%) of Scrum teams not being able to get anywhere close to the state of hyper-productivity.

One of the important roles suggested by Scrum is the role of the *Scrum Master*. While Coplien identified the Gate Keeper and Firewall patterns, unfortunately, the Scrum Master role is completely antithetical and counterproductive to the achievement of a hyper-productive state. In a normal Scrum team, the Scrum Master has basically two duties.

- Protect the team from the interference of management
- Ensure that the team focuses on making the right thing, while the team might be more concerned about making the thing right.

In a traditional organization, where there is dysfunctional management lacking understanding about the nature of knowledge-work, the introduction of these two aspects are beneficial. Improvements of maybe two or three times can be obtained easily through these and the rest of the Scrum practices and roles.

However, these two priorities do not exist in a hyper-productive organization with functional management who is very much aware of what is going on. A hyper-productive organization naturally aggregates the IQs of all people who have any kind of involvement in the delivery of the product or service that is being built or delivered. They *all* know what the *right thing* is, and they all strive to make the *thing right*. There is no division of roles between those who focus on the right thing and those who focus on doing the thing right. Everybody on the team knows that *both* of these must be achieved equally; and that all have to focus on both things equally by developing a collective intelligence supported by shared values. In a truly hyper-productive organization, where the CEO is truly a leader and not a manager (and likewise for any intermediary subordinate management positions that might exist) there is absolutely no need to protect the team from management.

The management of a hyper-productive organization will have an intimate and deep understanding of the dynamics of knowledge-work and will have fostered such a focused culture that they will never have to disrupt operations that are happening in the shop.

If events and circumstances are of such a nature that a disruption of operations is needed, then the team as a whole will have developed their own aggregate IQ and emotional intelligence to be able to take those decisions autonomously. Naturally, the inputs might come from the scouts that are out in the field or the suggestion and proposal might have been brought forth by the CEO. However, it will always have been framed and proposed in accordance to the decider protocol. A hyper-productive team is mature enough, and has sufficient understanding of the organization's Unity of Purpose and of the team's own shared vision that they will naturally approve of the right decision and then execute it in the right way. It will all be according to the preeminence of unanimity.

The CEO who does not have enough trust in his organization and thinks that his team is not able to act as described above, is simply *not* leading a hyper-productive organization and has missed entirely what his own role is therein.

THE SOLITARY PROGRAMMER

If the stereotype of the solitary geek programmer is still alive in your organization, make sure you understand it is only a stereotype and not a factual classification of personality traits. Most software engineers are rational, intelligent, and reasonable. They should be able to understand most situations that are happening in a business setting.

If, nonetheless, you truly have someone fitting that stereotype, then you should make sure he or she is not part of the team or the organization. There is no space for prima donnas or solitary geniuses on a hyper-productive team. If you happen to have such personalities on board, then get rid of them; they don't belong there unless they can be trained or rehabilitated to become good team members.

This advice might not be politically correct, but a hyper-productive team is like a military elite force or an A-league sports team. Not everybody can be part of it—not even on the bench. Mind well though, that this is not about elitism. It is about finding the people who are fit for the purpose of getting to a state of hyper-productivity. It is not about skills and abilities—though they do help and are taken for granted—it is more about a matter of attitude and emotional IQ. What matters is the individual's ability to develop a sense of deep belonging to the team and of acting in unison with all his/her peers.

THE LEADER IS PART OF THE TEAM

This applies to the leaders, too, starting with the CEO. So if you are a CEO, or are governed by a CEO who has more of the traits of a paranoid psychopath, then you will not be able to have a hyper-productive team. Sorry—but that kind of CEO doesn't have what it takes.

This is also one reason why Scrum is successful at suggesting that management should get out of the team's way. In that way the team will become somewhat more productive; because it can avoid the interferences and disruptions by management. However, such a team will never become hyper-productive. Hyper-productivity requires a deep and intense involvement of the leader. The leader has to feel a deep connection to the team as a whole, and gain the respect of all team members right there on the field, through acts and deeds. One of the most critical moments is when you select whom you want to have on board.

This also relates to how decision making is taken within the context of a *learning organization* (double-, triple-loop) and in particular, one that has effectively adopted the Thinking Processes of the Theory of Constraints.

PRIDE, FUN, AND SLACK

A related aspect, pertaining to the *sentiment* or *climate* in the work organization, is that of pride in workmanship.

It is important that the knowledge workers (like software developers) become deeply motivated because motivation bears a side effect on the quality of their work. Poppendieck (2007) describes the importance and consequences of pride in workmanship:

Pride builds commitment, and without mutual commitment a group really isn't a team. [...] To keep volunteers committed, the leader and later the [...] community must recognize, appreciate, and applaud good work.

There must be a balance between how much work is allowed on the project as such, and how much must be done on *polishing* workmanship. One possible approach is imitating *The Google Way* as reported by Mediratta (2007). At the time, engineers at Google could take 20 percent of their work time to attend to personal projects, as long as they were somehow related to the company. Any engineer with an innovative idea could give it a run. This approach is based on the obvious observation that people work better when they are passionate about what they are doing. In particular, programmers are most happy about programming, as Weinberg (1998) observed back in 1971:

Anyone who has ever seen a programmer at work [...] knows that programming itself, if the programmer is given a chance to do it his way, is the biggest motivation of programming.

This requires the appropriate *organizational culture*, where programmers are encouraged to *have fun*. Most companies do not have the predisposition to allow these kinds of concessions. In Demarco (1999) a section aptly entitled *It's Supposed to be Fun to Work Here* describes the common notion that work is presumed to be burdensome—if it is pleasant, it cannot be considered as work; and work should make one feel distressed. The notion is magnified by the stereotype that managers should ensure that people attend to their work, and not have fun—that it is all about exploiting workers to the highest degree, not allowing any space for having fun. The notion is deeply ingrained in most corporate cultures to the point that people feel guilt if they are having any kind of fun in the workplace.

Most companies will not have the resources to be as generous as Google. However the approach has merit and can be adapted. Creating space for staff to enjoy their craft and workmanship has far-reaching consequences, it creates slack in the organization. The benefits of slack have been described by Demarco (2002) as increasing an organization's agility. With slack, there is less personnel turnover, more flexibility to adapt to the future, and better capacity for judicious risk taking in place of risk avoidance.

While slack requires a cultural leap of faith and the investment of adequate resources, creating slack and letting go can amply compensate the business. Demarco (1999) recommends allowing for loosely stated responsibilities to give employees the power of defining their own work. The most spectacular cases are those where companies have self-motivated super-achiever employees who can freely determine their roles and work. Such individuals will generate extraordinary advantages for the companies they work for and they will abundantly reward the organization for the positions and degrees of freedom they are given.

It is not only a matter of creating the appropriate conditions, providing resources, and giving up control: it is also a matter of accepting the possibility of failure. Constantine (1995) sustains you must have good people, with suitable training, tools, and resources. Then you have to give them the freedom to achieve outstanding results. Yet that will not be done with the greatest efficacy because space must be allowed for creative experimentation, wherein failure is acceptable in order to contribute to organizational learning. In a way, creativity has a cost, and implies taking risks. People factors come first and being open to failure means accepting risks with your own people. Making space for and having trust in people is a trait of enlightened entrepreneurship.

REFERENCES

1. One should not forget the direct contribution of the Maltese people, too. The knights commanded were the best trained, and were all professional warriors, but there were 3,000 to 4,000 Maltese irregulars defending, plus various other soldiers from a variety of nations. Nonetheless, even at a ratio of 5,000 to 40,000, we are still witnessing a case of hyper-productivity.
2. Fellowship and covalence are used here as defined by Bob Marshal in his blog *Think Different* (http://flowchainsensei.wordpress.com/), and are parts of his *Rightshifting Model* (http://flowchainsensei.wordpress.com/rightshifting/) for improving the effectiveness of knowledge-work. The essence of the model is that knowledge-work effectiveness is a function of mindset.

10

THE THINKING PROCESSES

The Theory of Constraints (TOC) is notorious for a *way of thinking* known under the name of the *Thinking Processes*. In this chapter we will introduce the Thinking Processes. They include a number of tools, although we are interested primarily in how the Thinking Processes support root cause analysis and help in managing relationships with people because that is where they contribute their value in supporting the *Unity of Purpose* and *Community of Trust* patterns.

The Thinking Processes were already used in Goldratt (1992, first published in 1984). Later they were formalized in Goldratt (1990a) and Goldratt (1990b), and finally presented in a more comprehensive form in Goldratt (1994).

The Thinking Processes are used in many situations which are considered in the TOC. Their purpose is primarily to resolve operational and management problems. They support decision making and represent logical reasoning. The salient aspect is this: the Thinking Processes are founded on logic, and in particular on Sufficient Cause thinking, and Necessary Condition thinking (Scheinkopf, 1999). The Thinking Processes have a number of tools. In Cox (2010), Victoria J. Mabin and John Davis give a comprehensive overview of these tools. They are illustrated in Figure 10.1.

In Schragenheim (1999) we find several examples of how the Thinking Processes can be applied to management. The Thinking Processes offer a variety of tools for use in different situations. Some are primarily focused on finding the root cause of problems; others are more operational and focus on how to resolve the identified problems. The root cause analysis capability of the Thinking Processes comes to fruition in the context of risk management.

Originally, the Thinking Processes were developed to support the TOCs' process of on-going improvement; and specifically to answer the three fundamental questions:

- What to change?
- What to change to?
- How to cause the change?

Later developments by Goldratt and others as told by Dr. Alan Barnard in Cox (2010) added another initial question, *"Why change?,"* and a final question, *"How to measure the*

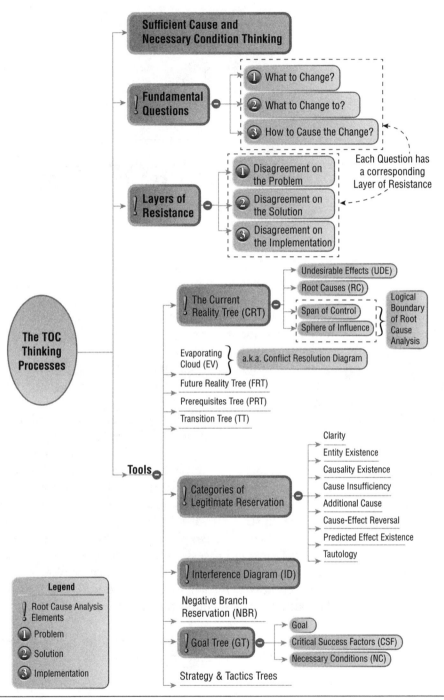

Figure 10.1   Overview of the Thinking Processes

change and achieve a process of ongoing improvement?"; though these last two questions are not as interesting as the first three for the purpose of supporting root cause analysis.

These three questions are the same questions you need to resolve once you have found the root causes of your problem. It is not only about finding the root causes, but also about doing something about them. The Thinking Processes also have this very important operational aspect: they help you in identifying the problem, finding a solution, and ultimately implementing the solution.

CURRENT REALITY TREE AND RELEVANT PROBLEM

The *Current Reality Tree* (CRT) is the tool of choice for conducting root cause analysis in the TOC. (While we focus on the CRT, we should not disregard the other tools offered by the Thinking Processes because they can be invaluable when formulating risk prevention, mitigation, and transference or avoidance actions.)

One of the most comprehensive treatments of the Thinking Processes is found in Dettmer (2007), wherein the CRT is introduced in terms of identifying the relevant problem first. If you fail to identify the relevant problem, then you would waste time, effort, and means on addressing the wrong problem. Not only would this be a waste of time, but the original, relevant problem would still be unresolved, and no real betterment would be achieved.

In complex situations, the real problems are not always evident. The suggestion is, therefore, to build a CRT—a logic tree which has the precise purpose of exposing unseen system-level problems in complex situations.

By using the CRT you gain confidence that you are directing your investigation toward the right problem, even if that problem may hide under several layers of cause and effect. The CRT depicts a logical structure, representing the current reality of the system you are examining. Given a set of circumstances, the CRT visualizes cause-and-effect connections between tangible conditions of the system, and their root causes.

Being an exercise in logic, the CRT is indifferent to arbitrary internal and external system boundaries: the investigation can persuade you to look outside of your normal domain of interest. Beware, though, of subjective biases; while the CRT can produce a faithful representation of cause and effect, it is not a complete picture of reality, but only of the part that is subjectively perceived and analyzed.

UNDESIRABLE EFFECTS AND ROOT CAUSES

When building a CRT, we are on the outlook for one or more *Undesirable Effects* (UDEs). UDEs can be thought of as problems though the intent of the terminology is to stress that they are effects. Being effects, they must have causes. Identifying the UDEs is the first step in constructing a CRT diagram. Dettmer (2007) describes an UDE as the most evident sign that something is wrong in a system. A UDE is something real including tangible negative consequences with respect to the system's goal (or partial goals, like critical success factors and necessary conditions).

You relate the UDEs via a logical chain of cause and effect to root causes (RCs), and identify the critical RCs producing a majority of the system's UDEs, including the worst ones. There can be more than one RC. You must select those generating the most negative impact in accordance with the TOC's principle of focusing effort where it can be most efficient. Once you identify the UDEs, then you progress from UDE to UDE, backwards through the chain of causes and effects visible in the tree, and eventually arrive at the underlying RC. RC are at the *root* of the logic tree. Notice that there might be numerous intermediate cause-effect entities between an RC and any specific UDE.

UDEs must have certain characteristics to qualify as *good* UDEs. Fedurko (2012) gives a list of several qualifying criteria for discerning a real UDE. A UDE must be an ongoing problem that is constantly present; in other words it is not a one-of-a-kind problem. It is more similar to common cause variation than to special cause variation. Being intrinsic to your situation, a UDE is better described in terms of a state of being rather than actions and transformations. A UDE should fall within your span of control if you are to successfully address it with your own means. You should be able to do something about a UDE; general adverse conditions (the weather is too harsh) are not UDEs. The description of a UDE should not be an expression of blaming or averting responsibilities. UDEs should never be based on unproven speculations or assumptions nor based on wishful thinking (i.e., identifying a false problem that can be resolved with the kind of solution you would like). The undesirability of a UDE should be self-evident with no further need to explain its negative consequences. For the purpose of clear identification, a UDE should not hide further cause-effect relationships. Finally, a UDE should not be subjective (subjective assessments are often given away by adjectives such as difficult, hard, poor, etc.).

SPAN OF CONTROL AND SPHERE OF INFLUENCE

We just mentioned above that a UDE should be such that you can effectively do something about it. For this purpose, we identify and focus only on the RC inside your *Span of Control* or *Sphere of Influence* as described by Dettmer (2007). The Span of Control is that part of the universe over which you have complete power to change anything. The Sphere of Influence is that further part of the universe over which you have some kind of influence; typically this means you need to persuade or gain the agreement of other people who have complete control over those parts.

Consequently, we do not track RC back into the remote external environment, where the possibility of exercising influence are nonexistent. Dettmer gives the wise advice:

> There's no point in working on something over which you don't have at least some influence.

When the RC has been found, depending on *where* it is, you can proceed in two ways:

- If the RC is in your own Span of Control, then you have found a system constraint and you can apply the *Five Focusing Steps* to improve the overall process (and avoid future recurrences of the problem).
- If the RC is in your Sphere of Influence then it is most likely a policy constraint (you are affected by somebody's decision), and you can apply the persuasion techniques that are an integral part of the Thinking Processes. Through such techniques you will gain agreement on the problem, the solution, and the resolution.

HUMAN FACTORS AND CHANGE MANAGEMENT

If you dig deep for the RC of your problems, often you will end up in your Sphere of Influence rather than in your Span of Control. Remember, there is no point going beyond your Sphere of Influence because you cannot have any impact there at all. By definition your Sphere of Influence is controlled by people other than yourself, therefore it is a place where (your) people skills matter.

Demarco (2003) stressed the importance of human factors in the context of risk management. Similarly, Agile methods stress human factors, too. However, of the many approaches in the software engineering literature, none give actionable advice and tools for dealing with human factors. The TOC does, and obviously, the approach starts with logic.

In answering the three fundamental questions (What to change? What to change to? and How to cause the change?), notice how they pertain respectively to the problem, the solution, and the implementation of the solution.

When you are trying to influence others, people might disagree on any of these, and in different ways. This is where you have to use the *categories of legitimate reservation* (CLR) in order to address the *layers of resistance*.

Categories of Legitimate Reservation

The CLR are simply a classification about reservations that might be raised (by yourself or others) from a purely logical perspective. There are seven of them:

- Entity existence
- Causality existence
- Cause insufficiency
- Additional cause
- Cause-effect reversal
- Predicted effect existence
- Tautology

Note that in order to apply the CLR, we further assume that all statements have sufficient clarity to be unambiguously interpreted. If any statement under consideration is ambiguous, you should agree on its meaning first.

Whenever there is a reservation, by recognizing which category it belongs to, you can better handle it. Notably the CLR have a technical role in constructing the logic diagrams and, in particular, the CRT as explained by Dettmer (2007), who refers to them as the *logic glue* that holds these trees together. The CLR are used while constructing the trees in order to assure the reasoning is robust and convincing. Then they can be used after the tree has been drawn, in order to review it. And, in particular, the CLR serve to critically examine the logic trees (or parts of them) presented by others. This is when the CLR gains more than a mere technical role and serve when you need to deal with others. They help to converse about objections and counterarguments in an objective manner. Hence, the CLR help in developing comprehension of the various viewpoints, and avoid adversarial conversations. This last point is particularly important when UDEs originate from people or worse, ingrained policies.

Policy Constraints

Policy constraints (like arbitrary deadline dates) are created by people. They are not limitations of the physical world. Paradoxically, they are much harder to break than physical constraints because often they involve clashes of egos, personalities, power plays, and so on.

This relates deeply to risk management, because of the necessary collaboration and/or understanding between people that is implied in resolving risks that are consequential to such policy constraints. Challenging a policy implies proposing a change. In Cox (2010), Efrat Goldratt-Ashlag explains:

> When we recognize that a change should be made, [...] we cannot pull it off without someone else's permission and/or collaboration. [...] getting buy-in is not a trivial task [...] Resistance comes in many forms.

When you perform root cause analysis, and find that the relevant root causes are in your Sphere of Influence, then you can solve such problems only by involving other people who supposedly you can influence.

In these instances, you must master debating and persuading to convince people to change, and resolve the problems you care about. You have to overcome resistance.

The Layers of Resistance

The layers of resistance are resistances to change that can be classified and confronted in a systematic manner. They are a simple means for recognizing *where* you might find disagreement when you engage in discussions with the individuals in your Sphere of Influence. There are three layers of resistance.[1]

- Disagreement on the problem
- Disagreement on the solution
- Disagreement on the implementation

The three layers of resistance correspond to the three fundamental questions that support the process of continuous improvement:

- What to change?
- What to change to?
- How to cause the change?

If change involves other people, you have to overcome their resistance; they might resist any one of those three questions, hence, the three layers.

While the layers of resistance deal with change generically, more specifically they also characterize problem resolution in the context of risk management. Knowing about the layers of resistance becomes critical when RC are found in your Sphere of Influence because then any problem, solution, or implementation has to gain the agreement of the people involved.

This is why the persuasion techniques of the TOC (which, unsurprisingly, are exactly the same techniques used in the TOCs' sales processes) are important when managing risk. The persuasion techniques allow you to exercise your influence in your Sphere of Influence. In fact, your mastering of these techniques may as well define how far out your Sphere of Influence really reaches.

The layers of resistance are the last tool of the Thinking Processes that we examine here. You might have to handle objections and reservations in any one of these layers. Knowing which layer you are dealing with will help you to use the appropriate tool of the Thinking Processes.

The CRT is the tool of choice for identifying and discussing problems. The Thinking Processes offer other kinds of trees and tools for the other two layers of resistance, such as the future reality tree, the negative branch reservation, the transition tree, the prerequisite tree, and the strategy and tactics tree. While we will not look at these other trees, what you will find as common ingredients in all discussions is how objections are raised; and you can handle them by knowing what kind of reservation is being raised.

REFERENCES

1. Actually, starting from these three layers of resistance, the Thinking Processes elaborate even more layers inside themselves, for a total of nine. These additional layers further expand on how to use the Thinking Process to overcome resistance to change. While the details of such techniques are important, they do not affect the present discussion, and are not examined any further. For more information, see the cited works by Dettmer and Cox.

11

THROUGHPUT ACCOUNTING

This chapter presents the topic of *throughput accounting* (TA), and in particular how TA can be employed in software engineering, although all of the ideas of TA can equally be applied to other fields of knowledge-work. What you should take away from this chapter is the notion that TA changes the priorities by which you make management decisions, compared to the common and widespread *cost accounting* (CA) approach. The decisions you make with TA are often the opposite of those you would arrive at via CA, yet they provide a greater positive impact on the financial performance of the organization.

TA is the approach supporting management accounting suggested by the *Theory of Constraints* (TOC). In Anderson (2003), we find the first application of TA to the field of software engineering. Anderson's ideas have been further expanded by Ricketts (2007), who applied the approach to the professional, scientific, and technical service businesses and, therein, information technology and software engineering.

Unfortunately, TA has gained a bad reputation within the circles of accounting professionals due to the fierce position taken by E. Goldratt against traditional accounting practices. Besides such politics, the reputation is undeserved. TA can effectively be added to the arsenal of management tools, often with spectacular effects on the bottom line.

Originally, it was the need to manage business systems in a more scientific way that led to the creation of TA. In fact, TA is defined by a few simple formulas, which might somehow remind you of the equations you find in physics.

TA is defined by the following arithmetic expressions:

- **Throughput**: TP = Revenue − Totally Variable Expenses
- **Net Profit**: NP = Throughput − Operating Expense
- **Return on Investment**: ROI = Net Profit/Investment

With only three variables to consider, TA becomes accessible to, and usable by, non-accounting professionals. Decision making is simplified. Bragg (2007) remarks that to make the correct decision, you need a positive answer to one of these three questions:

- Does it increase throughput (TP)?
- Does it reduce operating expense (OE)?

- Does it increase the ROI?

It really is as simple as this: with TA, positive business decisions can be taken if the action considered increases TP, decreases OE, or increases ROI.

In particular, ROI is determined only by three variables: TP, OE, and Investment (I). Since the TOC is concerned about producing the maximum result with minimum effort, a *leveraging priority* is defined among those three variables. One should favor, in order:

- Increase in TP
- Decrease in I
- Decrease in OE

This priority is contrary to what is customary in conventional cost accounting, which favors cost reduction above anything else. One key tenet of the TOC is this: reducing cost is limited, while increasing TP is potentially unlimited. An excessive focus on cost reduction will jeopardize the company's capacity to deliver and will decrease TP, with much more devastating consequences.

THROUGHPUT ACCOUNTING VERSUS COST ACCOUNTING

The order of focusing in TA is the opposite from that which is assumed in traditional CA, where the focus is on reducing costs, while any consideration about increasing TP is considered last. This is another technical reason why TA is at odds with CA. CA presents fundamental problems, as described by Corbett (1998):

> [...] cost accounting is based on the assumption that the lower the cost of a product, the greater a company's profit. As the product cost results from the products' use of the company's resources, one way of reducing the cost of a product is by reducing its process time on a resource.

This kind of thinking leads companies to seek local optimizations (i.e., reducing processing time on all resources); only to be deluded to find that the sum of the parts is less than the whole. The TOC focuses optimization efforts only on the *capacity constrained resource* because it maintains a systems thinking view, and aims at improving the economic performance of the business as a whole.

With focus on the constraint, the TOC favors optimizing the performance of one resource at a time; and not of all resources all the time. The analogy of the chain illustrates this—the whole chain gets stronger only by strengthening the weakest link. When focus is on TP, you have to adopt a systems thinking view, which is hindered by traditional CA. Minimizing overall resource utilization and unit product cost becomes the last resort and not the first, as sustained by CA.

Cost Accounting Is Not for Management Decisions

Using CA to make management decisions is a mistake because that is not its intended purpose. Smith (1999) explains that CA's main purpose is to comply to Generally Accepted

Accounting Principles (GAAP). However, that does not imply that CA data should also support management decision making—this is the underlying and common misunderstanding. Smith further observes that conventional CA already acknowledges that you maximize profit by selling the product with the highest contribution margin per unit of its scarce resource.

TA is not really new, it just renders practical an abstract accounting idea. Cost, or absorption accounting, has the only purpose of satisfying outside reporting requirements, but it is not the right tool for management decisions. Therefore, use CA for external reporting requirements, but TA for making management decisions.

Throughput Accounting Can Be Reconciled with Cost Accounting

Traditional accounting theory recognizes the underlying principle of TA. To reiterate, it is: sell the product with the highest contribution margin per unit of scarce resource. The key terms to understand are *contribution margin* and *unit of scarce resource*. Notice that the principle becomes actionable only through the systems thinking approach of the TOC. TA is just the numbers tool to make the principle practical from a financial point of view. (Other tools of the TOC contribute to more operational and logical aspects.)

A significant corollary follows: TA is part of the generally accepted accounting theory, and it can be reconciled with GAAP for customary external reporting needs.

The contraposition between TA and CA is more artificial and political than actual. The reconciliation between the two was certainly not helped by Goldratt's unmitigated positions and statements. He was known for uttering harsh statements targeted at CA (such as: "Cost Accounting is productivity's public enemy number one.").

The contraposition has been sustained even through technical arguments. In particular, observe that traditional CA provides artificial incentives to build inventories. This is the technical reason why TA has been poorly accepted by traditional accounting professionals. CA values inventory as a positive asset, while TA considers inventory as a negative liability, indicating a weakness or even a dysfunction in the whole organization. Work in process and inventory are negative liabilities. They limit TP and are indicative of deeper organizational and work-flow problems.

The duality is more artificial than real, and is also simple to reconcile as highlighted by Smith (1999). The effort of transforming absorption costs into decision-making data is futile, and there is an easier alternative: that of using a bridge to convert periodic direct costs into absorption costs. In fact, this approach is typical with small firms that have not adopted an advanced computerized system that can track costs by product at the smallest unit of time. This bridging approach is straightforward, requires no complicated software, and is known by all accountants.

What is the important conclusion? Reconciling TA with CA is a simple accounting exercise that any trained accountant can perform. The real challenge is often in making the accountants appreciate the overall operational benefit, and true bottom line impact of TA. A lesser challenge is recognizing that TA uses a different terminology for concepts which are already well known in traditional accounting.

Now that we've seen that TA can coexist with traditional CA, and that any dismissal of TA is mostly due to not understanding that it is already part of traditional CA, we can move on and see what this means for software engineering.

THROUGHPUT ACCOUNTING FOR SOFTWARE ENGINEERING

Software engineering is intangible, while the origins of the TOC are in the very tangible manufacturing industries. To acknowledge these differences, Ricketts (2007) identifies a *Throughput Accounting for Software Engineering* (TASE).

Ricketts defines a more extensive *Throughput Accounting for Software Businesses,* covering sales and research in addition to software engineering proper, and also distinguishes between selling a software product and a software service. He further distinguishes between TA for software engineering and other intangible service businesses, which are different because they are more labor based and less automated and reusable. For this discussion, TASE alone is sufficient. TASE is defined in terms of TP, I, and OE, as follows:

- *Throughput of Software Engineering* (TSE) is the rate at which money is generated by delivering working software to paying clients. It can easily be calculated as sales minus all direct costs, including packaging, installation, training, support, and so on.
- Investment is all amounts needed to put in place the software development systems and to discover, create, or elicit the requirements.
- OE is all amounts needed to transform ideas into working code. In practice, the salaries of software engineers, sales efforts, and administrative costs are all part of the OE.

The following performance measures are computed exactly the same way:

- **Net Profit**: NP = TSE − OE
- **Return on Investment**: ROI = NP/I

A simple view is sufficient to draw meaningful conclusions: NP is the difference between the revenue generated and the implementation cost; ROI is the ratio between NP and requirements gathering costs (and considering the cost of the software production system already amortized). To increase NP and ROI, you must increase TSE while decreasing I and OE. Ricketts (2007) suggests this is best done by collecting good requirements as quickly as possible in order to eliminate all waste that derives from requirements that are not deployed to, or used in, production. In practice, you should minimize time spent gathering requirements and planning, and minimize the scope of the project.

These principles, derived from the TOCs' systems thinking approach, and supported by TA, are comparable to what is endorsed by Agile and Lean processes. On the contrary, the application of these principles to traditional software processes is in conflict with the need to identify *all possible* requirements upfront.

Example: Decrease Operating Expense by Avoiding Feature Creep

You can reduce the OE by discarding requirements before starting implementation work, as described in Tendon (2010) where a value-based technique for triaging requirements expressed as user stories and estimated in terms of story points (as proposed by Cohn, 2005) is presented.

Each story point was associated with a corresponding estimated revenue value, which was recomputed after eliminating unnecessary stories. In an agile setting with a CA perspective, the production cost of a story point is always the same; the only way to increase value is to lower the cost per story point, or increase velocity/productivity. With TA, instead, increasing TP in terms of the story point's economic value is different. The stories worth less are eliminated. After eliminating a single story, you reduced the OE (the effort to produce the software).

From an Agile perspective, you have applied the principle of simplicity to *maximize the amount of work not done* of the *Agile Manifesto* (Beck, 2001). From a Lean perspective (Poppendieck, 2003), you applied the principle of eliminating waste.

By recomputing the value of the story point, the overall value of the project increases. Reducing scope, project duration, and time to market decreases; therefore ROI not only increases, but gets realized and collected much sooner.

Example: Decrease Investment and Operating Expense with Open Source Software

Adopting open source software is naturally a way to reduce I. You avoid developing all the equivalent functionality. The broader the open source solution, the more you decrease I. The narrower the proprietary extensions you develop yourself, the smaller the OE. Choose your market so that your proprietary development becomes as small as possible. Choose the open source project to maximize coverage of your requirements, and conversely minimize what you have to implement yourself.

Example: Increase Throughput by Targeting the Long Tail

When it comes to choosing a market, instead of targeting broad markets, you can increase the unit price of your sales by focusing on a market niche (i.e., the *long tail*). For instance, if you were in the CRM business, providing a solution targeted at certain professional categories with some unique features (such as complying with law requirement), you could command a higher price. Increasing sales price is a way to increase TP.

Combine this with the previous example: embracing open source software as a platform on top of which you can develop your own solutions frees up resources to develop other value-adding code. The custom code will add value appreciated by the market niche. With more resources, you can also have more frequent releases, which (if paid for) increase TP.

The key point: when there is the chance to free up resources, don't take this as an opportunity to lower costs by reducing head count. Instead, use the freed-up engineering capacity to develop further value adding functions or products. That's the significant, big difference that comes from focusing on throughput first and on costs last.

Considerations on Combining the Examples

The strategy of embracing an open source project decreases OE (as does outsourcing) because there is less work to be done in-house. At the same time (and unlike outsourcing), it also reduces I because you don't need a requirements gathering phase to define the part of functionality delivered by the open source software (apart from the activity of evaluating the fitness for purpose of the open source software), nor to invest in any additional equipment to support the development of the platform. By outsourcing the development of such functionality, rather than exploiting open source software, you still increase OE (but less than by doing the development in-house).

By choosing to target a long tail niche market and defining the scope of functionality covered respectively by the open source component and your proprietary development, you give the proprietary code a positive impact on ROI, according to TA. Choosing the open source allows you to reduce I. Limiting the scope of the proprietary code reduces OE. The strategy to target a niche market increases TP because higher prices can be commanded.

Adopting open source software is seen as I; with the very beneficial quality of being free. Though there is a component of OE, too, to cover the new kinds of activities that come with open source software. *Using* open source software is not a zero-cost operation. Only the acquisition is zero-cost. Consider the total cost of ownership, and at least the expenses for gaining the knowledge about how to use open source software. Often, it also means assigning development resources for integration, extensions, and maintenance of open source software. Time must be invested in tracking down problems, especially when support is not available (as is often the case with smaller open source software solutions). The sum of all the additional OE is negligible compared to the effect of the I we are focusing on. Recall: I appears as the denominator in the ROI ratio, while OE is only a factor in the numerator difference. Finally, consider that the work on the proprietary code is all covered by OEs.

SOFTWARE PRODUCTION METRICS IN THROUGHPUT ACCOUNTING

Ricketts (2007) suggests using the following metrics specifically for software production:

- **Production Quantity**: Q = client valued functions delivered in working code
- **Inventory**: V = ideas + functions in development + completed functions
- **Average Cost per Function**: ACPF = OE/Q

The ACPF was originally presented by Anderson (2003), who also defined the:

- **Average Investment per Function**: AIPF = I/Q
  Ricketts suggests that Q, V, and ACPF correspond to TP, I, and OE, respectively. However, we may consider this imprecise, and propose to add an **Average Throughput per Function** (ATPF) defined as:
- **Average Throughput per Function**: ATPF = T/Q
  The ATPF metric, rather than Q, is more correctly mapped to TP. Using just Q appears to consider cost (the implied assumption being that cost is proportional to quantity) as prevalent over TP.

As illustrated in the preceding example (about decreasing OEs by avoiding feature creep), the ATPF metric has important practical applications. To be precise, in the case cited in that example, the *average revenue per story point* was used; but revenue per story point/ function can be considered as a first approximation of ATPF. The TP per story point just subtracts a constant factor—the totally variable costs—from the revenue figure. Triaging stories and eliminating those worth less increases both numbers, so the effect on the decision making is unaltered by using the simplified metrics.

Take advantage of these software specific production metrics derived from TA. In particular, focus on increasing the ATPF and decreasing the AIPF. Consider the ACPF last.

THROUGHPUT ACCOUNTING'S EFFECTS ON DELIVERY

The different perspectives given by TA and CA with respect to software engineering are described in detail by Ricketts (2007). Traditional CA gives more weight to OE rather than TP or I. In a traditional setting, timesheets are used to track software engineering tasks, and tally the corresponding costs as value of the software that is being coded. This brings about the absurd consequence that the longer a software development effort lasts, the more CA will value the software as an asset. Hence, there is no economic incentive for early completion, even though it is well known that software requirements have more value the sooner they are delivered. Undelivered software or late software will inevitably become *shelf-ware*.

When using TA, the perspective is different, because there is no adding up of *added value*. TA will simply take notice of I at the start, and of TP at the end of the project. There is no need to use timesheets, because all work is covered by OE. This has the opposite valuation on project duration; the longer a project lasts, the more OE will increase, and hence, decrease its TP. In this way, TA provides a financial incentive to finish projects sooner, as that is what will maximize NP. This line of reasoning gives financial support to Agile/Lean processes that promote early completion and frequent delivery on the basis of technical reasons (to better capture and live up to the client's needs). TA creates incentives to complete projects on time, or earlier, for financial reasons. And it is really simple: record I at the start and TP at the end, while all effort is represented as a fixed running cost by OEs.

Throughput Accounting's Effects on Other Common Processes

TASE also provides a different viewpoint than CA on some common circumstances in software engineering, also well described by Ricketts (2007). For instance:

- Staff turnover will decrease OE but also TP on the constraint. The loss of TP can be many times larger than the cost of turnover, which would be the only variable noticed by CA.
- New hires will not affect TP, unless they occur on the constraint. So new hires will usually increase OE, yet give no effect on TP.
- Outsourcing will lower OE, but it might move the constraint. Outsourcing the constraint might result in less TP, with an impact many times larger than the corresponding cost saving.
- Protecting projects through buffering of various kinds (time, money, resources, and scope) will increase OE, but not TP. For instance, adoption of defined processes and maturity certification aim at reducing the extent of such buffers, but they themselves increase OE. This raises the question: Do they really make a tangible difference at the end?

CONCLUSION

The simplicity of TA's logic reveals a general strategic direction, which can be verified and validated with the simple metrics of TP, OE, and I. TA gives strong arguments to pursue (or not pursue) any strategy under consideration, even without estimating or calculating costs and revenues, but only through logic. TA's strength is in the simplicity of its approach to decision making when supported by its metrics; it is an advantage because it comes to a decision in less time.

TA can be used to take management decisions on all business processes, including turnover, hiring, outsourcing, choice of methodology, and so on. The trick is simply that of relating any decision to TP, OE, and I, in order to make an informed and financially sound decision.

12

HERBIE AND KANBAN

The previous chapter about *Throughput Accounting* hinted about the *Theory of Constraints* (TOC). In this section we will focus on the more practical, hands-on aspects of building a hyper-productive knowledge-work organization, and the TOC plays a critical role in our approach. Therefore, we will start by introducing the most basic ideas about the TOC, as they were originally described by Eliyahu Goldratt in his business novel *The Goal* (Goldratt, 1992).

THE STORY OF HERBIE

The first description of the TOC comes through the story about an overnight hike that a team of scouts set out on. They start their walk early in the morning, planning to hike through a forest to some remote place where they will set up camp and sleep overnight. Then they will walk back the morning after.

The trail in front of the team can be imagined as a long series of steps, like this:

The walk starts briskly. The terrain is not challenging and the trail is well-marked and easy to follow.

All scouts carry their own rucksack on their backs.

The terrain becomes more difficult, with undergrowth on both sides, forcing the hike into a single line.

As the terrain becomes more and more difficult, the line gets stretched longer and longer. The troop leader is concerned about keeping the team together, so nobody gets lost in the forest.

One of the scouts is a little overweight.

He also carries a backpack that is obviously overloaded.

At first, the overweight scout can keep his pace within the line. Slowly a gap develops in front of him, while he is holding back everybody behind.

Even if the troop leader encourages the team to close ranks, slowly, step by step, the little overweight scout loses his position, as those behind him overtake him to fill the gap in front of him.

Eventually he drops to the end of the line.

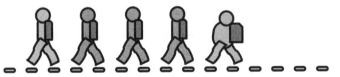

Finally, a gap develops and he stands out, far behind all the others.

That scout is Herbie. The troop leader calls him, *"Herbieeeee!"*

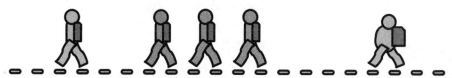

The troop leader shouts, *"C'mon, Herbie! Speed up!"* to encourage the scout to walk faster but he's already walking at the maximum of his capacity.

Eventually, the leader understands that Herbie's speed is determining the troop's ability as a whole to move faster; but Herbie can only walk at his own speed, which is slower than anybody else's. Herbie is determining the troop's throughput in terms of how much terrain they actually cover.

The troop leader gets the insight that whoever is moving the slowest in the troop is actually determining the overall throughput. That role can actually float from one scout to another; it depends on who is the slowest at that moment.

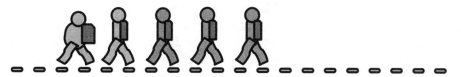

At that time, Herbie, obviously, has the least capacity for walking and his speed ultimately determines the speed of the entire troop.

The troop leader then puts Herbie in front of the line and commands: "Everybody stays behind Herbie!" and also gives instructions that nobody passes anybody else, but keeps to his position.

In that way the team can stay together and nobody's out of breath. Any gap that develops can easily be recovered, since everybody can walk *faster* than Herbie, who is at the front. Now at least, nobody will get lost in the woods.

However, time is running short and they risk not reaching their camp before dark. The troop needs to walk faster.

Herbie is not only overweight himself—he is also overloaded. Being fond of food, he carries along a six-pack of soda, some cans of spaghetti, a box of candy bars, a jar of pickles, and two cans of tuna fish. In addition, for the sake of being prepared (as a good scout), he is also loaded with a rain coat, rubber boots, a bag of tent stakes, a large iron skillet, and a collapsible, steel shovel.

The troop leader realizes that if they can take some of the load off of Herbie, he will be able to walk faster. So the leader commands: "Everybody carries a piece of Herbie's gear."

With the new arrangement the team can pace at double the speed they did before, while they are still able to keep together behind Herbie. They arrive to their night camp late in the afternoon, just before dusk. The troop leader reflects over the fact that Herbie was the key for governing the performance of the *entire* team.

HERBIE AND WORK IN PROCESS

The troop of hiking scouts is similar to a system that has to produce a product or deliver a service. The troop delivers *walked trail*—that is, the distance that the whole team has covered together. The head of the line begins work by processing the unconsumed trail in front of the troop, which is the equivalent of raw material, or work to be done.

When the first scout in line walks, he processes work and hands it over to the second one in line, followed by the next, and so on until the last one. Every scout is like an operation or a step in a production or delivery process. No matter in what order the scouts are lined up, they represent a series of dependent events, subject to statistical fluctuations on how fast they can walk. Statistical fluctuations will accumulate rather than average out, explaining why the line tends to get longer and longer. Not until the last scout has walked a step, can that step be considered as delivered.

All the steps between the first and last scout is the inventory or work in process. When the distance between the first and last scout increases, there is more work in process. The throughput of the system of walking scouts corresponds to the rate of walking (their speed).

Operational expense is the energy required by the scout to sustain the walk. Any time they hurry up to close a gap, operational expense increases because they consume more energy.

THE FIVE FOCUSING STEPS

The way the troop leader rearranged the order of the line and redistributed the load to carry is an example of the so-called *Five Focusing Steps* (5FS) of the TOC. The 5FS are the foundation of the process of ongoing improvement that characterizes the TOC. The 5FS are stated more clearly in the paragraphs that follow:

Step 1: Identify the Constraint—*"Herbie!"*

A production/delivery system is considered as a chain; and the chain has a weakest link. That weakest link is the constraint that prevents the entire system from performing more. The first step is to identify the constraint, so one knows exactly where to intervene. In the example, the weakest link was Herbie.

Step 2: Exploit the Constraint—"C'mon Herbie! Speed up!"

The second step is to exploit the constraint, in the sense that you must ensure that it is working to the maximum of its capacity. This is what the leader was doing when he kept on encouraging Herbie to walk as fast as he could.

Step 3: Subordinate to the Constraint— Everybody stays behind Herbie!"

The third step is to ensure that all other resources of the system subordinate to the constraint. By putting everybody behind Herbie, the leader made sure that the line was kept short, that nobody ran away in the front, and that they all arrived together at their destination. By means of subordination, overproduction is avoided while inventory and work in process is kept under control.

Step 4: Elevate the Constraint—"Everybody carries a piece of Herbie's gear!"

The fourth step intends to elevate the capacity of the constraint. By elevating the capacity of the constraint, the entire system will perform better; it will perform at the new level reached by the constraint. In the story, Herbie's walking speed was elevated by offloading his rucksack. As a result the entire team could progress faster through the forest.

Step 5: Repeat!

While not illustrated in the story, the final step is to go back to step one. In particular, this should happen if the elevation of the constraint actually breaks the constraint. This could happen, for example, if Herbie, without his load, could walk faster than someone else. In that case, that other scout would have become the new constraint of the team. Any time a constraint is elevated, it is possible that it will no longer be the constraint. Some other resource might take its place. Also note that a constraint may move because of other events, unrelated to Herbie himself. For example, another scout might develop a blister on his heel which is now slowing him down so much that he can't keep up with the rest, including Herbie.

The fifth step is also accompanied by a warning, suggesting you should not allow *inertia* to become a constraint. At times, complacency and relaxation takes over, and you are no longer actively looking for the real constraint.

The *Unstated* Step 0

Often a *Step Zero* is also listed: that of determining and agreeing on the *goal* that the system needs to pursue. Without agreement on the common goal, it is impossible to determine if any change is an improvement or not. In the case of the scouts, the goal was reaching the night camp before dark.

The *Secret* Step 6

On a more strategic level, a *Step 6* is considered whereby you deliberately redesign your system and decide where you want to place the constraint. By intentionally deciding where to place and where to maintain the constraint, all other subordination and elevation decisions become easier. By keeping the constraint in a given place, the whole system becomes simpler to manage because it remains stable. This is important, because (as we will see in other chapters) stability is also a prerequisite for being able to use *Little's Law*.

FROM STEPPING STONES TO THE KANBAN BOARD

Another critical component of our hyper-productive approach is the use of the *Kanban Method*, as originally taught by David Anderson—a pioneer in using the TOC in software engineering (Anderson, 2003). It is no surprise then, that the Kanban Method was deeply influenced by the TOC, as David Anderson (2012) says:

> What I didn't expect to find in Eli Goldratt's writings were the foundations of what we now call the Kanban Method; the foundations of an incremental, evolutionary approach to change and an explanation for why people resist change in the organizations and in their working practices. [...] It is clear [...] that the Kanban Method can be described as an evolution of the Five Focusing Steps (drum-buffer-rope) embodiment of the TOC, most heavily associated with Goldratt's work in the 1980s.

One way to see this association is to consider, again, a snapshot of the scouts' hike through the forest, like this:

We can make the association more evident by first enlarging the *stepping stones* of the trail, like this:

Then we just draw those stepping stones as a column underneath each scout, like this:

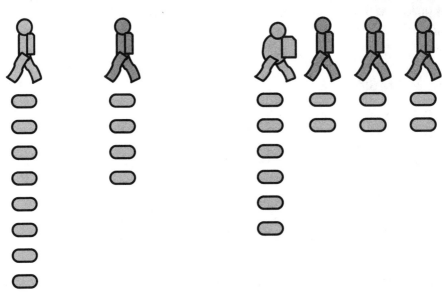

At that point, we space them out evenly across, and we have effectively produced a *Kanban Board*:

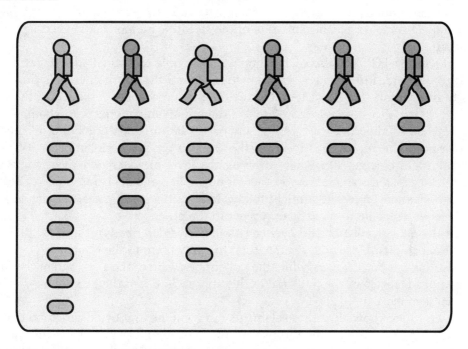

Such visualization represents the walking effort (work) that each scout has to perform. (For more information about Kanban Boards, refer to Anderson [2010]; we assume that a Kanban Board is a known tool.) This shows how tight the connection is between the TOC and the Kanban Board. Therefore, it stands to reason that all the tools and methods of the TOC can be applied to any work or process that is represented on or by a Kanban Board.

A PHILOSOPHY OF ONGOING IMPROVEMENT

One of the most important insights that inspired the creation of Scrum is that software development is an empirical process and it can be managed only through empirical process control methods, wherein feedback loops play an important role. Scrum tries hard to institutionalize such loops with its practices (daily stand-up meeting, sprint, stakeholder demo/show, retrospective, etc.).

In almost all significant process approaches, ongoing improvement through feedback loops and iterative activities play an important role. Some noteworthy improvement loops are:

- Deming's *Plan-Do-Check-Act*
- Shewart's *Plan-Do-Study-Act* cycle for learning and improvement
- Six Sigma's *Define-Measure-Analyze-Improve-Control*
- Colonel Boyd's *Observe-Orient-Decide-Act*

These feedback loops work great, not only on a tactical level where they allow organizations to steer their projects and activities in operational terms, but also on a greater scale, and on a strategic level.

The reconception phase of an iterative emergent process is discernible in all these loops; it invariably implies change. Change is going from a before to an after. It means deciding what to change and identifying what to change to, and how to make the change happen. They are all, in some way, an instantiation of the scientific method and, hence, in line with empiricism.

The 5FS of the TOC are also such a loop with a couple of distinct advantages. The first advantage is the idea of leveraging all activities around the constraints. This provides an ability to focus effort that is not found in the other approaches. Consequently, the second advantage is that once constraints are broken, the improvement effects are dramatic.

The Kanban Method does not impose any particular direction in its improvements efforts. Normally, the approach is to lower the work in process limits in order to discover where the rocks emerge (like when lowering the level of water in a river, you will see where the biggest rocks are). However there is no explicit and deliberate sense of direction of the improvement actions that might follow. In fact, it is possible that successive actions might be counterproductive, one with respect to the other.

Given the evident relationship between the 5FS (as described in the story of Herbie) and the Kanban Board, it would seem natural to apply them to the Kanban process. However, most Kanban practitioners, while they might be aware of the TOC and of the 5FS, do not take full advantage of the potential of this approach. Often the 5FS are used in a very superficial manner.

Later, we will see how all of these elements can combine to provide a method that thoroughly supports focusing on the throughput of the system. Having a clear focus on flow and throughput is a precondition to hyper-productivity, as we will see in the next chapter.

13

THE FINANCIAL METRIC SUPPORTING UNITY OF PURPOSE AND COMMUNITY OF TRUST

The story of Herbie is illustrative of the general concepts of the *Theory of Constraints* (TOC) and the process of ongoing improvement which is represented by the *Five Focusing Steps* (5FS). While the ideas of the TOC were originally applied to the factory floor, the story of Herbie contains another key to unlock hyper-productivity.

When the troop leader shouts, "Everybody stays behind Herbie!" (to subordinate to the constraint), and later, "Everybody carries a piece of Herbie's gear!" (to elevate the constraint), he is effectively instilling the two principles of *Unity of Purpose* and *Community of Trust* into the psychology and the minds of the boy scouts. At first, some might protest, but once the spirit of one for all and all for one starts to become internalized, the whole team's performance will increase.

Herbie alone, by being put in front of the line, will probably walk faster than if he kept lagging far behind everybody else. Herbie needs to trust his peers to let them carry his valuable gear. Herbie will become grateful to all others once they arrive at their destination. Once he is no longer the *constraint*, but someone else is, he will be more prone to reciprocate.

Therefore, we see the powerful connection between the 5FS of the TOC (when applied to people rather than to machines) and the noble patterns of Unity of Purpose and Community of Trust.

PROBLEM: CONFLICTING METRICS AND INCENTIVES

Nobody will doubt that a Unity of Purpose and Community of Trust are key ingredients in any company. Few will say openly that their organization is in any way lacking a unity of purpose and that it is not a community of trust. Even if it were not so, it wouldn't be politically correct to affirm otherwise.

The Unity of Purpose and Community of Trust patterns are cornerstone patterns for achieving hyper-productivity. Unfortunately, the vast majority of organizations are miserably lacking and deficient in this respect because of how organizations are structured and how they measure performance. In other words, the majority of organizations are structurally and behaviorally prevented from enjoying a Unity of Purpose and Community of Trust.

The inherent problem that prevents both the Unity of Purpose and the Community of Trust patterns from getting a foothold inside organizations becomes evident when it is time to make decisions. It relates to conflicts of interests and different agendas. The trouble is revealed even when simple and fundamental business decisions have to be made; decisions that one would expect to have unanimous support.

Decision Making That Creates Disharmonies

Let us illustrate the matter with a simple example. This example is credited to Prof. James R. Holt at Washington State University. We have to decide which product to build. Suppose we can choose between making four products: A, B, C, and D. Their selling price is as shown in Figure 13.1.

The company is growing. You cannot make the decision by yourself. You must delegate the decision making. You expect your team to make a wise decision, which is in the best interest of the company. We further suppose that the market is not limited, and that it will absorb any amount of products we can make. However, we do have limitations in our production capacity.

While the products might have different looks and appeals, knowing only about their selling price is not enough to make a good decision. We need to gather and/or derive some further information in order to make the decision. Figure 13.2 shows what information we might be interested in.

First we look at how long it takes to produce any single product, and list their respective build times. The product build times are, respectively, 36, 38, 35, and 35 minutes.

Next, we take into consideration what parts, components, and materials are needed to build any single product and sum up the material costs for building any single product. Respectively: $20, $25, $25, and $20.

Then we consider labor and calculate the labor cost incurred in building any one of the four products. The incurred labor costs are, respectively: $6.00, $6.33, $5.83, and $5.83.

Finally, we can calculate the gross profit of the four products, which results in, respectively: $24.00, $18.67, $24.17, and $26.17.

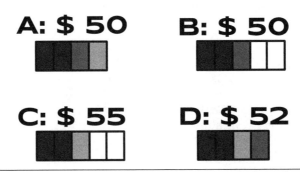

Figure 13.1   Four products and their selling price: which one should we sell?

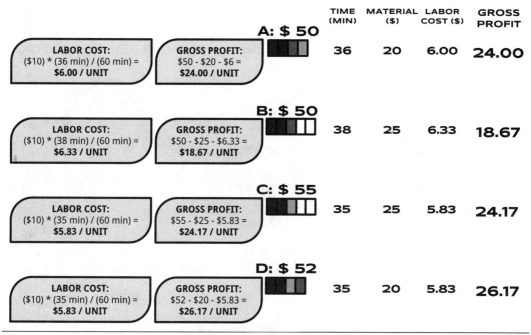

			TIME (MIN)	MATERIAL ($)	LABOR COST ($)	GROSS PROFIT
A: $ 50						
LABOR COST: ($10) * (36 min) / (60 min) = $6.00 / UNIT	GROSS PROFIT: $50 - $20 - $6 = $24.00 / UNIT		36	20	6.00	24.00
B: $ 50						
LABOR COST: ($10) * (38 min) / (60 min) = $6.33 / UNIT	GROSS PROFIT: $50 - $25 - $6.33 = $18.67 / UNIT		38	25	6.33	18.67
C: $ 55						
LABOR COST: ($10) * (35 min) / (60 min) = $5.83 / UNIT	GROSS PROFIT: $55 - $25 - $5.83 = $24.17 / UNIT		35	25	5.83	24.17
D: $ 52						
LABOR COST: ($10) * (35 min) / (60 min) = $5.83 / UNIT	GROSS PROFIT: $52 - $20 - $5.83 = $26.17 / UNIT		35	20	5.83	26.17

Figure 13.2   Considering time, material, and labor cost, we calculate the gross profit. Production times are in minutes. Resource costs: $10 per hour, working 8 hours per day.

The decision seems quite natural: we pick the product with the highest gross profit, meaning that product D should be chosen. It is at this point where the undermining of the Unity of Purpose and Community of Trust patterns really happens. The decision might seem rational and completely in line with the business objective of maximizing profit.

When the company grows, it will add more staff and specialize it by function. You will have sales, engineering, support, marketing, and so on. The problem is that each department has different objectives and interests, which may or may not be in conflict with another. Figure 13.3 highlights the diverse and conflicting perspectives that people might have.

For instance, if Sales and Production departments were to make the choice of product, it would be different than the one obviously chosen by the Accounting unit. So the choice is no longer so obvious:

- Accounting would keep the original choice, as it optimizes profit.
- Sales would prefer the product that gives the highest sales commission.
- Production would pick the product that gives the best resource utilization figures.

Even if a choice is mandated by executive management, the practice might roll out differently. So while management might decree that product *D* should be sold at the end of the month, Sales comes in with an urgent order of product *C*. Or maybe the head of Sales makes friends with the head of Production and will ask him or her to produce more of product *C* in exchange for selling more of product *B*; that way both Sales and Production

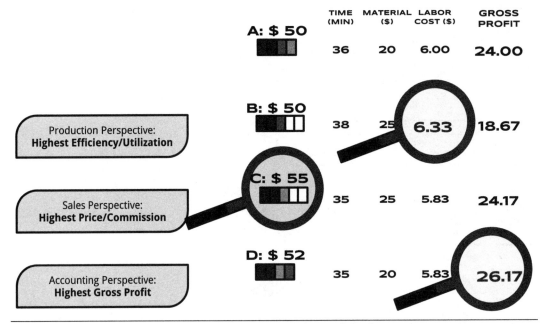

	TIME (MIN)	MATERIAL ($)	LABOR COST ($)	GROSS PROFIT
A: $ 50	36	20	6.00	24.00
B: $ 50	38	25	6.33	18.67
C: $ 55	35	25	5.83	24.17
D: $ 52	35	20	5.83	26.17

Production Perspective: **Highest Efficiency/Utilization**

Sales Perspective: **Highest Price/Commission**

Accounting Perspective: **Highest Gross Profit**

Figure 13.3   Conflicting views between Accounting, Sales, and Production

are happier, while the accountants will grumble over why the company is not pursuing the maximization of profits.

Different incentives and metrics create internal tension and conflicts. Production, Sales, Accounting, etc., will have different (hidden) agendas, because they are judged by different metrics and driven by different incentives. It is impossible to have Unity of Purpose and to build a Community of Trust in the presence of different metrics that establish different incentives.

Unfortunately, the vast majority of companies foster precisely such conditions. Often these partial interests are hidden under the more politically correct term of optimization. Actually, they are all local optimizations and truly do not benefit the business as a whole. Local optimizations are the source of all internal conflicts and tensions that hide within organizations and that give rise to hidden agendas, mistrust, and the prevalence of the command-and-control management style.

What about your company? Do you recognize that your company is driven by local optimizations, with different metrics and different incentives? If so, give it up! You will never achieve organizational hyper-productivity. First, you must focus the entire organization on a system-wide common metric and align the personal interest of all single individuals.

SOLUTION: ADOPT A SYSTEM-WIDE METRIC

To develop a systemic view, it is necessary to stop chasing local optimizations. The simplest way to do so is to start focusing on flow; that, in turn, is most easily achieved by answering a simple question: how much can we make per day?

The qualification *per day* changes the perspective radically. To be able to answer the question, different information is needed; information that can be gained only by examining the system as a whole.

IMPLEMENTATION: FOCUS ON FLOW

We know that we have a production or delivery process, which may be similar to that shown in Figure 13.4.

We see that product *A* is built by taking two darker pieces to perform some work on them; then a medium shade piece is assembled with the next step in the process; and finally a light piece is added with a last bit of work. This is done similarly for the other products.

In short, we are able to visualize how the production process rolls out. (Naturally, this also applies in the case of services, where we would focus on an analogous delivery process rather than on a production process.)

Once we know what the production/delivery process looks like, we need to find resources. For example, we hire two workers: Mr. X and Mr. Y. We know they cost us $10 per hour and that they will work 8 hours per day: Mr. X and Mr. Y are assigned to operate parts

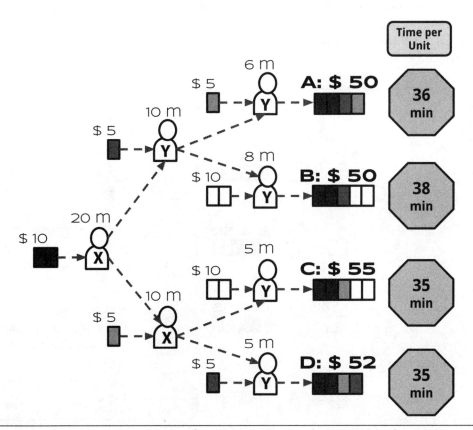

Figure 13.4 Process overview with specific resources (Mr. X and Mr. Y) assigned to process steps, with materials and times. Focus is on time needed to build a single unit.

of the process, according to their qualifications, skills, and abilities—maybe after an initial period of training. In the example, Mr. X will be able to perform two steps of the process, while Mr. Y will be able to perform five steps.

Next, we consider where in the process the raw materials, parts, and components are worked on and assembled into the final product, and further qualify the costs of material. The costs add up to what was already listed in the materials cost in the first calculation.

For product A, we have $10 for the two darker shaded parts, $5 for the medium shaded part and $5 for the light part; which adds up to $20, as listed in the material column. The same holds for the other products. We see the breakdown of costs in their constituent components.

Likewise we map out how much time each step in the process takes. We see that Product A needs 20 minutes of work in the first step of the process, which is performed by Mr. X. Then Mr. Y takes over and works 10 minutes on the second step and another 6 minutes on the third step. The total adds up to the 36 minutes. We thus gain an understanding about which resources (Mr. X or Mr. Y) are active at any step of the process, which materials they use and how long it takes, as illustrated in Figure 13.5.

With this knowledge we can compute how much time is needed by each resource to produce each product and, consequently, the maximum number of units per day that can be produced.

Mr. X is the constraint in the making of all four products. He always works *more* than Mr. Y. By looking at the maximum amount of time that Mr. X can work on any given product, we calculate the maximum number of units that can be produced per day, as shown in Figure 13.6.

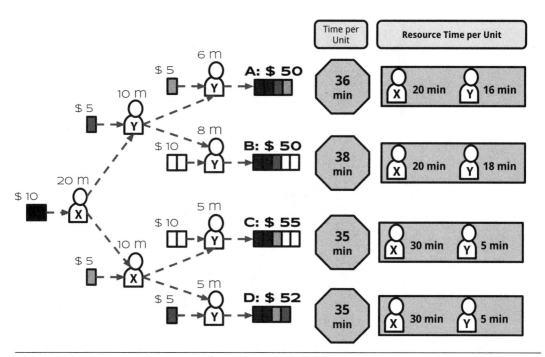

Figure 13.5   Resource time per unit for each resource involved

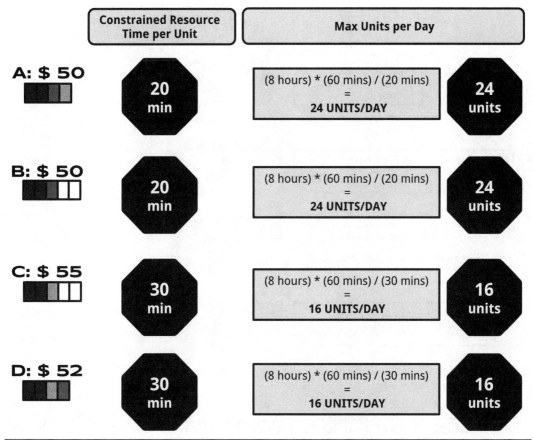

Figure 13.6   Calculation of maximum number of units per day (operational throughput) based on constrained resource time per unit

For instance, if we consider product *A*: Mr. X works 20 minutes to produce one unit. The question is: how many 20-minute periods can fit in an 8-hour workday. The answer is 24. In this way we can find that we have a production capacity, respectively, of 24, 24, 16, and 16 units per day.

The maximum units per day refers to how many units of a certain product we can produce with the *current* process and resources.

The totally variable cost (TVC) is the cost incurred in producing every single unit; in this simple case it is the cost of material. We consider the operational expense the cost of the resources for the reference period (one day in this example). This cost is incurred by the company whether the resources are producing or not; in this case it corresponds to the labor cost of the two workers (Mr. X and Mr. Y). We calculate the maximum possible throughput per day for each of the four products and subtract the TVC from sales.

Now, we subtract the operational expense to find the daily net profit, resulting in, respectively, $560, $440, $320, and $352 per day, as highlighted in Figure 13.7.

After giving due attention to the constraint that is limiting the production capacity and to the effect of the time dimension, we see that the net profit per day changes the decision

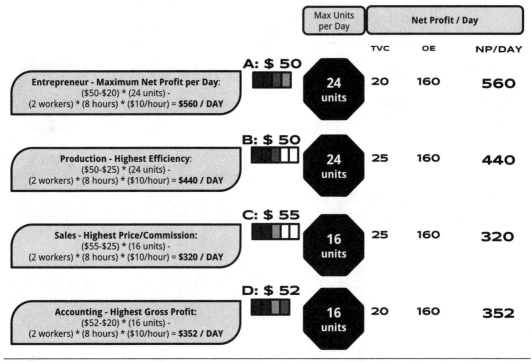

Figure 13.7   Calculation of maximum net profit per day (financial throughput) based on the maximum number of units per day

quite dramatically. We can now focus on the right choice—Product *A* gives the highest throughput per day, as you can see in Figure 13.8.

This choice gives us 60% more money per day than the original, obvious choice of Product D, the product that gave us the highest gross profit. We did not have to use any more data to make this decision. We can compare the two cases by looking at the tables of numbers that we used to make the calculation, as shown in Figure 13.9.

In the original case, based on traditional cost accounting (CA), we looked at time (minutes), material (in dollars) and labor cost (in dollars) to compute the gross profit. In the revised case, based on constraints accounting, we looked at capacity constrained resource production in terms of units per day, the TVC and the operating expense to compute the net profit per day.

By focusing on flow and calculating the financial throughput represented by the four products, we can arrive at a better decision. Product *A* is the best choice. By opting for Product *A* you will obtain an increase of 60% in daily net profit, compared to choice *D* which was aiming at providing the biggest gross profit. This example shows not only that constraints accounting suggests different choices, but also that such choices can have a significant impact on the bottom line.

In both cases we used a table of 16 numbers. The difference lies all in what these numbers represent, and in their interpretation. What is more important than the mere fact that the new choice is economically much better than the other ones—which by itself would be a decisive factor in most companies—is that with this new viewpoint, we overcome the differences of interests that we had originally.

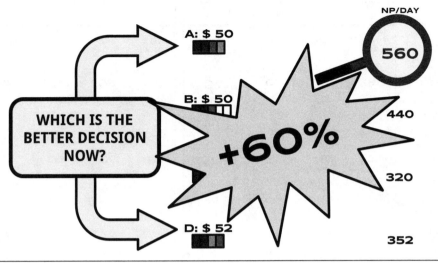

Figure 13.8   Product *A* provides the maximum net profit per day!

	Cost Accounting				Constraints Accounting			
	TIME (MIN)	MATERIAL ($)	LABOR COST ($)	GROSS PROFIT	UNITS/ DAY	TVC	OE	NP/DAY
A: $ 50	36	20	6.00	**24.00**	24	20	160	**560**
B: $ 50	38	25	6.33	**18.67**	24	25	160	**440**
C: $ 55	35	25	5.83	**24.17**	16	25	160	**320**
D: $ 52	35	20	5.83	**26.17**	16	20	160	**352**

Figure 13.9   Numbers supporting decision making

The original viewpoint highlighted in Figure 13.10, was sustained by the CA mindset, and *each wanted his own*. Accountants would pursue products with the maximum gross profit. Likewise, salespeople would favor the product with the highest commissions, while the production department would pick the product that resulted in the highest utilization.

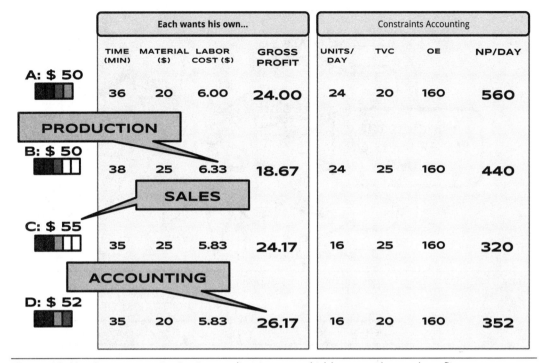

	Each wants his own...				Constraints Accounting			
	TIME (MIN)	MATERIAL ($)	LABOR COST ($)	GROSS PROFIT	UNITS/ DAY	TVC	OE	NP/DAY
A: $ 50	36	20	6.00	**24.00**	24	20	160	**560**
PRODUCTION								
B: $ 50	38	25	6.33	**18.67**	24	25	160	**440**
SALES								
C: $ 55	35	25	5.83	**24.17**	16	25	160	**320**
ACCOUNTING								
D: $ 52	35	20	5.83	**26.17**	16	20	160	**352**

Figure 13.10   Cost accounting instigates disagreement, hidden agendas, and conflicts

In short, the traditional CA mindset is a root cause of conflicts of interests and hidden agendas. CA is what foments disagreement whether or not that disagreement is verbalized and stated in the open. In most companies, it would not be politically correct to explicitly reveal and sustain what each one really wants. Instead, compromises are reached and soft language is used to cover these inherent conflicts.

The vanguard viewpoint, shown in Figure 13.11, is based on constraints accounting, and aligns all partial self-interest with the direction of the company. You would encourage the accountants to pursue sustainable daily cash flows, rather than hypothetical gross profits. You would grant commissions to salespeople based on the daily throughput that they are able to produce. You would award bonuses to the production teams based on their producing products that maximize the daily (financial) throughput, rather than resource utilization.

In short, all people would be focused on one and the same metric which in this case is net profit per day thereby nurturing a strong Unity of Purpose and setting the foundations for building a Community of Trust. Everybody knows they share a common objective and can trust that those other people in the company are working in the same direction.

You will not get Unity of Purpose and a Community of Trust by only adopting a flow-focused viewpoint and using constraints accounting rather than CA. However, you will have avoided the most common mode of failure that structurally prevents these two fundamental patterns from developing holistically at the organizational level, and you will have avoided the common trap of CA and local optimizations. You will have reached the preconditions to achieve hyper-productivity.

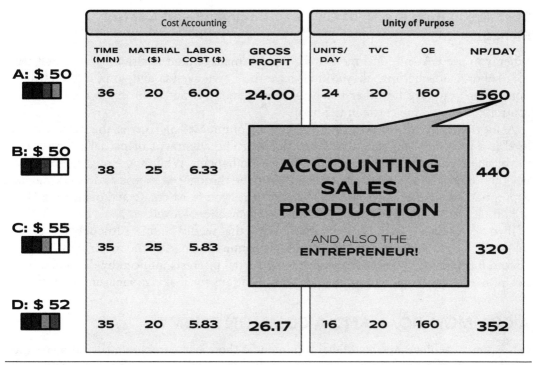

	Cost Accounting				Unity of Purpose			
	TIME (MIN)	MATERIAL ($)	LABOR COST ($)	GROSS PROFIT	UNITS/ DAY	TVC	OE	NP/DAY
A: $ 50	36	20	6.00	**24.00**	24	20	160	**560**
B: $ 50	38	25	6.33					440
C: $ 55	35	25	5.83					320
D: $ 52	35	20	5.83	**26.17**	16	20	160	352

ACCOUNTING
SALES
PRODUCTION

AND ALSO THE
ENTREPRENEUR!

Figure 13.11   Constraints accounting creates agreement and Unity of Purpose, and aligns self-interest with the company direction

If you adopt constraints accounting as the main metric for company performance, it is essential that you make this clear to everybody in the company. You want everybody to know what they are measured against, and make sure they all truly pull in the same direction.

COMMAND-AND-CONTROL MANAGEMENT

Many in the Agile/Lean community resent the "old fashioned" command-and-control management style, believing it derives from a nostalgic attachment to Taylorism; that is, the factory management methods originally defined by F. W. Taylor in his famous book "The Principles of Scientific Management" (1911). Well, that view is naive.

In most companies, the command-and-control management style has nothing to do with the survival of Taylorism. Instead, command and control is an intrinsic, structural characteristic of companies that are driven by the local optimization mindset, induced by resorting to CA for making management decisions.

Such companies are structurally incapable of exhibiting Unity of Purpose or developing a Community of Trust. Under such circumstances, where different parties have different interests and agendas, the only way for executive management to move toward their desired direction is to exercise a strong command and control, though that will never bring about the alignment, unity, and trust that is necessary for attaining superior organizational performance.

Cost Accounting Is a Root Cause of Command-and-Control Management

When you use CA and local metrics for making management decisions, you cannot trust your subordinates because they will all have their own agenda and go in different directions. Then you have no other means of management, if not resorting to command and control, to keep all the cattle in the herd.

Achieving Unity of Purpose and building a Community of Trust at the organizational level is a must for achieving hyper-productivity. The alignment of partial interests with the business's interest is a precondition for this to happen. While some might debate over whether or not the suggested approach of using the throughput metric to do so is the most appropriate, the takeaway from this chapter is that you must create and maintain a Unity of Purpose and a Community of Trust at the organizational level.

If you can achieve them through other means, that would be fine. Although, it is doubtful you will ever succeed in doing so without eliminating one of the major root causes of discord in the majority of organizations—the partial interests induced by discordant metrics, rooted in the usage of CA and local optimizations for making management decisions.

A COMMON GOAL AND A COMMON ENEMY

It is easier to achieve organizational alignment if there is a common goal and a common enemy—constraints management gives us these. The common goal is represented by the global throughput metric. The common enemy is the constraint of the system. The constraint gives the focus and the leverage for the whole organization to improve in harmony toward one common direction.

When an organization starts to think in these terms, it will establish the preconditions that lead to a Unity of Purpose and Community of Trust. Naturally, for these two noble patterns to truly develop, a lot more is required by both the leaders and the followers in the organization.

For instance, in the next chapter, we will see that the *Kanban Method* is founded on nine core values, some of which are: understanding, agreement, respect, transparency, and collaboration. We encountered other eminent values in earlier chapters, for instance: openness, dialogue, tolerance for failure, accountability, and others.

It is very unlikely to find anybody who would openly deny the worth of such values. But one thing is what people say, and another is what they do.

What is important to fully appreciate is that any attempt at developing these other values before setting the preconditions will remain a vain exercise in lip service. They will receive the same espoused and politically correct support as the maximizing profit goal that was seen at the beginning of this chapter. Then, behind the scenes, the hidden agendas driven by the different metrics will set the real stage and reveal the real forces that come into play and into conflict with one another.

The greatest effect of having a common goal (throughput) and a common enemy (constraint) is that the espoused theory of action will be made to coincide with the theory of action in use: *what people say is what they mean*. Without a common goal and a common enemy, the two foundational patterns of Unity of Purpose and Community of Trust, which are the necessary preconditions to achieve hyper-productivity, will not be allowed to exist.

14

THE KANBAN METHOD, FLOW, AND THROUGHPUT

We have mentioned earlier that *Scrum*, while worthwhile, is not conducive to hyper-productivity because of the dysfunctional role of the *Scrum Master* who is actually isolating the development team from the rest of the organization. A hyper-productive organization cannot afford to have isolated parts. All parts must work toward the same goal (the *Unity of Purpose* pattern), and must trust that everybody knows their role and what is best for the organization and everybody who is part of it (the *Community of Trust* pattern).

Scrum further undermines the fundamental noble patterns by the weird characterization of *Chickens and Pigs;*[1] effectively institutionalizing an *Us versus Them* mentality, which is antithetical and not conducive to hyper-productivity.

The *Kanban Method* (or *Kanban* for short) is better equipped than Scrum for reaching hyper-productivity. If nothing else, Kanban will unleash more powerful conversations within the entire organization. Such conversations will be more encompassing of roles outside of the team proper. In fact, it is more appropriate to consider Kanban as a generic management philosophy that impacts the management of the organization as a whole, even though its origins are in the management of software development and information technology operations. Kanban is better at instituting systems thinking and installing an adaptive and evolutionary capability in the organization.

There appears to be a controversy in the industry about the name of "Kanban" since many practitioners of *Lean* (in the sense of *Lean Manufacturing*) have taken issue about characterizing the Kanban Method with the word Kanban.[2] While it is true that there are differences between the Kanban Method and the Kanban system originally used in the Toyota Production System, the similarities of mechanisms and intents far outweigh the differences. The main point is to avoid overproduction. The Kanban Method works and delivers. Kanban allows you to successfully manage any immaterial process. So attention should not be around what it is named or not named. Attention should be given to the patterns that emerge from the adoption of this method—how those patterns can evolve to induce improvements, and then evolve even further to reach hyper-productivity. In fact, as we will see hereafter, even better effects can be achieved when merging together the essence of the original Kanban system with the Kanban Method.

Kanban is quite flexible with very few prescriptions to get started; consequently, it is very easy to get started. It is also easy to combine Kanban with other methods, approaches, or theories. In fact, Kanban promotes using other theories and models to improve the process as part of its core values. Kanban has been combined with Scrum (Scrumban), Crystal, Extreme Programming (Xanpan), and Cynefin. In the second part of this book, we propose other combinations that take advantage of the *Theory of Constraints* (TOC), and its many tools (such as, drum-buffer-rope, Critical Chain, and Thinking Processes).

GETTING STARTED WITH KANBAN

We assume that you have familiarity with the essential concepts of Kanban. If not, refer to:

- The original work of David J. Anderson (2010).
- The excellent introductory text by Marcus Hammarberg and Joakim Sunden (Hammarberg, 2013).
- The practical field guide by Chris Achouiantz (2013).

Though the technical aspects of setting up a Kanban system and visualizing it with a Kanban board—with work in process (WIP) limits, class of services, etc.—are at the heart of the method, it is worthwhile to see what the preconditions are for a successful implementation of the principles, practices, and values. Furthermore, an understanding of the perspective (the *Kanban Lens*) and the purpose and intent (the *Kanban Agendas*) is helpful.

The Four Founding Principles of Kanban

Getting started with Kanban is truly easy, as it is just a little prescriptive. In fact, reduced to its essence, Kanban can be realized as acting according to its four founding principles:

- Start with what you do now
- Agree to pursue incremental, evolutionary change
- Respect the current process, roles, responsibilities, and title
- Encourage acts of leadership, at all levels

The Six Core Practices of Kanban

Since Kanban does not require big changes, but starts from the current operational conditions of an organization, the entry threshold is very low. These four principles are not operational; they just invite you to start by agreeing that the four principles should be of guidance. Then, when it is time to get more operational, six core practices are suggested:

- Visualize
- Limit WIP
- Manage flow
- Make policies explicit
- Implement feedback loops (organizational level feedback loops)
- Improve collaboratively, evolve experimentally (using models and the scientific method)

Again, we will not look further into the principles and practices as the given references explain them exhaustively.

The Nine Values of Kanban

In the blog post *Introducing Kanban Through its Values*,[3] and in his book *Kanban From the Inside* (2014), Mike Burrows presents Kanban not through its technical aspects, but through a value-based description. His nine values are:

- Understanding
- Agreement
- Respect
- Leadership
- Flow
- Customer Focus
- Transparency
- Balance
- Collaboration

It is interesting to observe how five of these values (Understanding, Agreement, Respect, Transparency, and Collaboration) are manifestations of the Community of Trust pattern; while three values (Flow, Customer Focus, and Balance) can be framed as manifestations of the Unity of Purpose pattern. The remaining value, Leadership, is naturally connected to both patterns.

Kanban is an excellent platform on top of which you can build a hyper-productive organization, precisely because of these values. This is the reason why we choose to adopt Kanban as the method of choice to move an organization into a hyper-productive state.

The Kanban Lens

Kanban is really a reference model of thinking wherein there are a few enabling core concepts which have also been given the nickname of the Kanban Lens.[4] It is through this lens that one can look at an organization from a perspective that is revealing and inspiring. This perspective (or lens) invites one to consider the following:

- Service-orientation
- Service delivery involves work flow
- The work flows through a series of knowledge discovery activities

The third point is powerful. It implies that the *steps* involved in a work flow do not necessarily represent work performed by a particular role, as is customary in a manufacturing setting and as is often understood. The steps represent a change in the state of a work item with respect to what knowledge has been created or acquired about it. Furthermore, because knowledge creation or discovery is often performed through collaborative activities, the steps might be performed by a number of collaborating roles, rather than an individual (role).

The Three Kanban Agendas

If the perspective of the Kanban Lens is adopted, then enacting the principles and practices through such a perspective will effectively create purposeful actions. That purposefulness is represented by *Kanban's Three Agendas:*[5]

- Sustainability
- Service-orientation
- Survivability

Sustainability relates to not doing more than what is materially possible; it corresponds to the *sustainable pace* often invoked in Agile and the principle of avoiding over-production of Lean and of the TOC. Service-orientation is about fostering a Community of Trust by improving reliability (in terms of due-date performance and consistent flow times). It is by means of service-orientation that reliable service level agreements may be instituted between the organization and its clients. Survivability relates to how an organization can better survive in a competitive marketplace by attaining a greater ability to rapidly adapt to change, which can be related to the idea of always having a clear definition of the organizational goal (as per the TOC).

LINKS BETWEEN THE THEORY OF CONSTRAINTS AND KANBAN

As we mentioned earlier in the story of Herbie, a strong connection can be made between Kanban and the TOC. The TOC developed a whole body of knowledge—the Thinking Processes—that are a critical part of any contemporary implementation. David Anderson (2012) says:

> Goldratt's Thinking Processes emerged in the mid-1990s and are now widely regarded by that community as representing the main body of the method. [...] [Goldratt] developed the Thinking Process as a systematic approach for managing change.

It is revealing to see how David Anderson looks at the development of the Thinking Processes with respect to what eventually became the Kanban Method:

> Coming to a similar conclusion about the problem with change, I chose not to pursue the Thinking Processes, which define an outcome known as the Future Reality Tree (FRT) and a managed change program known as the Transition Tree. Instead I chose to develop an evolutionary approach that does not define an outcome or prescribe a transition plan. It pursues a guided-evolution approach based on a scientific understanding of the flow of work and the implementation of safe-to-fail experiments that evolve the existing process in a series of steps. [...] We could think of the Thinking Processes and the Kanban Method as evolving from a common ancestor, the Five Focusing Steps. The slight irony is that the Thinking Processes do not offer an evolutionary approach, but rather

a planned transition to a defined outcome, whereas the Kanban Method follows the implied evolutionary approach inherent in the original Five Focusing Steps.

One can still see how the *Five Focusing Steps* (5FS) are at the basis of Kanban's event-driven risk identification and issue escalation policies, as we will illustrate shortly. However, apart from this obvious use of the 5FS, none of the deep body of knowledge of the TOC is used in Kanban. This is by deliberate choice.

We will see that there are parts of the TOC that can improve how Kanban is put into practice. By completely disregarding anything beyond the 5FS, we are indeed looking at a case where the *baby was thrown away with the bathwater!*

While it is true that the entire armory of tools of the Thinking Processes might not be entirely aligned with the idea of an evolutionary approach (since they aim at defined outcomes), there are parts therein which are very powerful. We will see how the Thinking Processes can be used in a way that is entirely aligned with the evolutionary process improvement approach championed by Kanban.

We illustrated earlier the importance of the throughput metric (as it is used in constraints accounting, i.e., money per day) as a means for aligning personal interests with the company direction, to nurture the Unity of Purpose pattern and set the foundations to build a Community of Trust. The throughput metric is a way to focus on flow. One of Kanban's primary means of improving is, indeed, to focus on flow. Furthermore Kanban highlights the importance of throughput, though it is expressed as the amount of work (rather than money) delivered per period of time. Hence, the reasons to consider Kanban from the perspective of the TOC is reinforced. They share one of the strongest drivers, therefore, we will build this bridge between the two disciplines by focusing on flow.

A LITTLE ABOUT FLOW AND THROUGHPUT

Focusing on flow naturally leads us to consider *Little's Law* (1961, 2008, 2011), which states the relationship between throughput (TP), WIP, and flow time (FT) as follows:

$$TP = WIP/FT$$

Little's Law is valid only under some well-defined conditions. First, it must be understood that the variables involved represent long-running averages and do not express a linear relationship between exact values. It also requires that the units involved are consistent; and above all, that the system is stable. One condition of stability is that all work entering the process must flow through until it is done and then exits.

A very common situation (in most companies) is that work is pushed into the system, rather than being pulled. This condition is illustrated in Figure 14.1. (Notice that in all diagrams that depict the ideal linear relationship between WIP and FT, TP is represented by the *slope* of the lines. The sharper the slope is, the higher the TP.) It is very similar to the situation of Herbie, at the beginning of his story. When the boy in front of Herbie—let's call him Bluey—creates more walking steps than Herbie can keep up with, a gap develops between them. Similarly, when demand for work is greater than available capacity, work in process increases. In the context of knowledge work, this is often the case when there are more work requests than the capacity to implement them.

A precondition to be able to transition from a push policy to a pull policy is that work is balanced. When Herbie was put in front of the line, nobody could run away. More

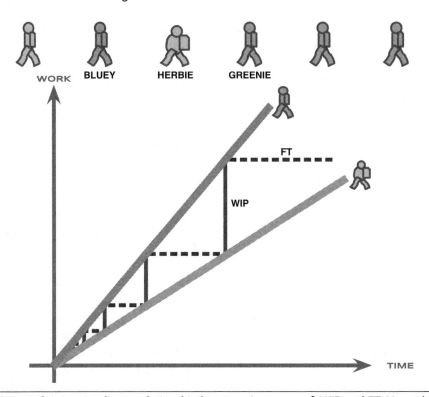

Figure 14.1   Little's Law is a linear relationship between (averages of) WIP and FT. Here, demand (Bluey's line) is greater (the slope is steeper) than capacity (Herbie's line). Herbie is the system's overall capacity. He falls further and further behind. FT (the dotted horizontal lines) gets longer and longer. WIP (the vertical lines) gets larger and larger.

schematically, the same effect can be achieved even without putting Herbie in front, yet forcing Bluey to walk at the same speed as Herbie. In practice, you do this by limiting WIP in order to balance demand to capacity, thus avoiding overproduction (of walking steps). This is illustrated in Figure 14.2, where demand is balanced to the capacity.

Having a balanced system is a precondition for the applicability of Little's Law. This is the main reason why it is so important to limit WIP. By limiting WIP, we can enable pulling. Naturally, the mechanism by which pull is implemented might vary (and we will soon suggest one). The important idea to understand is that once demand is balanced to capacity, the capacity can be used as the driver—as the pacing element that pulls in work into the system. When capacity is available, new work is pulled into the system. When capacity is not available, no new work is pushed into the system.

THE CONSEQUENCES OF VARIATION

Naturally, all this is much easier to apply in manufacturing where you have homogeneous work items and where machines are the processing agents.

In immaterial processes, like software development, there is a lot more variability involved. There is variability in the size and nature of work items, and variability in their arrival rates. While many Kanban practitioners worry about how to manage the variability

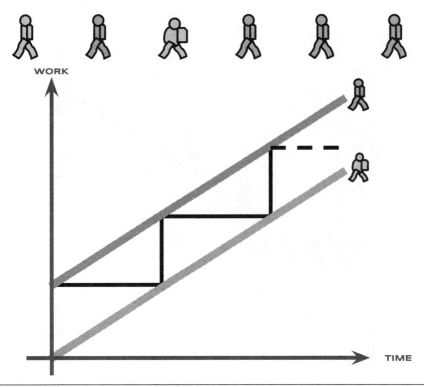

Figure 14.2   By limiting the amount of WIP, you can balance the demand against the capacity. Both lines have the same slope. FT and WIP remain constant. Herbie is still the system's capacity, but now he leads the line, and everybody else keeps up with his pace.

in the work items, the greatest source of variability lies in the process agents—it is a matter of people.

Let's refer to Herbie's walk in the woods from Chapter 12, and examine the case of variation or *Murphy* (in the sense of *Murphy's Law*—if anything can go wrong, it will) hitting Bluey (the scout walking in front of Herbie), Herbie himself, and Greenie (the scout behind Herbie).

When Murphy hits Bluey, Bluey will stop his walk temporarily; then he can resume at a higher pace than Herbie. Remember that Herbie is the slowest boy in the line. Bluey has more capacity than Herbie. Bluey can outpace Herbie, until he recovers the terrain he lost due to the encounter with Murphy, as illustrated in Figure 14.3.

By definition any non-constrained resource has more capacity than the constrained resource. So, as long as you know where the constraint is, you can be reassured that any other resource has the capacity to recover from any disruption that might come along. (Of course, this assumes that the disruption does not last long enough to affect Herbie himself—in this case the constraint would have moved to where the disruption occurred.)

Naturally, the same holds when Murphy hits Greenie. Greenie has extra capacity (compared to Herbie), so he too, can recover any terrain he lost, as can be seen in Figure 14.4.

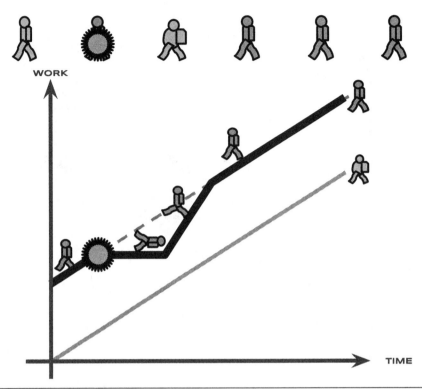

Figure 14.3 When variation (Murphy) hits a noncapacity-constrained resource (Bluey) upstream of the constraint, that resource will have extra capacity and be able to sprint and recover, as it will be able to outpace the capacity-constrained resource (Herbie).

The only significant difference is that Greenie can only recover to the point where he runs into the back of Herbie. In other words, the advancement of Greenie is literally limited by the presence of Herbie. Bluey, on the other hand, could run away and create a gap between himself and Herbie; though we will see shortly how to prevent that from happening. The key point is always the same: Bluey and Greenie can always outpace Herbie.

Things are different when Murphy hits Herbie himself. In this case, when Herbie recovers from Murphy's beats, he has *no extra capacity*. Herbie will never be able to make up for the terrain that he lost and WIP will inexorably increase. You can see this clearly in Figure 14.5.

THE MIRAGE OF BALANCING THE FLOW

The consequence of variation on the processing agents is that WIP will increase even if you attempt to balance the line because anytime that variation affects the constraint, the constraint will not have sufficient capacity to recover.

Any attempt at balancing the line to the apparent capacity of the constraint will balance demand to a pace that is less than the real capacity of the constraint. This happens when you are balancing against the *average* capacity of the constraint, as shown in Figure 14.6.

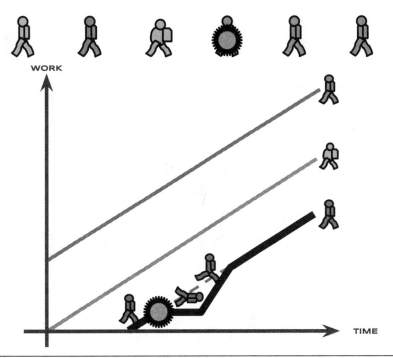

Figure 14.4   When variation (Murphy) hits a noncapacity-constrained resource (Greenie) downstream of the constraint, that resource will also have extra capacity and be able to sprint to recover and catch up with the capacity-constrained resource (Herbie).

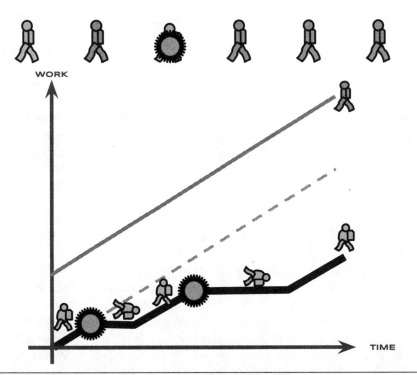

Figure 14.5   When variation (Murphy) hits the constraint (Herbie), the constraint will not have any extra capacity, and will be unable to recover. WIP and FT will increase again.

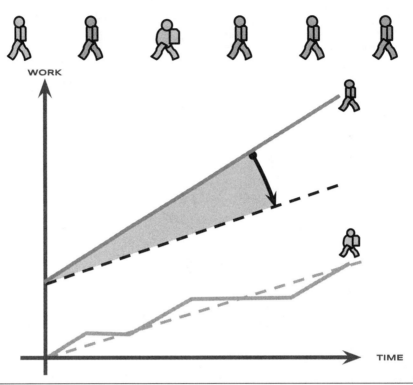

Figure 14.6   Do not balance against the average capacity of the constraint (Herbie); you will waste the constraint's maximum capacity when it is available

In other words, whenever you perceive that you have a balanced line, you are actually wasting capacity, and that capacity is wasted on the constraint; the most precious resource whose capacity you need to protect. Whenever you see a balanced line, there is ample room for improvement on the constraint.

Not only is it important to know where the constraint is in the system, but it is also vitally important to understand at what capacity it is able to operate and then regulate the release of work (rather than balance the work) for the entire system to that capacity. This is the very idea of subordination of the 5FS. Everybody should walk *behind* Herbie.

So there is this contradiction: balancing against the actual capacity of Herbie will always create an ever increasing inventory of WIP (when Murphy hits Herbie). On the other hand, balancing against the average capacity of Herbie will waste Herbie's capacity when it is available. In other words, limiting WIP through balancing is ineffective. Another mechanism is called for.

This is where the TOC suggests using (metaphorically) a rope, to tie Bluey to Herbie, so that he cannot run away. This is one of the key components of the drum-buffer-rope scheduling mechanism of TOC. We will find out more about it later.

For the moment, the important thing to notice is that work is released into the system only if Herbie is able to handle it. When Herbie is idle, work is not released. When Herbie is processing, work is released at whatever pace Herbie is keeping. When Herbie accelerates, more work is released. Conversely, when Herbie slows down, less work is released. You can see this mechanism in Figure 14.7.

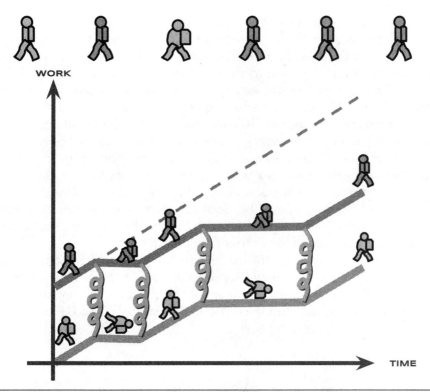

Figure 14.7   Limit WIP with a rope: tie Bluey to Herbie, so Bluey doesn't run away when Herbie is hit by Murphy

Work is limited in relation to the current capacity of the constraint. Releasing more work than Herbie's capacity would create excess inventory in the form of WIP. Releasing less work would waste Herbie's capacity. In other words, this is like a dynamic balancing that is always gauged exactly on Herbie's current capacity.

Naturally, if the constraint changes (and moves off of Herbie), the *end points* of the rope will have to be adjusted accordingly.

Two related questions are: when do we need to release new work into the work flow and how can we ensure that Herbie always has enough work? The two issues are answered with a drum and a buffer—but we will examine the details of this later, when we look into how we can realize the drum-buffer-rope scheduling mechanism directly on a Kanban board in Part 2.

WHERE TO IMPROVE

Professional athletes train very intensely to weed out all variability from their movements, so that they can perform to the best of their ability when they enter a competition. Many practices have a similar function—to reduce variability (like stand-ups, retrospectives, etc.). However, humans are not machines, and there are many reasons that cause variability in performance. It is only through a deliberate process of continuous improvement that such variability can be reduced; just like an athlete strives to improve.

This gives rise to the extremely important question of where one should improve. Referring again to the story of Herbie, it should be quite obvious. If you improve the performance of Bluey or Greenie, the overall performance of the system will remain entirely unaffected because it is still limited by the constrained capacity of Herbie. The only positive effect is that Bluey or Greenie would have an even higher capacity to recover after encountering Murphy. This is illustrated in Figure 14.8.

This is beneficial in two ways. First, it would allow for longer downtimes of either Bluey or Greenie (as long as the downtime does not affect Herbie, of course) because they would be able to recover more quickly. Second, they actually raise the bar for Herbie. Later, we will explain how, sometimes, this is a way to control the constraint, in the sense that we keep the constraint in its current place, helping the system to remain stable. While these are two important benefits, it should be clear that there is no direct gain in terms of TP (business value) of these improvements (though they might improve responsiveness, time to market, and cash flow due to the shorter flow times).

In order to gain TP and improve the business performance of the system, it is necessary to improve Herbie. If the improvement is gained on Herbie, the benefit will propagate to the entire system. Both Bluey and Greenie should be able to keep up with the new, faster pace of Herbie (if they cannot, then the constraint has moved). This is illustrated in Figure 14.9.

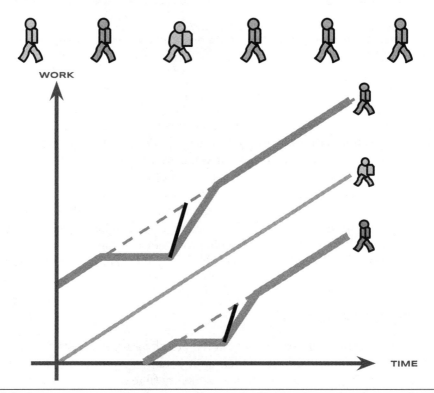

Figure 14.8 Improvements at the non-constraints are ineffective. Improving the capacity of Bluey or Greenie will only improve their capacity to recover, but it will not improve the system's overall TP, which remains constrained by Herbie.

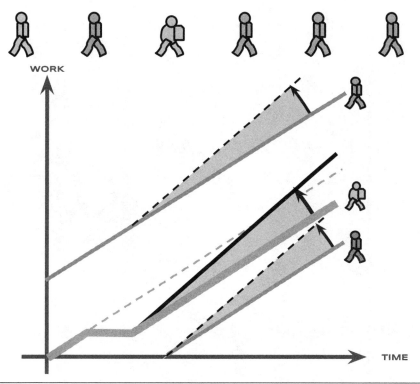

Figure 14.9   Improvements at the constraint are effective. Improving the capacity of Herbie will not only improve his capacity to recover, but also his maximum sustainable capacity. Therefore, improving Herbie will also increase the system's overall TP (as long as Bluey and Greenie can keep up with the improvement, too).

Consequently, the conclusion can be drawn that improvement initiatives should focus, first and foremost, on Herbie—on the constraint of the system. This is the very essence of elevating the capacity of the constrained resource in the 5FS.

Naturally, this does not mean that improvements on the non-constraints should be ignored or disregarded, but focus should be primarily on improving the constraint, as illustrated in Figure 14.10. In fact, improvements on the non-constraints can be beneficial when they effectively raise the bar for the constraint. If Bluey and Greenie improve their capacity, then Herbie needs to improve even more before he becomes a non-constraint. This is an important consideration: the objective is not to eliminate the constraint—because there will always be one—the objective is to manage the constraint.

In any case, you will want to keep the constraint in a well-defined place because then it becomes easier to manage, and consequently, so does the entire process. If your elevation of the constraint causes the constraint to move somewhere else, then you should be ready to repeat the 5FS so you can improve even further. However, each time the constraint moves, you are introducing instability in the system; and you need to investigate to find the new constraint.

You can apply the power of Little's Law only when the system is stable and the system is stable only when the (average) input is balanced to the (average) output. One of the best

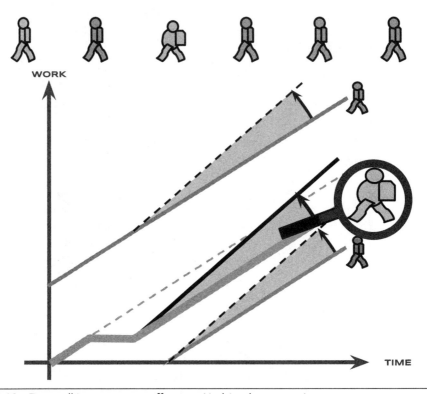

Figure 14.10   Focus all improvement efforts on Herbie, the constraint

ways to keep the system stable is to always know exactly where the constraint is. In that way, you can let the assumptions underlying Little's Law guide your policies. Constraints management is one of the most powerful ways you have at your disposal to keep the process in a stable condition.

We will now see how this element is missing in those implementations of Kanban where there is a strong focus on limiting WIP by limiting the amount of work that is allowed in each state (i.e., a column of the Kanban board) and, that is to say, the majority of implementations.

REFERENCES

1. The *Chicken and Pig* story was used in Scrum to characterize the distinction between people who had an active role in the Scrum process (the *pigs*) and all others (the *chickens*, which are typically seen as all *managers*) who do not have an active role in delivering products. The characterization is obviously divisive, and even derogatory. In 2011, the labels were taken out of the official Scrum guide, although the original heritage and culture still remains vivid in the Scrum community.
2. Alexei Zheglov described the controversy and diversity of terminology in his blog post *The Seven (or More) Meanings of Kanban,* which can be found online at: http://learningagileandlean.wordpress.com/2013/08/07/seven-meanings-of-kanban/

3. The blog post *Introducing Kanban through its Values* is available online at http://positiveincline.com/index.php/2013/01/introducing-Kanban-through-its-values/
4. The *Kanban Lens* was first described by David Anderson in his blog post available online at: http://www.djaa.com/kanban-lens
5. The *Kanban Agenda* is described by David Anderson in his blog post at: http://www.djaa.com/kanbans-3-agendas

This book has free material available for download from the
Web Added Value™ resource center at *www.jrosspub.com*

15

UNDERSTANDING THE IMPACT
OF A CONSTRAINT

In this chapter we will revisit throughput accounting, or more precisely, we will look into the significance of *constraints accounting* (Caspari, 2004). The purpose is to gain a deeper understanding of the magnitude of impact that a constraint can have on business operations.

CHOOSING BETWEEN TWO PROCESSES

For the sake of illustration, let us consider a small software house that engages in custom-software development. The business owner has asked his people to examine their operations and come up with suggestions for improvements. Two proposals are ultimately contending for a positive verdict: *eXtreme Programming* (XP) and *Behavorial Driven Development* (BDD). What the two approaches prescribe and how they work is irrelevant in this discussion, as we are focusing only on the business consequences of choosing one or the other. Besides, the business owner is not versed in technicalities, so those acronyms bear little significance for him—they are simply considered as names with which you can refer to the two different processes.

The two options come with similar investment requirements. Both would need an investment of 5,000 EUR to purchase new equipment (office furniture, workstations, computer hardware, etc.). The two options are summarized in Table 15.1. The question is which option should be taken.

PROPOSED INVESTMENT	Current	XP	BDD
Furniture / Workstation / Hardware		5,000.00	5,000.00

Table 15.1 The proposed investment is the same for both cases under consideration

THE LEAN PERSPECTIVE

After a fierce debate that leaves the question unanswered, someone from the marketing department asks if it might not be possible to measure and compare one approach against the other; and maybe do some kind of comparative testing. The business owner likes the idea, but wonders how the two options can be measured without actually carrying them out. The suggestion is to call in a Lean process expert to quantify the approaches in order to make a significant comparison.

After doing detailed value stream mapping the expert runs statistical simulations to gain a quantitative understanding of the two alternatives. He comes back with his metrics. He discovers, through historical data, that the current process was exhibiting (on average) a flow time of 7 working days to deliver a work item.

In this case a work item can be considered as a user story, a use-case, etc., which, according to Kanban practices, has been classified according to a class of service that is associated with an average delivery time. Naturally the example is a simplification, as it considers only one kind of work item, which is assumed to have a (reasonably) consistent size. (In the real world the situation would be different, but the overarching principles exposed through this example would still remain valid.)

The runs of several thousands of simulations showed that XP would reduce that average flow time to 6.7 working days, while BDD would increase it to 7.3 working days. The Lean process expert wholeheartedly recommends choosing XP over BDD. The findings are summarized in Table 15.2.

THE ACCOUNTING PERSPECTIVE

The business owner, being wise, asks his accountant to look into the figures and confirm that the recommendation made by the Lean process expert is sound.

The accountant starts by looking at the data he knows about: the overhead (expenses) on a yearly basis; how many work items were delivered (on average) every year; the price of each work item; the average acquisition cost of each item (i.e., the cost of finding a requirement); the hourly wages; and so on. The initial data appears in Table 15.3.

Then the accountant starts making some calculations on the back of an envelope. He wants to figure out what is most convenient to do on a daily basis.

The daily labor rate of one resource (the process always had exactly one employee working at any given stage) is the hourly wage (22 EUR) times the hours per day (8), resulting in 176 EUR per day. The overhead expense per day is computed by dividing the yearly overhead (150,000 EUR) by the number of working days during the year (240),

AVERAGE FLOW TIME (DAYS)	Current	XP	BDD
Days	7.00	6.70	7.30

Table 15.2   Compared to the current (average) flow time, the (average) flow time is shorter for the XP option, but longer for the BDD option

INITIAL DATA	Current
General Expenses / Year	150,000.00
Work Items / Year	75.00
Average Item Price	16,000.00
Average Item Acquisition Cost	80.00
Hourly Wage	22.00
Work Hours / Day	8.00
Work Days / Week	5.00
Work Weeks / Year	48.00
Work Hours / Year	1,920.00
Work Days / Year	240.00
Daily Wage	176.00

Table 15.3   Initial data typically used in a cost-accounting based investment appraisal

resulting in an expense of 625 EUR per day. Thus, the total daily expense, including labor and overhead, is 176 + 625 EUR = 801 EUR per day.

These figures were the same for each of the two cases, XP and BDD, as shown in Table 15.4.

The next step is to determine the cost of a single work item. It takes an average of 7 working days to deliver a work item. Thus, the work item incurs a labor cost of 176 EUR × 7 = 1232 EUR. Similarly it incurs overhead costs of 625 EUR × 7 = 4375 EUR. Furthermore, the acquisition cost of 80 EUR has to be considered (the acquisition cost is what you pay to discover, or define the requirements). Adding these numbers together (1232 + 4735 + 80), the standard unit cost is determined as 5687 EUR. In other words, any single work item costs the company 5687 EUR.

The same calculations are done for both cases, considering the difference in the average flow times. The results show that XP can be associated with a standard unit cost of 5446.70 EUR, while BDD comes in at 5927.30 EUR. The derivation of the standard unit cost is shown in Table 15.5.

The standard unit cost variation, compared to the current situation, is easy to find. XP has a standard unit cost of *minus* 240.30 EUR (than the current case), while BDD has a standard unit cost of *plus* 240.30 EUR. (The two cases have the same magnitude because it is the monetary quantification of the *minus* 0.3 days and the *plus* 0.3 days on the flow time of the two cases that distinguishes the difference; the time variation happens to be of the same magnitude—0.3—and changes only in sign.) The standard unit cost variation is shown in Table 15.6.

LABOR AND OVERHEAD RATES (DAILY)	Current	XP	BDD
Labor	176.00	176.00	176.00
Overhead	625.00	625.00	625.00
Total Charging Rate	801.00	801.00	801.00

Table 15.4   The daily charging rate is the daily cost as determined by wages and overhead costs; every day the company incurs this amount of cost

STANDARD UNIT COST	Current	XP	BDD
Acquisition	80.00	80.00	80.00
Direct Labor	1,232.00	1,179.20	1,284.80
Overhead	4,375.00	4,187.50	4,562.50
Standard Unit Cost	5,687.00	5,446.70	5,927.30

Table 15.5   The standard unit cost represents how much a single item costs to produce. It is composed of the charging rates multiplied by the flow time (the production time) of the item, plus any additional costs needed to make the item (such as raw materials, requirements gathering, etc.).

STANDARD UNIT COST VARIATION	Current	XP	BDD
Standard Unit Cost Variation		-240.30	240.30

Table 15.6   The variation in standard unit cost is calculated for the two options

Taking the standard unit cost variation (+/− 240.30 EUR) and multiplying by the number of units produced (75), the annual cost variation is determined as −18,022.50 EUR for XP and +18,022.50 EUR for BDD. Naturally the accountant is quick to discard BDD as it implies an increase in cost, while XP comes with a cost saving. This is shown in Table 15.7.

To further reinforce his conclusion, the accountant performs a quick (approximate) calculation of the internal rate of return and of the payback period of the investment to adopt XP. The net cash flow corresponds to the cost savings; the investment is 5000 EUR. The calculation shows an amazing 360 percent return on investment and the payback period is just over 100 days, or approximately 5 months. This result is shown in Table 15.8. Naturally, the accountant wholeheartedly recommends the adoption of XP.

ANNUAL COST VARIATION	Current	XP	BDD
Cost Variation		-18,022.50	18,022.50
Cost Variation First Year		-13,022.50	23,022.50

Table 15.7 The variation in standard unit cost is used to compute the variation in annual costs. Notice that the numbers show costs; a negative number corresponds to a cost saving, while a positive number is a cost increase.

INTERNAL RATE OF RETURN	Current	XP	BDD
Net Cash Flow		18,022.50	
Investment		5,000.00	
Internal Rate of Return		360%	
Payback Period (Days)		101.26	

Table 15.8 The internal rate of return and the payback period show that the XP option is the favorable one by considering the cost savings effect on cash flow with respect to the investment needed. The values are not computed for the BDD option since it would incur a cost increase, and not a cost saving.

THE CONSTRAINTS MANAGEMENT PERSPECTIVE

The business owner is happy to receive such good advice from the Lean process expert, corroborated by the numbers provided by the accountant. He breaks the news to his senior developer, Herbie, who has been with the company from the very beginning. He sees from Herbie's expression that he is not happy. So he asks why, after stating again how good the choice is (it reduces flow time and provides a real positive impact on the bottom line, with good internal rate of return and a short payback period). He is even more surprised when Herbie—whom he respects for his great technical skills and past contributions—says that the choice is really throwing away money rather than making any. So in a patronizing tone, he challenges Herbie to show him that the Lean process expert and the accountant were mistaken.

Herbie, having lived through many such wise business choices in the past, takes the chance to explain his viewpoint now that the business owner was willing to listen to him.

It is true that the XP option has a lower flow time, but neither the Lean process expert nor the accountant had taken into consideration the effect of the system's constraint. By breaking down the flow time into its constituent parts (the work-states of analysis, development, and test), Herbie points out that in the current situation he, himself, is the constraint. On average a work item takes 3.20 days on his desk, while it takes only 1.8 days upstream in analysis and 2.0 days downstream in test. Obviously he is the constraint. These numbers are shown in Table 15.9.

The XP solution would actually increase the time required by Herbie from 3.20 to 3.40 days for each work item. In other words, the constraint would become loaded even more. On the other hand, the BDD solution would lower Herbie's load from 3.20 to 2.70 days for each work item (yet he would still remain the constraint of the system). This fact alone is enough for Herbie to draw his conclusion, but he knows too well that he has to convince the business owner with more hard data, and especially, he has to convince the accountant with money numbers.

Herbie starts to show his boss that the impact of the change has to be examined in terms of how things change for the constraint. While the number of working days in a year is always the same, the fact that Herbie's (the constraint's) time on the work items varies actually changes the *capacity* of the entire system. The accountant wrongly assumed that the capacity was a given (75 work items per year) and made calculations accordingly, but capacity changes because the flow time on the constraint changes. In the case of XP, capacity decreases from 75 work items per year to 70.59—the 240 days divided by the 3.40 days per work item. Conversely, in the case of BDD, capacity increases to 88.89—the 240 days divided by 2.70. All this is illustrated in Table 15.10.

AVERAGE FLOW TIME (DAYS)	Current	XP	BDD
Total Flow Time	7.00	6.70	7.30
- Analysis -- Bluey	1.80	1.50	2.40
- Development -- Herbie	3.20	3.40	2.70
- Test -- Greenie	2.00	1.80	2.20

Table 15.9 The (average) flow time is broken down into corresponding (average) flow times of the single resources involved. Notice that in the current situation, the development state (*Herbie*) is the constraint because it employs more time than any other work-state.

CAPACITY IMPACT / YEAR	Current	XP	BDD
Available Work Days	240.00	240.00	240.00
Flow Time on "Herbie"	3.20	3.40	2.70
Capacity	75.00	70.59	88.89

Table 15.10 The variations in flow time on *Herbie* determine the real impact on the capacity of the team in terms of how many items (on average) can be produced per year

The throughput in terms of money per work item is the same in all three cases: The work price minus the totally variable cost, or 16,000 EUR minus the 80 EUR for the cost of acquisition, resulting in 15,920 EUR, as shown in Table 15.11.

The XP option produces 70.59 minus 75.00, which equals 4.41 work items less each year. Multiplying those 4.41 work items by the unit throughput of 15,920 results in 70,235.29 EUR less each year. Conversely the BDD option produces 88.80 minus 75, which equals 13.89 work items more each year. Multiplying those 13.89 work items by the unit throughput of 15,920 results in 221,111.11 EUR more each year. This is shown in Table 15.12.

The business owner is astonished, but Herbie continues with the numbers, even considering the effects of the investment and of the operating expenses. Herbie shows that the net cash flow on the first year is a negative 75,235.29 EUR for the XP option, while it is a positive 216,111.11 EUR for the BDD option.

What the accountant had computed as a positive 360 percent internal rate of return for the XP option is actually a 1404 percent *loss* on investment; and the BDD option that had been discarded on the basis of increasing costs is a 4422 percent *return* on the investment. This finding is shown in Table 15.13.

What is originally seen as a simple decision and minor improvement costing 5000 EUR returning an annual benefit of approximately 18,000 EUR, in reality, would cause a net loss of over 75,000 EUR the first year alone, and over 70,000 EUR every year thereafter.

THROUGHPUT / WORK ITEM	Current	XP	BDD
Work Item Price	16,000.00	16,000.00	16,000.00
Variable Cost	80.00	80.00	80.00
Throughput	15,920.00	15,920.00	15,920.00

Table 15.11   The throughput (revenues minus total variable costs) per unit is the same in all three cases

TOTAL THROUGHPUT VARIATION	Current	XP	BDD
Capacity Variation		-4.41	13.89
Throughput Variation		-70,235.29	221,111.11

Table 15.12   While the throughput for each unit is the same in the three cases, the amount of units that can be produced varies in consequence of the different flow times. Taking into account the variation in capacity, the total throughput variation per year is computed. The conclusions are the opposite of those derived by using a cost-accounting approach.

VARIATIONS IN TP, I, OE, ROI	XP		BDD	
	First Year	Subsequent	First Year	Subsequent
Throughput (TP)	-70,235.29	-70,235.29	221,111.11	221,111.11
Investment (I)	5,000.00	no change	5,000.00	no change
Operational Expenses (OE)	no change	no change	no change	no change
Cash Flow (TP-I-OE)	-75,235.29	-70,235.29	216,111.11	221,111.11
ROI ((TP-OE)/I)	-1,404.71%		4,422.22%	

Table 15.13 The variation in total annual throughput determines a significant difference in terms of return on investment for the first year, and in terms of cash flow for the first and subsequent years

BOTTOM LINE PROFITABILITY	XP	BDD	Range
Cost Accounting (Standard Cost)	13,022.50	-23,022.50	**36,045.00**
Constraints Accounting (TP, I, OE)	-75,235.29	216,111.11	**291,346.41**

Table 15.14 The range on the (first year) bottom line profitability calculated by the two approaches (cost accounting and constraints accounting) differs by one order of magnitude. Not only are the conclusions opposite, but the real profitability impact is ten times larger than what cost accounting would lead you to believe.

Comparing the two choices, we discover a bottom line profitability effect that spans almost 300,000 EUR. This is shown in Table 15.14.

What is worse is that the cost accounting metrics induces selecting the option that actually makes you *lose* money and will make you discard the option that brings the real profit. The business owner is astounded, and reconsiders his decision. (*Note:* In addition to the financial throughput effect in this particular example, the better choice is the one with the longer flow time. In most cases where Kanban is used, there is often an effort on reducing flow times. This example highlights that flow time reduction is not always beneficial, unless it specifically includes flow time reduction on the constraint. Also note however, that there might be other reasons for reducing flow time. One is when service time needs to be improved in order to increase customer satisfaction. Another is when you need to increase the capacity of the non-constraints in order to maintain the current constraint in its place.)

CONSTRAINTS ARE ARCHIMEDEAN LEVERS

Naturally the previous example must in no way be interpreted as a value statement of either XP or BDD. The two techniques were used only for the sake of illustration. In a real world scenario, the true measures of flow times would determine which of the two options actually improves the constraint; and the constraint is always dependent on the particular situation and context you are examining.

Similarly, the example should not be deceitfully represented to mean that flow time reduction is bad and flow time increase is good. There is no way to tell if a positive or negative flow time variation is good or bad unless you carefully analyze its impact on the constraint. A variation (whether positive or negative) on total flow time will have a positive impact on throughput only if it involves a reduction of flow time on the constraint. As this example illustrates, that can happen even if it means increasing total flow time.

The point to understand is that the effect of any decision must be measured in terms of its impact on the system's constraint. Constraints are lever points, whereupon one can exercise an Archimedean lever in terms of financial results. The previous example, even though devised for the purpose of illustration, shows this very clearly.

Constraints Management Is Key to Throughput Performance

It follows that knowing exactly where the constraint is in the system becomes paramount. This is the main reason why work-state work in process (WIP) limits (as classically used in Kanban) can be a danger because they give so many false positives about where the constraint really is. With work-state WIP limits it becomes impossible to exercise effective constraints management and, hence, very unlikely to gain the lever effects that would benefit your decisions otherwise. Work-state WIP limits might give the impression of achieving improvements, while in reality they are a random walk into the future. In that randomness, real improvement is coincidental when the real constraint happens to be affected by the intervention. What is worse is that the randomness causes an artificial system instability. We will see the details about these problems and their solutions in Part 2 of this book.

This is one of several reasons why it is preferable to have a well-known constraint in a well-known place, rather than elevating it's capacity so that the constraints move to some other undefined and unidentified place in the system. As long as the constraint is under control, then it is possible to control and manage flow. When it moves, you will have an unstable system and you have to start over again (Step 1: Identify the constraint)—chasing and pinning down the new constraint. This period of instability between the elevation of an old constraint and the identification of the new one usually has very bad effects in terms of flow.

Constraints and Service Level Agreements

In Kanban, classes of service are naturally associated with average flow times in order to be able to maintain service level agreements (SLAs) with stakeholders and customers. Because work-state WIP limits can adversely affect the systems stability, they artificially increase the average flow times which are used as the basis for establishing SLAs. In other words, this artificially induced system instability will make the organization settle for less competitive SLAs than what the organization is truly capable of sustaining. Keeping the system stable is paramount for setting aggressive service levels without straining the system and without reducing reliability (more about this can be found in Part 2).

Constraints and Investment Decisions

A strong focus on constraints management will also give clear guidance in terms of when an investment should be undertaken. Investments should be aimed exclusively either to establish necessary conditions of operations or to elevate constraints. The first kind of investment is usually taken when a business is starting up. Often they are one-time investments. The second kind of investment (to elevate the constraint) is taken in the light of achieving a considerable increase in profits, which are inevitably associated with the elevation of a constraint.

It is important to realize the corollary—money should not be spent in order to subordinate to or to exploit the constraint. Subordination and exploitation are simply the reconfiguration of current resources and policies, which do *not* require any investment. However, subordination and exploitation can significantly impact the company's profit because of the increase in the throughput they produce. This is one way that constraints management improves financial performance *without* requiring new expenses.

When a decision is taken to effectively elevate a constraint, it is often worthwhile to consider elevating the capacity of other resources too, *only* for the purpose of keeping the constraint where it was previously. It is like raising the bar for Herbie, while Herbie still remains the constraint. The intent is to prevent moving the constraint to somewhere else in the system; the purpose is to avoid the instability that comes out of moving the constraint. So the general advice is to aim investments not only at elevating the constraint, but also to actively keep the constraint in the same place while doing so. As long as the system remains stable, then the assumption of Little's Laws can be applied and aggressive SLAs can be maintained.

When using WIP work-state limits, it is never clear if you are confronting the real constraint or not. You might be induced to spend money and invest in elevating some false constraint. You will not only have zero impact on the system's real throughput, but you will also impoverish the company of the spent investment.

So the key point becomes the following: if work-state WIP limits can be so counterproductive, what else can be used? How can we handle constraints in a way that is coherent with the visual management paradigm promoted by the Kanban Method and yet enable all the constraint management techniques for improved organizational performance which are typical of the Theory of Constraints? You will find the answers in Part 2.

16

THE (SUPER-) HUMAN SIDE OF FLOW

The previous chapters have examined what affects flow from different perspectives:

- The flow of information and ideas (for example, through Pattern Theory)
- The flow of work (for example, through Kanban and Theory of Constraints)
- The flow of cash and capital (for example, through constraints accounting)

This final chapter will focus on flow from a psychological perspective, and examine how the mental state of flow is a fundamental, if not the most important, component in the pursuit of hyper-productivity.

FROM HAPPINESS TO HYPER-PRODUCTIVITY

A common desire of most of us is to achieve *happiness* in all aspects of our human condition. Psychologist Mihaly Csikszentmihalyi has done a lot of research on what makes people feel happy—considering their backgrounds, life experiences, professions, environment, personality traits, and many other variables. The surprising common denominator, the one thing that seemed to recur over and over again, notwithstanding the many other differences, was that people experienced happiness when they were in a mental state of flow.

The mental state of flow is significant not only for producing a state of happiness, but also because it is the state in which the highest level of individual and team performance can be found. Therefore, it is important to know about the psychological aspects of flow, how to produce such mental states of flow, and how to use them proficiently—both to increase people's happiness and to produce superior performance.

Csikszentmihalyi (2008) suggests that the path to happiness begins with "achieving control over the contents of our consciousness." Life is full of uncontrollable, external forces. Yet there are moments when we experience control and mastery of what happens. These moments, which are the ones remembered as moments of happiness, are the moments of extreme efforts, both physical and intellectual, in the endeavor to achieve something difficult. Artists, athletes, professionals, and just about anyone who is stretching the limits goes through the experience of flow. In fact, most breakthroughs in the arts, sports, science, and technology have been brought about by someone going through a state of flow. Being in a state of flow means being hyper-productive, and going beyond what were previously thought of as limits to human abilities. Hence, we realize the importance of understanding what the state of flow is, not only in the pursuit of happiness, but more specifically in the pursuit of what makes us most productive, or hyper-productive.

Naturally, this applies to business, too. Kotler (2014) mentions a ten-year McKinsey study reporting that executive managers were five times more productive when in a state of flow. When individuals working in a team all get to a state of flow the effects compounded. That is why the Borland Quattro Pro engineers described in the case at the beginning of this book could be 50 times more productive than industry averages.

THE MENTAL STATE OF FLOW

Csikszentmihalyi (2001) defined the mental state of flow as the condition in which someone is so deeply immersed in what they are doing that their perception of the world changes dramatically. Focus is extreme on the activity and in the moment; action and awareness merge; self-consciousness is lost; there is a sense of deep control; temporal perception is distorted; and the activity, in and by itself, is intrinsically rewarding. The state is described as *flowing* in the sense that every decision, movement, etc., comes effortlessly and leads *fluidly* to the next one with no hesitation and no interruption. In this state, extremely difficult problems are resolved at a very high speed.

The experience is so intense that it is described as moments of ecstasy and euphoria. Attention is so concentrated on the activity that there is none left to elaborate other signals (so, for instance, self-consciousness is diminished, or even completely lost). The activity itself is perceived as effortless, spontaneous; it just happens and flows. There is great clarity in understanding what needs to be done, and how the activity is progressing. Equally there is complete conviction that the activity can be done, even if it is challenging and might appear as impossible for onlookers. There is a great sense of satisfaction and serenity in doing the activity—it becomes rewarding in itself, providing the highest degree of intrinsic motivation.

Kotler (2014) explains that the experience of flow is primarily mental, and can be considered as altered brain functions induced by the release of five neurochemicals: norepinephrine, dopamine, endorphins, anandamide, and serotonin. The common thing between these five neurochemicals is that they all impact performance and self-reward. The interesting twist is that the mental state of flow is the only condition where these five powerful neurochemicals are all released at the same time. That explains why performance and sense of satisfaction and happiness are so greatly magnified when in flow.

Another key point is that these neurochemicals vastly enhance motivation, learning, and creativity—which are obviously key elements for hyper-productivity to emerge.

FLOW TRIGGERS

Kotler is spearheading the Flow Genome Project (http://www.flowgenomeproject.co/), where flow research is conducted on a broad scale. In particular, the objective is to be able to harness flow and make it happen as a routine process in all endeavors of humanity—including, of course, the business and professional setting.

Kotler (2014) describes how research has found that there are specific *flow triggers* that one can put into action to facilitate the happening of flow. There are 17 triggers grouped in four categories:

- Environmental
- Psychological
- Social
- Creative

Let's study them in more detail.

Environmental Flow Triggers

Environmental triggers are in the external environment (while the others pertain more to the internal, psychological sphere). They include:

- **High Consequences:** When the stakes are high, focus becomes sharper. Focusing helps with getting into flow. The greater the risks, the more focused the action and the greater the flow. Risk can be physical, but also emotional, intellectual, or social. This relates powerfully to the prowess of being open toward accepting failure, and allowing for experimentation, exploration, and discovery. Also, this is why flow often happens in situations of emergencies, crisis, and immediate danger.
- **Rich Environment:** Novelty, unpredictability, and complexity capture attention and concentrate awareness. This trigger can be put into action through environmental design, for instance, to facilitate employees being exposed to such elements. For example, having daily standup meetings will create deep and rich interactions, and discussions about the surprises of the day.
- **Deep Embodiment:** This happens when there are multiple sensory streams, all perceived simultaneously. It is typical for athletes while practicing challenging sports activities, yet it can be realized in other settings. In the case of knowledge-work management, all techniques that result in visualization extend the sensory experience. A project buffer fever chart (see Part 2, Chapter 20, Figure 20.11) makes the project status immediately visible. Moving sticky notes on a Kanban board involves the sense of touch—physically moving the cards implies coordinating sight and touch, while thinking about what the move signifies.

Psychological Triggers

The psychological triggers are those originally identified by Csikszentmihalyi.

- **Intense Focus:** Any activity that produces flow is characterized by long periods of uninterrupted focus. Environments and activities that require multitasking inhibit flow. Focus must be on the single task at hand, with no distractions. Flow is reached as a solitary effort (though there is a *group* variation of flow, as we will see shortly).

- **Clear Goals:** When goals are unclear, doubts and questions have to be resolved before any action is taken. Conversely, if goals are clear, the mind already knows what needs to be done. There is less, or even no, space and time for doubts and hesitation. The emphasis is on the clarity of the goals—it is through clarity that quick and resolute action becomes possible. It is clarity and immediacy of the goal that make action and awareness merge. The goal should relate to the now—the actual situation that is unrolling—and not some desired future state, which would be just as distracting. Attention must be brought into the moment, with the clarity of an immediate, challenging, and attainable goal.
- **Immediate Feedback:** A clear goal identifies what to do. Immediate feedback about how we are progressing (or not) helps us to focus on the moment, too. Delayed feedback will induce the mind to wander with hypothesis, searching for validation about how the action is progressing. A wandering mind is detrimental to the focus on the present that is needed for the best performance. In a business setting, the tighter the feedback loops, the higher the performance. That's why practices like daily scrum meetings work.
- **Challenge/Skills Ratio:** This element is one of the most significant findings of Csikszentmihalyi. There must be a specific ratio between the challenge and the skills required—that's where the so-called *flow channel* can be found. If the challenge is too high, then action will be blocked by anxiety and fear of failure; if it is too low, attention wanders away into boredom or even apathy. Similarly, one must feel confident to have mastery of the skills needed to reach the goal. Flow is best reached when skills required are just a bit higher than what is needed in the ordinary (so that one stretches), yet not so difficult as to become unattainable. The challenge needs to be just above what you ordinarily are capable of so that the uncertainty of the outcome keeps attention fixed in the now.

Social Triggers

Going from single individuals to teams, we encounter what is called *group flow*. The easiest way to relate to this is with team sports when they are exhibiting peak performance, where all members of a team seem to be at the right place at the right time, and do the right thing almost "automagically". All the individuals are in a state of flow; but also, the whole group acts as a single agent in a state of flow. Group flow is particularly interesting when searching for what can explain extraordinary organizational performance—where a group of people coordinate to progress at an incredibly high pace toward a common and significant goal.

- **Serious Concentration:** When an individual is in flow, focus is of essence. When a group of people reach the state of flow, their concentration must be at its sharpest. Things move quickly. Attention must be given not only to the action taking place, but also to where the other members of the group are and what they are doing (and in sports, also to the position and movements of all opponents). It is almost as if a sixth sense develops, whereby everybody just knows where they have all other team members at the same time. In a business setting, this group awareness can be facilitated simply by walling off the team from the rest of the organization so that the team can fully concentrate on its own teamwork without unnecessary distractions.

- **Shared, Clear Goals:** The *Unity of Purpose* pattern, which in this book has been presented as a guiding principle for achievement of hyper-productivity, and the shared vision enabled by Jim McCarthy's Core Protocols address the need for the organization and the teams to have clear and shared goals. The whole idea of *The Goal* (Goldratt 1992) underpins the Theory of Constraints. In Chapter 13, we saw how constraints accounting can express a shared goal in terms of financial objectives. Clarity and sharing of such goals are of essence for teams and organizations to act and perform in unison and with high performance.

- **Good Communication:** Communication obviously supports flow inasmuch as it provides immediate feedback. Naturally, communication is bidirectional. It is not only about telling, but also about listening. Listening skills are heightened in teams that flow. People become more engaged in the activities by paying attention to what the other members are communicating, and immediately build on top of that.

- **Equal Participation and Skill Level:** As mentioned in an earlier chapter, high performance teams will not work with prima donnas or individuals who are dominant or arrogant, or who deem they might not learn anything from the other members. Similarly, all team members must have comparable skills, so that the border of the impossible is at the same point for all, and all can work together to cross that line. If the team members do not have comparable skills, they will be positioned differently in the challenge/skills ratio despite having to work toward a common goal. Unless skills are comparable, the more-skilled will be bored, and the less-skilled will be frustrated.

- **Risk:** This trigger is similar to the individual one, but with the added dimension of social interaction. The team must be open to the potential for failure, and failure can be not only in the actions to be performed, but also in the patterns of communication and interaction that happen between the team members. In either case, the risk of failure must be accepted, and seen as a means to innovate. In particular, innovations in the team dynamics can go a long way to improve the team's future performance.

- **Familiarity:** The more a team works together, the greater the shared and common knowledge they have. It is the construction of tacit knowledge, because everyone becomes more and more familiar with the other team members, and how they individually relate to the team as a whole. In other words, the more *familiar* members become with each other, the less effort they need to spend on communicating, debating, and decision making. Many of the fundamental decisions will be embedded in the team's tacit knowledge, and when communication is needed, the more team members are familiar with one another's communication styles, the more effective the communication.

- **Blending Egos:** This is, in a way, a consequence of equal participation. No one is there to dominate the other team members. But there is more to it. With equal participation and familiarity, repeated performance will develop the ability to think and act with one mind. The contribution to the thinking or the action of any one individual becomes the starting point for the next one, as if they were guided by a single mind that effortlessly coordinates and synchronizes thoughts and actions. Often, this is also a means for innovation, as one individual often builds in new ways on top of what the partners have contributed.

- **Sense of Control:** At the individual level, being in control is part of flow, as it gives that sense of mastery that, in turn, gives satisfaction and happiness. The same is still true when an individual is part of a team. Yet, there must be acceptance to relinquish part of that control to the other team members. This means that being in control is no longer possible and is replaced by a broader sense of control that is exercised by the team as a whole. Naturally, this also means that team members must trust each other. The noble pattern of the *Community of Trust* is again at the foundation for building a team that can be in a state of flow.

- **Always Say Yes:** A further manifestation of the Community of Trust is being ready to accept the contributions of the other team members and build further on that. This is similar to the first rule of improvisational comedy, where the previous participant's line is accepted in full, then built upon. This has both the beneficial consequence of allowing for innovative paths to be taken, and more importantly, not to frustrate anybody by backing out of their contribution. It makes everyone more willing to contribute toward the shared common goal, as each one knows their effort will be taken care of by the next member that picks up the ball. This keeps the team moving forward, often through paths of unexpected creativity.

Creative Triggers

- **Creativity:** Creativity, in itself, is a flow trigger. An environment that fosters creativity naturally allows flow to develop more easily. Creativity is all about a novel association of ideas, often based on pattern recognition. Creativity is also about risk-taking and being open to the possibility of failure. When presenting new ideas we must be prepared that they might not work, or might be rejected. Both pattern recognition and risk-taking release neurochemicals that underly the experience of flow. Because flow leads to results that were inconceivable before, it naturally leads to novel ways of resolving difficult intellectual problems or physical challenges.

THE STATE OF FLOW AND ORGANIZATIONAL HYPER-PRODUCTIVITY

Flow can enhance individual performance many times, and also help teams reach their peak performance. There might be limits as to how much flow might scale; however, as there are cases of entire organizations being hyper-productive, one must assume it is possible to extend the state of flow from individuals and teams to entire organizations. That is why it is beneficial to give attention to this concept of being in a state of flow, and learn how to make it happen in a broader organizational context.

Part II

Hyper-Productive Scrum and Kanban: Applying the TameFlow Perspective

---

17

CHALLENGES OF WORK-STATE
WORK IN PROCESS LIMITS

One of the core practices of Kanban is the practice to limit work in process (WIP). As we saw in Chapter 14, *The Kanban Method, Flow and Throughput*, limiting WIP is necessary to get to a stable state that enables pull, and allows us to reason in terms of Little's Law.

Having a stable state improves the long-term average flow time and enables the maintenance of service level agreements and policies based on classes of service. Limiting WIP is the most fundamental process management practice of Kanban. It is probably the single most powerful practice that can quickly produce tangible performance improvements.

Yet, it is also a practice that is full of traps and pitfalls.

PROCESS MANAGEMENT AND PROCESS IMPROVEMENT IN KANBAN

Naturally the first hurdle limiting WIP is the counterintuitive concept of doing less in order to deliver more. It is only by gaining a systems thinking viewpoint and understanding the nature of flow, and the consequences of having interdependent work stages, that one can appreciate the significance of limiting WIP.

In a typical Kanban implementation, limiting WIP is achieved by limiting the amount of work that can exist at any given stage—in simpler terms, by putting a limit on the number of items that can reside in any column of a Kanban board. This is a perfectly sensible way to limit WIP. It helps the team to close the ranks and keep the lines tight (the line between Bluey and Herbie stays short).

However, limiting WIP is much more powerful than just allowing for delivering more by doing less and keeping the work team together. In fact, limiting WIP is one of the fundamental mechanisms that can be used to determine where to focus any attempts at improving the process itself.

Kanban excels at managing the huge variability that is typical of knowledge-work because it is based on event-driven risk management. The basic idea is that when something goes wrong, (i.e., there is risk materialization), evidence of the problem will show up on the Kanban board, as shown in Figures 17.1 and 17.2.

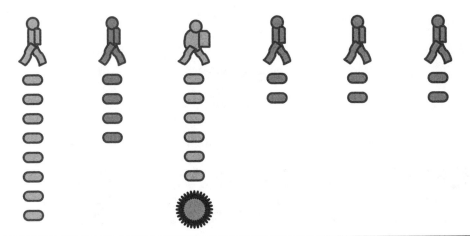

Figure 17.1 Event-driven risk management is the basic process-management and process-improvement mechanism in the Kanban Method.

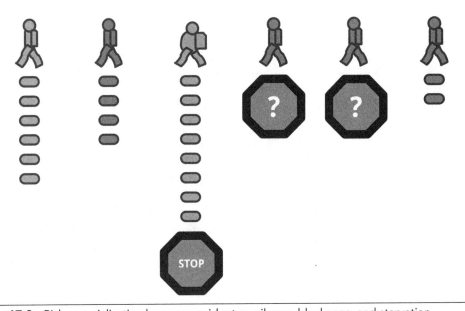

Figure 17.2 Risk materialization becomes evident as pileups, blockages, and starvation

On a Kanban board the most common signs that risk is materializing show up as either pileups (i.e., queues) or starvation. A problem will cause the disruption of the flow of work. Queues will form at (or in front of) the work-state which experiences the problem. At the same time, the work-states downstream of that one will run out of work, to the point where they might actually become completely starved of it.

Often this approach is described as *event-driven risk management*. Problems are confronted in a reactive way as soon as there is evidence of their materialization.

A simple, but incorrect, interpretation of this situation is to consider the column with a pileup as the *constraint*. The reason why it is wrong to consider the pileup as an indication of a constraint is that often the risks that are detected in this way are due to special cause variation. Common cause variation is inherent in the process itself, while special cause variation has external origins. We will examine special cause and common cause variation more in-depth later.

Naturally, one needs to investigate and resolve the reason why the pileup occurred, but considering the corresponding column as a constraint while it is not will prevent you from benefiting from the vast process improvements that become possible only by addressing the real constraints.

In other words, having the view that queues on the Kanban board reveal constraints will not allow you to reach a hyper-productive state; to do that, you need to be able to identify and then address the real constraint. (We will see how to do this, in practice, in the following chapters.)

In this simplistic view, such work-states may be erroneously mistaken as constraints; but in reality they are bottlenecks. Bottlenecks are not the same as a constraint. This is a venial error though.

What really matters is that the organization actually reacts to some problem of which there is evidence on the Kanban board. The ensuing investigations and discussions often result in decisions and changes that effectively improve the situation.

When this pattern of reacting to the evidence of problems that is manifested on the Kanban board becomes systemic, the organization will undergo more profound changes. Further improvements will be undertaken, one at a time, as problems are given away by the configuration on the Kanban board.

This is the huge value of Kanban—it enables an evolutionary improvement of its processes; it is effectively a Kaizen, a stepwise, cooperative, and collective refinement and improvement of the process.

Typically, when it is evident that there is a problem, the reaction might take on many forms:

- Reflective Introspections
- Retrospective
- Root Cause Analysis (Five Whys)
- Team Swarming
- Kanban Katas (as proposed by Håkan Forss)
- Five Focusing Steps
- Changing policies
- Changing class of service (escalating, expediting, etc.)
- Changing the (column) WIP limits

While the *Five Focusing Steps* of the Theory of Constraints (TOC) are sometimes invoked, their applicability in this situation is very doubtful because, as we will discuss hereafter, the problems encountered do not (ordinarily) reveal the *real* constraint of the process, but just a temporary bottleneck of the work flow.

THE RATIONALE BEHIND WORK-STATE WIP LIMITS

Limiting WIP enables pull. While Kanban does not specify *how* WIP should be limited, it has become almost a de facto standard operating procedure to limit work per work-state. In other words, a WIP limit is set for each column on the Kanban board. The number of items in any work-state (such as analysis, development, testing, etc.) is predetermined and that limit must be respected. Whenever the limit is exceeded, it is taken as a sign of trouble and intervention is required, as illustrated in Figure 17.3.

The reason to limit work per column comes from the idea that in doing so you can react more quickly when risk materializes. WIP limits per work-state also intend to establish the expected (it is a policy) capacity, or work that could be done, by that particular state. From a constraints management point of view, this makes little sense, as one would be more concerned about the capacity of the entire system, rather than the capacity of the single work-state; and the system capacity is determined solely by the constraint. Policy driven work-state WIP limits make it harder to find the real constraint. In fact, this is a situation that the TOC would characterize as the policy itself being the true constraint, and policy constraints are the most difficult to break.

Policies notwithstanding, the rationale of work-state WIP limits is to detect signs of pileups, starvation, and blockages, as early as possible. Such signs would appear earlier on a Kanban board with WIP limits per column. This provides leading indicators of any bottlenecks that are forming.

Unfortunately, they are also causing such bottlenecks to form. That is, they are the source of limitations that prevent a Kanban system with work-state WIP limits from performing even better. We have to stress this point—introducing work-state WIP limits will undoubtedly improve the performance of the organization; yet it will also put a cap on that improvement. In other words, it is possible to gain even more.

Kanban intends to use these leading indicators to encourage discussions about what to do. Furthermore, the setting of WIP limits is driven by policies and/or by staff liquidity criteria. Even so, the mechanism by which change is initiated is the breaking of a work-state WIP limit.

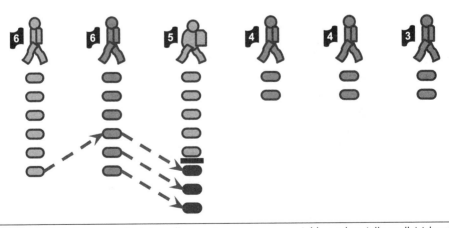

Figure 17.3 WIP limits on work-states allow us to react more quickly and to (allegedly) identify the constraint. Downstream states are not necessarily and immediately starved once a WIP limit is reached, but progress is blocked upstream.

Column WIP limits work wonders when one is starting off with Kanban. First, they do somewhat regulate flow and enable pull—which alone is a good enough reason to use them because they will give rise to a significant increase in performance (compared to any earlier practice). Second, and more important, with the periodic disruptions of operations that happen when WIP limits are reached or exceeded, the organization gets into the habit of having discussions about any part of the system in order to improve it.

These stoppages, due to WIP limit busting, are similar to the *andon* signaling of Lean Manufacturing—the signaling that just about anybody on the factory floor has the power to turn on in order to stop the line if a problem is detected. The real value of work-state WIP limits is in making the team work together to resolve a problem that impedes overall progress.

THE POSITIVES OF WORK-STATE WIP LIMITS

It is obvious that work-state WIP limits bring about beneficial effects, especially compared to the status quo ante, the state of affairs before their adoption. There are many significant cases of successful Kanban implementations, which all started by applying the Kanban principles and practices, and inevitably the particular practice of limiting WIP through column WIP limits.

There are even cases of success at scale in very large organizations, like Chris Achouiantz's work at Sandvik resulting in the *Kanban Field Guide*, Håkan Forss and Erik Shön's work with Ericsson, Gerber and Engel's work with SAP, and many others.

A great deal of these success stories can be attributed to the mechanisms and interactions that derive directly from the adoption of work-state WIP limits. In brief, they are:

- **Open Discussions.** The engendering of open discussions that derive from frequent and explicit signals provided by reaching work-state WIP limits, and their public and common visibility; discussions that would be entirely ignored and avoided without such explicit signals.
- **New Modes of Interaction and Communication.** The discussions following the busting of a column WIP limit will nurture new cross-functional, cross-team, cross-departmental and even cross-organizational conversations that would otherwise not take place. In other words, they are wiring new modes of interaction and communication into the organization. This is very much unlike other approaches (typically, like Scrum, but not only) that impose predefined patterns of interaction and communication, actually dictating when and who has the right to speak. This is in direct support of the noble patterns of *Unity of Purpose* and *Community of Trust*.
- **Self-Reflective Introspection.** More important than the signals themselves, is that the organization learns the essential skill of how to look for, react on, and finally act upon the signals. This creates a state of mindfulness, of self-reflective introspection, which is the basis for building a double-loop learning organization. Unlike Scrum, where self-reflection is a predefined event (in the Retrospectives), in this instance the exercise is performed on the spot, when problems occur; much in line with the *andon* cord-pulling of Lean.
- **Positive Organizational Habits.** Because breaking of work-state WIP limits occurs very frequently, these reflective activities become a habit and, most of the time, the

activities involve reflection and introspection about the process being used (in addition to, naturally, the problems about the work being done). Such reflective habits strengthen the foundation for double-loop learning, which, in turn, is key in gaining superior organizational performance.

- **Team Building.** Teams are shaped and reinforced through common struggles. Positive team behavior will crystallize more and more each time a work-state WIP limit is reached, and the team needs to think and decide together to resolve the issue.
- **Natural Swarming.** Just thinking and taking decisions about problems together is usually a great improvement over other approaches, but the true benefit comes when the team actually acts together to resolve problems. A positive swarming behavior develops naturally when reacting to work-state WIP limit breakages. This is unlike other approaches where swarming is dictated (often with the artificial excuse of being lean and caring about one-piece-flow). Swarming that develops naturally is more effective and efficient than any imposed behavior. The benefit is not so much in the swarming behavior as such, but in its natural, organic development made possible by the frequent, recurring breakage of column WIP limits.
- **Organizational Learning.** Already mentioned above, but this is worth stressing again due to its importance. Through the effects of work-state WIP limits, the organization learns how to learn. This is an essential skill that becomes critical once you aim at higher performance levels. At that point, the organization will no longer be expected to follow prescribed recipes but to apply its own (collective) insights in confronting and resolving its challenges.

We will refer back to these positive aspects in the remainder of this chapter. Notwithstanding these positives, there are also challenges with work-state WIP limits, and it is well worth understanding them because therein lies a key for unlocking even better organizational performance.

THE CHALLENGES WITH WORK-STATE WIP LIMITS

The challenges of work-state WIP limits are not obvious. They may become evident if one relates to core practice #6 (see page 151), and, in particular, tries to resort to the TOC as a supporting model for improvement. When adopting any such additional model, one has to be prepared that there might be new insights, even critical insights, that will require you to reconsider some aspects of the core Kanban practices, or at least of the ways that such practices are commonly pursued. This is such a situation.

There are two cases wherein the TOC perspective is beneficial.

- **Shallow and Immature Kanban.** While Kanban might seem easy on the surface, often the organizational context and culture will work against its successful implementation. In particular, when the organization does not already have a distinct clear *North Star* (a sense of direction and purpose), shallow implementations of Kanban will not provide all the benefits they could. In these instances the Kanban values, agendas, and lenses are not developed sufficiently to guide the transformation. In these instances the adoption of the TOC mindset, with the pragmatic and clearly-defined goal of maximization of financial throughput, can provide that missing sense of purpose that is vital.

- **Deep and Well-functioning Kanban.** Conversely there are cases where the adoption of Kanban goes very well, yet, the results thereof are not entirely satisfactory. Either the improvements happen too slowly, or they do not impact the critical success factors that the company cares about, such as increasing throughput.

The second case is important. A great many successful Kanban implementations achieve spectacular results in reducing flow times. This is possible in many ways; all of which do not necessarily impact on the constraint of the underlying work process. Consequently, even if the organization will be capable of delivering their things faster, they will not be able to deliver more of them. This was highlighted in an e-mail exchange with Kurt Häusler, who said:

> Kanban's background in maintenance and product development might focus on lead time where being quick to market is important, but many companies just need more things to be done in less time (rather than faster) and cheaper, which is where improving throughput comes in.

Without an explicit focus on the constraint, which comes from the TOC perspective, improving throughput might be very difficult even when Kanban is well implemented, and delivers improvements in terms of reduced flow times. As we will see next, the use of work-state WIP limits is really a hindrance for this.

THE NEGATIVES OF WORK-STATE WIP LIMITS

In this section we are going to expose the negative aspects of using work-state WIP limits. Highlighting that there are negatives with work-state WIP limits does not diminish their value, nor that of the Kanban Method in general. The *TameFlow* approach is not an alternative to the Kanban Method. It is, in fact, a natural evolution of the sixth core practice:

> **Core Practice #6:** Improve collaboratively, evolve experimentally, using models and the scientific method.

The *TameFlow* approach is the result of using the TOC as the reference model when striving to use the Kanban Method and trying to improve by using models. When one applies the Kanban Method with an experimental and scientific mindset, one should also be prepared to improve, even if that means letting go of precepts that are otherwise founding and fundamental in the initial stages.

The *TameFlow* approach is the outcome and result of the evolutionary change promoted by the Kanban Method, exercised with the TOC as the reference model in Core Practice #6. It is through this evolution that the following problems with work-state WIP limits have been identified.

Thirteen Problems with Work-State WIP Limits

It is obvious that any organization or team that decides to adopt Kanban is interested in improving its processes and performance. By learning to use Kanban with work-state

WIP limits, organizational performance will improve dramatically. However, and maybe because of such positive outcomes in such situations, it might be difficult to realize that performance can be increased *even further* by moving beyond the use of work-state WIP limits.

The use of work-state WIP limits is the principal reason why Kanban teams are *not* able to reach a hyper-productive state. The reason is to be found in the numerous problems and drawbacks that are associated with work-state WIP limits. These problems and drawbacks can be summarized as follows:

- Work-state WIP limits hide the real Herbie (constraint). For instance, column WIP limits might signal that Bluey is having problems, despite the fact that, in reality, Herbie is still the real constraint. The organization will try to make fixes to remove the perceived constraint on Bluey. Unfortunately, the intervention is on a non-constraint, and therefore, with a TOC mindset we know that it will not deliver any improvement in terms of higher throughput. (Note: the intervention may reduce the overall flow time, but it will not increase throughput.)
- As a consequence of the previous point, work-state WIP limits give too many false positives of problems that are not really problems, but are problems that have been self-inflicted by the very act of setting the work-state WIP limits. As mentioned in the previous point, the signal on Bluey diverts attention away from Herbie, the real constraint.
- Work-state WIP limits promote excessive trial and error. Finding a balanced set of work-state WIP limits can be difficult. Practitioners, especially those who are inexperienced, will try to play with the column WIP limits to find out what works. (Note that this is not what is recommended by experienced Kanban practitioners; yet it is what happens in practice.) Rather than measuring the effects in terms of throughput of the whole system and deciding accordingly, this approach proceeds without guidance and without a specific goal in mind—the goal of increasing throughput. Often, in these cases, work-state WIP limits are determined according to the comfort of the various column-owners, rather than as a consequence of a quantitative assessment of what is happening in the system (by measuring flow times, WIP and throughput).
- Playing with work-state WIP limits is a way of tampering with the system. Tampering was defined by Deming (1993) as a waste of productive time that causes loss of focus.
- In particular, the focus that is wasted is the focus on the real constraint, and attention is diverted away from throughput of the entire system, and put on one of its work-states.
- Work-state WIP limits risk becoming local optimizations. Instead of being concerned about how work flows through the entire system, team members working in specific columns become concerned about finding the appropriate WIP limit for *their* column. Instead, the effort should be on setting a WIP limit for the entire system in order to favor the overall flow, without damaging throughput.
- Because only one column can be the constraint, it follows that the majority of interventions (on the other columns) are actually a waste of effort and resources. Fixing a non-constraint (like Bluey or Greenie) is waste. The only reason to be concerned with non-constraints is when you want to improve flow times, but not when the concern

is about throughput. Fixing the constraint (Herbie) gives the real gain. Again, this must be considered as unnecessary waste, considering that those bottlenecks were created artificially. (There is a distinction between a bottleneck and a constraint.)

- Work-state WIP limits introduce artificial bottlenecks where there should not be any. This point is quite perverse, because it can give the false impression of resolving process problems, while those process problems were not there at the beginning. It is a trap that will make one consider as improvements what are really wasteful actions. With work-state WIP limits, one should be extremely careful about such self-inflicted bottlenecks, especially since they can be avoided in the first place.

- Work-state WIP limits hinder and disrupt true flow. The team is constantly interrupted and has to engage in local firefights with whatever column breaks its WIP limit. While these interruptions have the positive effects described earlier, they must also be recognized for what they are—mostly unnecessary. Furthermore, firefighting is not sustainable especially if the fires are set artificially, arbitrarily, and on purpose. The intent of limiting WIP (in general) is indeed that of keeping the team tightly together, but work-state WIP limits do so at the risk of stopping Bluey (or Greenie) every so often, when in reality they do not need to stop at all.

- Work-state WIP limits render directionless the evolutionary approach enabled and promoted by Kanban. This is because the intervention to resolve a breakage on one work-state (for example Bluey), might be canceled out entirely by the next one on a different work-state (for example Greenie). In other words, the evolutionary improvement becomes more like a random walk, rather than guided by deliberate effort. Naturally, this should find guidance in the Kanban Agendas and in change fitness assessment, but this might be very difficult in immature Kanban implementations, and inconsistent in mature ones which might lack the discipline of using the appropriate metrics to make such decisions. The TOC perspective gives very clear directives in both cases.

- Work-state WIP limits bring about the moving constraint syndrome. Chasing the breaking WIP limits becomes a *Whack-a-Mole Hysteric Hysteresis* game. When constraints are constantly moving in the system, it is a sure sign that the real constraint is not known, and above all, is not managed. This is a well-known topic in the TOC literature, and there are many ways to deal with the problem. We will discuss one shortly.

- If improvements do develop, then those improvements occur by accident and happenstance; they originate from those interventions that just happen to affect Herbie, the real constraint. The fact that they involve the real constraint is merely coincidental, as a lucky combination of column WIP limits that happen to expose the real constraint, in that particular circumstance. It is not done by deliberate and thoughtful choice. Later we will elaborate on the distinction between a bottleneck in the work flow and a constraint in the work process. If you do not know where the constraint is in your work process (work-state WIP limits do not show this), then any improvement in throughput must have happened by coincidence. You could not deliberately target the constraint in the work process because you did not know where it was. You were acting on some bottleneck in the work flow, which—by happenstance—coincided with the constraint in the work process. Unfortunately, this effectively reinforces the conviction that the approach is always valid because it does produce tangible and positive throughput improvements after all. Sadly, the majority of the interventions are completely ineffective (for increasing the system's throughput), and they must be considered waste. It is much wiser to make a deliberate effort and focus interventions where they are needed—on the real Herbie. It is worth noting that this effect might escape attention precisely because positive results and improvements will indeed ensue; but these results and improvements come from (1) the open discussions that are provoked about problems; and (2) the coincidental fact that, at times, they truly affect the real constraint.

- Finally, work-state WIP limits induce instability in the system, and this has dire consequences, as we elaborate in the following section.

Induced Instability

With work-state WIP limits we have artificial bottlenecks, and we get artificial hiccups in the flow—in other words, we are making the whole system more unstable than what it already is through its inherent variation. Notice that the instability we refer to here has nothing to do with the consequences of changes to the system that one might introduce for the very reason of improving the system itself. It is obvious that when you introduce changes, you will have to face some instability; but that is another kind of instability altogether—one that you are expecting and that you are prepared to manage. The instability we are concerned about here comes as a consequence of the artificial bottlenecks induced by work-state WIP limits.

This induced instability effectively disrupts the applicability of Little's Law. It is ironic that limiting WIP is justified by the need of getting to a stable state so that Little's Law applies, but work-state WIP limits break this condition, rather than promoting it.

Furthermore, when the system is in an unstable state, most variability will come from special cause variation. Thus any opportunity to identify, let alone improve on, common cause variation will be lost. A system is stable when it is affected only by common cause variation. Therefore, if one is able to keep the system in a stable state, you will have two significant advantages: you can apply Little's Law and you get the opportunity to identify common cause variation. We will see how important this is in Chapter 20, *Improving While in the Flow*.

To be able to exploit Little's Law, it is necessary to keep the process at a stable, steady, and sustainable state before and after any improvement. Jump-starting a new column improvement every other day does not help to improve systematically. Continuous disruption of flow hinders continuous improvement.

Just as there is a conceptual distinction between shallow- and deep-Kanban, the same can be said about constraints management. The shallow version applies the Five Focusing Steps blindly, addressing the queues on the Kanban board and effectively inducing the moving constraint syndrome. The deeper version strives to *know where the constraint really is* and then to *keep the constraint in place*. By keeping the constraint in a known position, the entire system can be managed much more reliably, and the promises made with classes of service can be delivered more consistently. In such a system, it becomes much easier to live up to the team's service level agreements.

There is one exception when one needs to improve a non-constraint. The only reason to improve non-constraints is to ensure that the constraint remains in the same place because only with a stable constraint will you have a stable system. This implies that any improvement on a non-constraint must be done with explicit deliberation; with the precise understanding that you want to raise the bar for the capacity-constrained resource so that it continues to remain the constraint.

Work-State WIP Limits Are Useful when Starting

The above list of negatives about work-state WIP limits should not be taken as a reason to rule them out. Work-state WIP limits are invaluable when starting out with Kanban because they will prepare the team and the organization to have open discussions about problems that are revealed through the visualization of work on the Kanban board.

This is an essential skill that needs to be well honed and exercised before moving to the more sophisticated methods that will be explained later. So to summarize, when starting off with Kanban, you should use work-state WIP limits. Once you feel comfortable with the patterns of interaction and communication that emerge within the process of visualizing disruption of work flow, you will be ready to abandon work-state WIP limits and move on, as we will see in the coming chapters.

When you introduce Kanban for the first time in an organization or in a team, you should always start by using work-state WIP limits. This is important because it instills the habit of discussing the problems within the process in a collective way.

It is essential to gain this habit before trying to move on to the more advanced method described later in this book. Chapter 18, *TameFlow-Kanban: The Throughput Focused Kanban*, will replace work-state WIP limits with another mechanism, which gives more subtle and less disruptive signals about where problems are materializing. The team needs to be well trained in achieving a collective effort in resolving process problems before it can work with this alternative.

Therefore, always start with work-state WIP limits. They will teach the team about swarming and developing productive ways to communicate and interact when solving problems together. Once the team knows how to do this, you can move on to the more advanced method. Work-state WIP limits give you immediate signals conducive to positive team behavior. In the more advanced method, the signals will be more subtle; the team might need to be collaborating already, just to recognize these signals.

Using work-state WIP limits is an essential part in the organizational *learning process* that teaches the team to think with a collective intelligence. Work-state WIP limits must be used as *training wheels* and they should be taken off once the organization has found the balance and is ready to speed up.

Evolutionary but Directionless Improvements

Because work-state WIP limits effectively hide the true constraint and actually induce moving bottlenecks, it becomes very difficult to improve toward a well-defined goal. Kanban is known to support evolutionary changes (with many small J-curves) rather than a big monolithic change (with one big J-curve). Evolutionary changes are certainly easier to control than big monolithic ones. However, every step might not go in the same direction as earlier ones. For example, think about the improvement you make on one column that ends up nullifying earlier improvements you might have made on other columns. These improvements resemble more of a random walk, rather than a concerted effort of many steps toward some discernible goal of significance. These improvements are local in scope (determined by the broken work-state WIP limit) and do not take into account the system as a whole. This is a direct consequence of having WIP limits defined per work-state. Kanban does enable evolutionary change, but work-state WIP limits may divert its progress toward a clear goal. (Note however that in a mature implementation of Kanban, a general sense of direction is provided by the Kanban Agendas.)

It becomes of essence, therefore, to find a way toward continuous improvement that keeps the evolutionary spirit of Kanban, but that gives a clear direction to all efforts. The guiding light is to be found in identifying the real constraint of the system, and then focusing all actions for improving around the constraint, as exemplified by the Five Focusing Steps.

Flow-Time Reduction Is Important

It must be stressed that all of the above negative remarks about work-state WIP limits relate to the possibility of increasing the system's throughput, which can only be achieved by improving on the constraint. In most organizations, there is a lot to gain by improving flow times. Flow times can be reduced dramatically by pursuing the limiting of WIP and improving flow time efficiencies. You can do this by value-stream mapping, and looking for the wait times of your WIP; even better if you start measuring it.

Any reduction of flow time will not affect throughput unless it also, and specifically, involves the constraint of the work process. Therefore, you must make a deliberate effort to identify the constraint, and make decisions accordingly.

When starting with a Kanban implementation, it is always good to start with work-state WIP limits (for all the positives described at the start of the chapter), and make all improvements that are possible in terms of limiting WIP and reducing flow times. It is only then—when you get to a point that further improvements seem very difficult—that you can switch gears and use the *TameFlow* approach to nail down the constraint in the work process and aim at improving the system's throughput.

Work-State WIP Limits Create Bottlenecks and Ignore the Real Constraint

By constantly creating new work flow disruption, work-state WIP limits effectively introduce bottlenecks in the work flow. The idea of identifying the constraint by looking at where work piles up (or where the local WIP limit is exceeded), gives the wrong signals.

It is important to realize that a system can have several bottlenecks, but only one constraint. In the hiking scout's metaphor, when Bluey has a temporary halt, he is a bottleneck in the flow of work: fewer steps are taken by the troop as a whole. As long as Bluey's stop does not last to the point that it affects Herbie, it will not have affected the troops overall progress. (And if it does, you will notice it because Herbie will have to stop.) Yet Herbie remains the troop's constraint, even when Bluey halts for a moment. It is Herbie's speed and not Bluey's temporary hiccup that prevents the troop from progressing at a higher pace.

This gives rise to some subtle misconceptions. For instance, in a Twitter conversation with David Anderson, he offered the following viewpoint:

> To maintain a bottleneck in one place requires too much slack in knowledge work [...] the bottleneck is prone to move around rapidly.

The perception that bottlenecks move around is definitively true on a Kanban board with work-state WIP limits, but that is an effect that is induced by the very fact that you are using work-state WIP limits.

Piling up of work in queues is certainly a sign that a bottleneck is forming (even in the absence of work-state WIP limits), as Reinertsen (2009) teaches. Therefore, as we will see, it is of the essence to keep an eye, and react quickly, on the formation of queues (and we will see how to do this without work-state WIP limits).

However, a bottleneck is not necessarily the constraint of the system. A system can exhibit a multitude of bottlenecks, yet there will be only one constraint. Using queues is ideal to identify the (temporary) bottlenecks that form because of some event. The bottlenecks that are identified in this way are due to special cause variation. In fact, Kanban excels at identifying problems due to special cause variation, and that is what enables the event-driven risk management approach.

The important realization that one has to come to grips with is that Kanban does not take into consideration common cause variation. Unlike manufacturing, (where one uses techniques like Six Sigma to minimize variation), in knowledge work there is much more common cause variation. Improvements that work off common cause variation are much more effective than those that work off special cause variation, but this implies that you have to employ methods that effectively expose common cause variation. Kanban deals only with special cause variation and therefore misses what is maybe the greatest opportunity to arrive at a hyper-productive state.

We will see how to handle common cause variation in Chapter 20, but before we can do that, we must learn more about bottlenecks and constraints and how to find the real constraint on a Kanban board.

Bottlenecks Are Not Constraints

The constraints management viewpoint makes a clear distinction between bottlenecks and constraints. Jacob (2009), describes the difference as follows:

> A bottleneck [...] is a resource that cannot consistently or reliably meet the demands placed on it. So its output is typically less than demand. This is in contrast to a primary constraint, which is the resource most likely to become a bottleneck if not properly managed.

A constraint is thus a managed bottleneck. A bottleneck becomes a constraint once you ensure that you do not create a greater demand than what it can handle, through explicit and deliberate management. Out of the many possible bottlenecks in the system, the constraints management precept is to choose the bottleneck with the least capacity and turn it into a primary constraint. It is that bottleneck that, once managed, will become the primary constraint of the system—the constraint that determines the overall capacity of the entire system.

Another way of thinking about this is that bottlenecks typically have some physical manifestation (showing up as queues and starvation in a work flow), yet a constraint is whatever mostly prevents the organization from achieving its goal. In particular, a constraint does not have to be of a physical nature. A constraint can also be immaterial.

Examples of such immaterial constraints are policy constraints, whereby ineffective and counterproductive ways of working are institutionalized by policies rather than lack of capacity or capability. Another example is attention. Goldratt has often stated that the biggest constraint of all is management attention. Managers and executives have only a limited amount of brain power with which they have to deal with all the challenges they are confronting. Their attention is spread thin, to the point that it might very well become the most limiting factor for making effective and efficient progress towards the company's goal.

FINDING THE PRIMARY CONSTRAINT ON A KANBAN BOARD

The principal problem with WIP work-state limits is that there is no reliable way to clearly distinguish the bottleneck with the least capacity from all others. Consequently, it is not possible to manage it and turn it into the system's primary constraint. Let's see how we can do that.

The Guidance of Flow Time

In Kanban there is a sophisticated and well accepted use of (average) flow times. For instance, classes of service for the sustenance of service level agreements (SLAs) are often defined in terms of confidence levels in average flow times. The basis of such SLAs is, in the long term, the stability of average flow times. It is important to realize that Kanban fully recognizes this; average flow times are much more stable than the extreme variability you find on a daily basis in the queues on the Kanban board. The real constraint of a Kanban process can be found by examining average flow times, rather than looking at queues.

By using (average) flow times as the basis for identifying the single primary constraint (as we will explain in the next chapter) instead of using queues, which work well for identifying temporary bottlenecks, we can effectively employ the process of ongoing improvement that is based on the Five Focusing Steps of the TOC.

Since (average) long-running flow times have a more stable nature than (temporary) queues, they will allow the improvement investigation to go in the direction of identifying the primary constraint in the process with respect to common cause variation.

What Is Next?

In Part 1, Chapter 15, *Understanding the Impact of a Constraint*, we learned why it is so important to find and manage a constraint. The next chapter, *TameFlow-Kanban: The Throughput Focused Kanban*, will present a way to forgo work-state WIP limits in order to improve the overall *flow* of work through the system and avoid the related problems. The chapter on understanding common cause variation will highlight why it is so important to identify common cause variation for the purpose of improving your process. In Chapter 20, we will see how we can identify common cause variation when it is affecting the work process.

Finally, in Chapter 21, we will see how we can find many sources of common cause variation and then choose the one upon which we can intervene to improve our overall process.

In particular, the next chapter will highlight how important it is to identify and manage the real constraint of the process. After seeing what the business impact of a correctly identified and managed constraint might be, there should be no doubts about its importance, and therefore, the need to improve Kanban in order to not only deal with the bottlenecks in the work flow, but also to properly deal with the constraint of the work process.

18

TAMEFLOW-KANBAN: THE THROUGHPUT FOCUSED KANBAN

In this chapter we will suggest a number of practical changes to Kanban. The intent is to support an enhanced variant of Kanban that specifically supports smoother flow and increased throughput. We call this variant, *TameFlow-Kanban*.

We have discovered how important it is, from a business perspective, to be in control of the constraints. Unless we know where the constraint is located in our system, it will not be possible to exercise constraints management; and consequently it will not be possible to reap the huge benefits of the Archimedean lever that comes from managing the constraint.

Without constraints accounting and focus on financial throughput, you will not be able to align the organization and set the preconditions to realize the noble patterns of *Unity of Purpose* and *Community of Trust*—and, of course, to achieve hyper-productivity.

There are many aspects that contribute to hyper-productivity, but unless the structural impediments are removed from the root, hyper-productivity will never be attained. In Part 1, we highlighted how these structural impediments are a consequence of using conventional metrics, typically based on cost accounting. To align the entire company in a structural way on one single metric, it is necessary to move over to constraints accounting and be very focused on measuring financial throughput.

Alas, this is possible only if we know where the constraint of the system is. It is therefore paramount to know where the real constraint is, and to manage it accordingly.

In the previous chapter we saw how the conventional way of defining work-state work in process (WIP) limits (that is, WIP limits on the columns of a Kanban board) is counter-productive to effectively identifying, let alone managing, the constraint.

To recap, some of the negative consequences of work-state WIP limits are:

- They are local optimizations
- They hide the real constraint
- They promote unwarranted trial and error
- They induce tampering with the system

- They produce a lot of waste in terms of unnecessary fixes
- They can improve the system, but only by happenstance, not by deliberate and directed action
- They induce artificial bottlenecks
- They hinder flow
- They work against the evolutionary improvement spirit of Kanban, because they render the improvements directionless
- They make the system unstable

It is therefore necessary to find ways to regain the systems perspective without defining WIP limits on the work-states; and yet having some means of limiting WIP in order to enable *pull* and to keep the system in a stable state in order to be able to apply *Little's Law*. We must also overcome these challenges and yet keep intact the visual management paradigm that is characteristic of Kanban boards.

Finally, we will introduce further execution control features that come from the Theory of Constraints (TOC) project management practices. We will also learn how to perform effective root cause analysis in order to find where one can intervene to improve the constraint.

FINDING THE REAL HERBIE

The accounting example in Chapter 15, *Understanding the Impact of a Constraint*, showed how considering flow time could be a misleading metric. In fact, the example illustrated the case where by choosing the option that reduced flow time delivered worse business results than either the original situation or the alternative option that increased flow time. To add even more confusion, that alternative option which increased flow time delivered the best business performance.

All this is definitively counterintuitive and, as we saw, it can only be explained by taking into account the constraint of the system.

In that specific example, any improvement in flow time did not have any positive business impact. It was only by breaking down the flow time per work-state that it was possible to identify the real constraint—the Herbie in development. Only by improving the flow time at the constraint could we identify the option that provided the best business value. The exercise suggests exactly how we can identify the constraint of the process.

Because flow time is an easy metric to gather, we have an easy way to find the *Herbie* in the overall process. We just need to plot a bar chart of the (average) flow time employed by each work-state, as shown in Figure 18.1. Naturally, the highest bar will clearly point out which work-state is the real Herbie.

In order to visualize the situation, we simply rotate and lay down the bars of the bar chart, placing them flat underneath each column header on the Kanban board. To add further emphasis, we can shade them all in while making the bar identifying Herbie black, as shown in Figure 18.2.

Naturally, one disadvantage of using flow time for the purpose of identifying the constraint is that it is a lagging indicator. We will see later how, through other techniques of the TOC, we can get leading indicators about problems in the process.

Figure 18.1   A bar chart of the (average) flow times for each work-state will reveal which work-state is the constraint

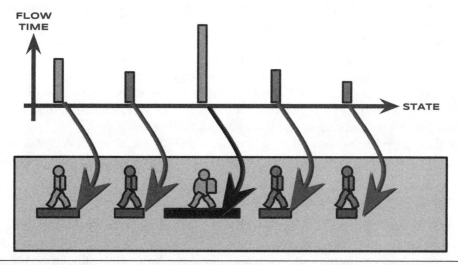

Figure 18.2   Visualize the constraint with shaded time bars under the work-state headings on the Kanban board—all bars are "gray" except for the one showing the constraint which is "black" (Herbie)

One should also consider that given the choice between over-reactive indicators (as those provided by WIP limits on work-states) and lagging indicators (as flow times), the latter are preferable, especially if you want to pursue long-term, systemic improvements. Even better leading indicators are those that reveal problems affecting the entire system's capacity to deliver as expected, and such that it is possible to tune their level of reactivity. We will find such indicators in Chapter 20, *Improving While in the Flow*.

THE NEED FOR THE *Real* KANBAN

Practitioners of Lean Thinking have been known to criticize the Kanban Method, as it does not faithfully reproduce the original Kanban pull signaling mechanism made famous by the Toyota Production System (TPS). While the objection might have some grounds, there are more similarities than differences between the two approaches. Certainly, the intent of both approaches is the same—namely to enable pull.

Paradoxically, in order to enable pull by means of visual signals on the Kanban board, Kanban introduced work-state WIP limits. Yes, precisely those column WIP limits which we have been criticizing are indispensable in making pull possible at all.

Pull is enabled not only because of the limitation of WIP, but also because of the clear visual effects and clues that result from it. Columns without WIP limits can contain an un-limited number of cards. By putting a WIP limit on a column, we literally limit the number of cards that can fit therein. Just as important is what you don't see: when there are fewer cards than the WIP limit, you have empty slots to be filled up with new cards. This is how the pull-signaling semantic is realized through the WIP limit. What does this mean? When there are fewer cards than the allowable WIP limit in a column, the empty slots are effec-tively a pull signal. The empty slot signals pull—it gives permission to take on more work.

Now, if we take away WIP limits on columns, we are also taking away any empty slots that signal the need to replenish the work flow. (Of course, using an infinite number of empty slots doesn't work, as WIP would continuously increase; just like when Bluey was walking further and further ahead of Herbie as we read about in Part 1.)

Even if we decide not to use WIP limits on columns, we still need to somehow impose a limitation on WIP in the entire system because of the need to keep the system in a stable condition (so that we can reason and manage with Little's Law).

Both of these problems, the pull-signal semantic and the limitation of WIP, can be solved very simply by resorting to the original Kanban system, as it was implemented in the TPS.

Toyota Production System Kanban

Let us first examine the pull semantic—what is used to signal that work has to be *pulled* to feed a downstream step in the process. In the TPS a very simple solution was found by using empty boxes that were sent upstream. The boxes were not really empty, they con-tained a card—a Kanban card. The empty box signaled the need to work (the process is hungry) and the card in the box detailed what kind of work was needed.

To make an extreme oversimplification and for the sake of illustration, imagine that a customer orders a new car. The process would start off at the last workstation with an empty box containing a card upon which is written *Car*, along with other details pertaining to the make and model. That last workstation would need to assemble an engine, a body, and four wheels. So it sends off, upstream in the production line, three empty boxes containing the three cards—*Engine*, *Body*, and *Four Wheels*. The upstream workstations, upon receiving the boxes, would in turn, send off other empty boxes with cards specifying what they would need. At the end, in front of the *first* workstation in this production line, the boxes would hit the materials store. Finally somebody would put the requested pieces into the boxes and send them back to the requesting workstation. That workstation would assemble the component it received from its upstream providers, and then fill the empty box that was sent to it by the workstation downstream. The whole process continues like this back to the *last* workstation that makes the final assembly and outputs the requested car, as illustrated in Figure 18.3.

As you can see from this example, there are two aspects that must be handled. One is the specification of what needs to be done—that is written on the card. The other is the signal to pull in work from an upstream workstation; that signal is given by the (empty) boxes. This system is similar to how shelves are replenished in a supermarket. Empty shelves indicate pull, and the labels describing the goods indicate what needs to be placed on the corresponding shelf. In fact, the American supermarket was what originally inspired Toyota to implement this system.

Real Kanban on a Kanban Board

On a Kanban board, the cards always play the same role as they communicate what needs to be done. The empty slots in the WIP-limited columns signal the pull.

In TameFlow-Kanban we will still keep the cards unchanged, but we will forgo the WIP-limited columns, so we will not have empty slots to signal pull. Instead, we introduce

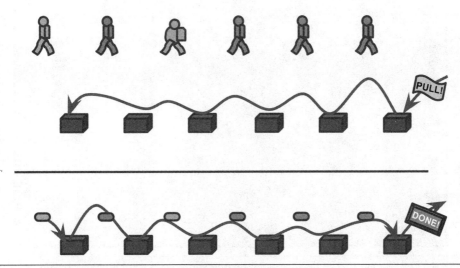

Figure 18.3   The original Kanban of the Toyota Production System

a new physical and visible element, the intention of which is to represent the empty boxes used in the original Kanban system.

Instead of boxes, we will use visible tokens that we will affix on the cards, as shown in Figure 18.4. One way to do this practically is to use magnets (provided the Kanban board has a metallic base) to keep ordinary cards in place on the board, rather than using sticky notes. We will call these visible tokens *Kanban tokens*. (Of course, they don't have to be magnets, as suggested; they can be any physical and visible element that you put on or around a card.)

We will limit the WIP for the entire process simply by limiting the number of Kanban tokens that we use across the entire board. There will be no WIP limits on any single column. Work is limited simply throughout the system in its entirety.

While the description that follows will focus on just one kind of Kanban token for simplicity of illustration, you should use different kinds of Kanban tokens (for instance, with different colors), in order to represent different kinds of work items, or different classes of service. (Every class of service should have its own system-wide WIP limit and, hence, its own kind of Kanban token; though in the examples and illustrations we focus on one class of service only, in order not to clutter the illustrations.) The key point is that any set of Kanban tokens must contain a finite number of tokens, in order to limit that kind of work through the system. This is the key mechanism for limiting WIP in this approach.

This bears some similarities with Constant Work In Process (ConWIP) systems, but with two significant differences. First, there is a different set of tokens (and hence a different limit) for each class of service. (A ConWIP would maintain the same limit across all classes of services). Second, as we will see shortly with the introduction of the constraint

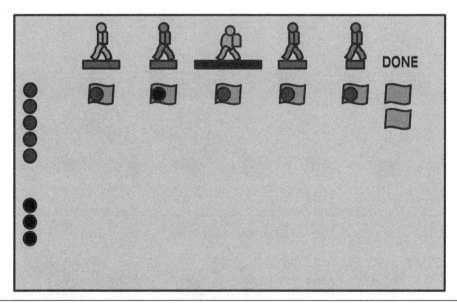

Figure 18.4 Put *Kanban tokens* (for example, magnets) on the cards. Limit WIP by limiting the number of Kanban tokens. Use different tokens (or colors) for different classes of service. Leave free unengaged tokens at the front of the board.

buffer, this limit may vary dynamically (in advanced applications) according to the signals that we gain from monitoring the buffer.

The rules for using the Kanban tokens are simple. Initially they are all lined up on the left side of the Kanban board, signaling that capacity is available (pull). When a card is released into the work flow, it is associated with a Kanban token. The Kanban token follows the card all along the Kanban board. When the card finally arrives at the last column (the "DONE" column) of the board, the Kanban token is released and moved back to the pool at the beginning of the board, as shown in Figure 18.5.

Naturally, when all Kanban tokens are used on a board, no further cards can be released into the work flow; at least not until some card exits the board and its corresponding Kanban token is released back into the pool, signaling that capacity is available again.

The mechanism is fairly simple and very visual. It models the original Kanban system more faithfully. The major advantage with respect to conventional Kanban boards is that it avoids the WIP limits on columns.

DRUM-BUFFER-ROPE

When reasoning according to the TOC, Step 2 of the *Five Focusing Steps* (5FS) is to *exploit the constraint*. In the story of Herbie, Herbie was constantly encouraged to walk at the maximum of his ability. A consequence of thinking in terms of exploiting the constraint is to strive to avoid letting the constraint be idle for reasons that do not depend on the constraint itself.

For instance, in the hiking metaphor, if when walking the single trail Bluey stops for some reason and stays still long enough to make Herbie stop too, then we know that Herbie will

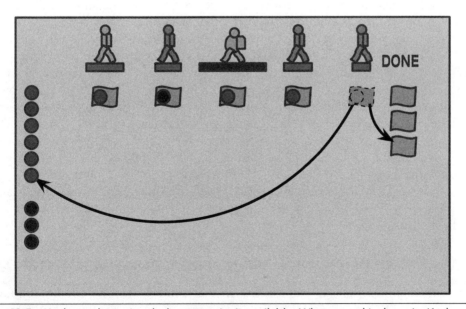

Figure 18.5 Kanban tokens signal when capacity is available. When a card is done, its Kanban token is returned back to the pool of Kanban tokens at the front of the board.

never be able to recover the time that was lost by Bluey. Bluey will have the extra capacity to walk away from Herbie, but Herbie will not be able to recover his lost time.

Naturally, if Herbie needs to stop for his own reason, the natural thing to do is to stop Bluey from advancing, and wait until Herbie is ready to move again. In the story, this was achieved by placing Herbie at the front of the line. In a work process, though, often we do not have a choice of where to place Herbie. Herbie might inevitably be somewhere in the middle of the line, and needs to stay there due to the nature of the process.

There are two problems to deal with. The first is to prevent Herbie from stopping unnecessarily when Bluey needs to stop and the second is to stop Bluey from walking away when Herbie needs to stop.

In the TOC, these problems are resolved with the so called drum-buffer-rope (DBR) scheduling method. The idea is simple and is made up of three parts:

- A **drum** is used to signal the beat of Herbie's steps. Whenever Herbie takes a step, a drum beat tells Bluey that he can take a step too. Bluey will always keep in front of Herbie, at the distance determined by the
- A **buffer** (of work) is placed in front of the constraint. Imagine that Herbie is always walking 20 steps behind Bluey. If Bluey has to stop, he can stand still for at most 20 of Herbie's steps before his stop affects Herbie's progress. (Naturally the size of the buffer has to be determined in a good way. There are many ways to do that, but we will not go into those details here, while introducing the concept.)
- A **rope** is tied (metaphorically) between Herbie and Bluey. Whenever Herbie has to stop, Bluey is prevented from walking away. In practice the rope is the WIP limiting mechanism in DBR.

In order to implement these ideas, we simply place a buffer of cards in front of Herbie's column on the Kanban board, as shown in Figure 18.6. This buffer must not be confused with the "done" or "ready" columns that are often seen on Kanban boards between columns. Even though in practice they can coincide on the Kanban board, it is important to distinguish between their different functions. The done or ready columns are simply placeholders for work in transit between one column and the next. The buffer is a flow control mechanism.

The number we write on top of the buffer does not represent a work limit—it represents the size of the buffer. For example, if we have identified the buffer size as three, we will strive to always keep that amount of work items in the buffer. Whenever there is a work item pulled from the buffer by Herbie, the buffer will free up an empty slot. This is similar to the empty slot we see in WIP-limited columns. But the interpretation will be very different; the level of consumption of the buffer will be used to take important and informed steering decisions, which are not present on the conventional Kanban board, as we will see soon.

DRUM-BUFFER-ROPE WITH VISIBLE REPLENISHMENT SIGNAL

In our case, we already have a WIP-limiting mechanism consisting of the limited number of Kanban tokens. We are effectively replacing the rope with the Kanban tokens. The effect

Figure 18.6   Place an appropriately sized buffer in front of the constraint

is the same as that of a rope, because Bluey will be prevented from walking too far away from Herbie.

However, because the Kanban tokens span the entire board, and not only the distance between Bluey and Herbie, there will be more slack compared to a proper rope. This slack is beneficial because it can absorb more variability in unforeseen places in the work process, especially downstream of Herbie. Naturally, we want to be able to detect when problems happen behind Herbie, too. We don't want Greenie (a resource downstream of the constraint, Herbie) to be left behind, should he encounter difficulties or stop. Since Greenie has more capacity than Herbie, we know he can stop to absorb variability, then recover his pace and close the gap back to Herbie.

If Greenie is developing a greater problem, we must quickly notice it. For this purpose, we introduce another token, which we will call the *replenishment* token. There will be as many replenishment tokens as there are Kanban tokens; each Kanban token will be associated with a replenishment token. Visually we can represent this by putting a replenishment token on top of each Kanban token, as shown in Figure 18.7. (The physical means and visual representation of the replenishment token may vary as you wish. We find it amusing to use a token shaped as *Pacman*, conveying the idea of *hunger*, the *Pacman* signals that Herbie is getting hungry.

The replenishment token is associated with a Kanban token, and the Kanban token is associated with a card. The replenishment token will travel along with the Kanban token and the card until it arrives at the buffer in front of Herbie. When Herbie pulls a card from the buffer, the Kanban token will remain with the card and continue its journey till the end of the board, but the replenishment token will be detached and placed back at the beginning of the board.

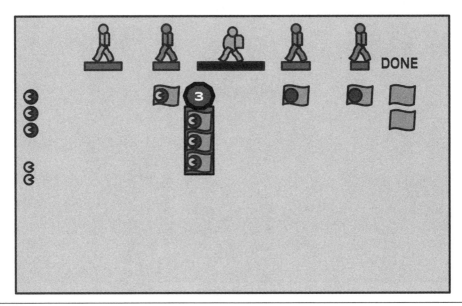

Figure 18.7 Each Kanban token is associated with another token—the replenishment token (the *Pacman*)

The Replenishment Token Is the Drum Beat

When a replenishment token returns to the start of the board, it is effectively functioning as the drum beat, signaling to the system that Herbie has taken a step forward; that there is capacity being made available in the system; and that the work flow needs to be replenished. In practice, the pull action is signaled not only by the empty spot that is freed in the buffer, but also by this replenishment token returning to base.

It is important to realize that the empty spot freed up in the buffer could, or could not, percolate all the way back to the beginning of the board, depending on whether or not some upstream state is busy or blocked. Maybe it could be just a temporary problem or impediment, but the empty slot signal would stop in its tracks there. The fact that the upstream states might have temporary stoppages should not cause any worry because they have the capacity to recover (with respect to Herbie's pace). Knowing that Herbie is still progressing is important; even more important is knowing that Herbie might be progressing toward some problem or impediment.

When a replenishment token returns back to the front of the Kanban board, it is effectively signaling immediately that capacity is being made available on or through the constraint, without the need to wait for the empty spot to propagate all the way to the beginning of the Kanban board, as shown in Figure 18.8. The replenishment token signals that *Herbie is getting hungry*, and that new work should be released into the work flow. We want to release new work so that the states upstream of the buffer don't run out of work, thus ensuring that the buffer remains full.

The replenishment token enables on-demand replenishment: it is a leading signal that shows that free capacity will soon be available. New work should be released into the work flow; it can be selected according to an on-demand replenishment policy as recommended by Kanban.

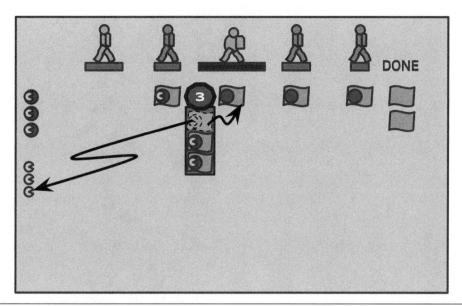

Figure 18.8 Whenever the capacity-constrained resource pulls a card from the buffer, the replenishment token (alone) goes back to the pool in front of the board. The Kanban token remains attached to the card. This is the drum beat that signals the need to replenish the work flow.

Capacity in the System versus Capacity on the Constraint

As mentioned, the Kanban token will continue to travel with the card all the way downstream of Herbie. Once a card reaches the final, or *Done* column, the corresponding Kanban token is detached from the card and placed at the beginning of the board where a free replenishment token will be reattached to it, as shown in Figure 18.9. Naturally, there will always be a free replenishment token available because the number of replenishment tokens is equal to the number of Kanban tokens.

This return of the Kanban token to the front of the Kanban board signals that there is capacity being made available in the system (and not only on the constraint as indicated by the replenishment token). Therefore, when a Kanban token returns to base, it is a sure sign that new work must be released into the work flow sooner, rather than later; otherwise flow will be disrupted.

We must focus on keeping the constraint as busy as possible (exploitation rule of the 5FS); but we must also make sure that the entire system has enough work so that it can subordinate to the constraint. The replenishment tokens give signals about the former, while the Kanban tokens give signals about the latter.

The Replenishment Pull Rule

Even if a replenishment token's returning to the beginning of the board gives the signal that there is capacity at the constraint and that it is necessary to release new work into the flow, work will not be allowed to enter the flow unless there is a Kanban token available. This is illustrated in Figure 18.10. This rule constitutes the WIP limiting factor entering

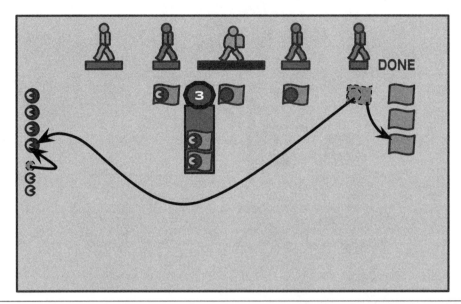

Figure 18.9 When a card is done, its Kanban token is returned back to the pool in front of the board, and a free replenishment token is reattached to it. This signals that capacity is available in the system

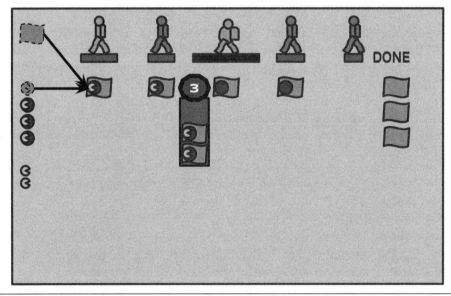

Figure 18.10 This is the replenishment pull rule—a new card may be released into the work flow only if there is a free Kanban token with a replenishment token. A replenishment token alone is not sufficient to allow for a new card to be released

into play—it regulates the amount of WIP throughout the entire system and is not limited to any single column.

The configuration of the Kanban tokens before, inside, and after the buffer, combined with the configuration of replenishment tokens at the front of the board, can be interpreted in order to better manage work execution with emphasis on keeping the work flowing through the constraint and through the whole system.

Focusing on flow also affects how work should be considered by the non-constraints. A good metaphor is the relay race. When a work item is released into the work flow, it should be treated like a relay race baton: everybody should work on it as fast as possible. Ideally, the only point where the baton will be waiting for processing is in the buffer in front of Herbie. The more work is limited; the closer one gets to this ideal. Naturally, the non-constrained resources will have idle time; but remember that the objective is not to keep resources busy; it is to make work flow through the system as smoothly as possible. The only resource which needs to be utilized as much as possible is (obviously) the constraint.

Buffer Signals

To facilitate the smooth flow of work through the system, we must react quickly when problems arise—especially those problems that affect the constraint's ability to keep on working. While we use flow time to identify the constraint, flow time is a lagging indicator. We need something that can show us the imminent materialization of problems *before* those problems become visible as increased flow time on one or more work-states.

To this end, we consider how work actually flows (or doesn't flow) through the buffer. We divide the buffer into thirds as illustrated in Figure 18.11. When the buffer is full, we consider it as "green", indicating everything is under control.

When the buffer becomes two thirds full, we consider it as "yellow" as shown in Figure 18.12. A yellow buffer is an early indication that something might be going wrong upstream of Herbie. This is when you should start looking into what is happening upstream of Herbie and see if there is evidence of problems.

When the buffer becomes one third full, then we consider it as "red" as shown in Figure 18.13. A red buffer is a sure sign that there is a problem upstream. Investigation is no longer sufficient. It is time to act. The investigation conducted while the buffer was yellow will give precise indications of where to intervene. We will see later how, through the TOC root cause analysis techniques, we have an excellent tool to identify what causes the problem and, thus, know how to intervene.

The buffer in front of Herbie is obviously a buffer of work (i.e., it contains work items). Later we will learn how to control the work flow even better by means of another kind of buffer, a time buffer. The basic technique will be the same—dividing the buffer into zones and monitoring how the buffer is filled up or consumed. In either case, the sizing of the buffer is a critical element. A buffer that is too small will trigger signals too often. A buffer that is too large will trigger signals too infrequently. The behavior of the buffer, and thus the triggering of the signals, is also affected by the WIP limit that is allowed. Therefore, (and unlike a ConWIP system), dynamic calibration of the WIP limit (per class of service) together with the size of the buffer can be considered as parameters you can control to fine tune the reactiveness of the leading signals, thus, overcoming the overreactive nature of the signals produced by work-state WIP limits.

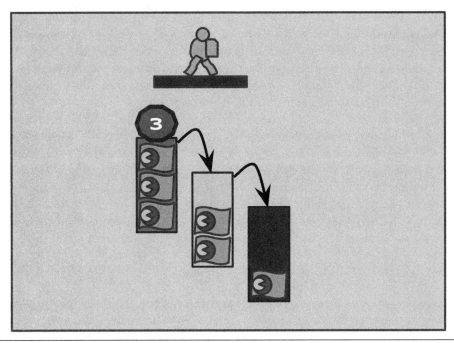

Figure 18.11   The buffer is ordinarily "green" (on the left). It becomes "yellow" (middle) when it is two-thirds full and then "red" (on the right) when only one-third full. These are the buffer signals.

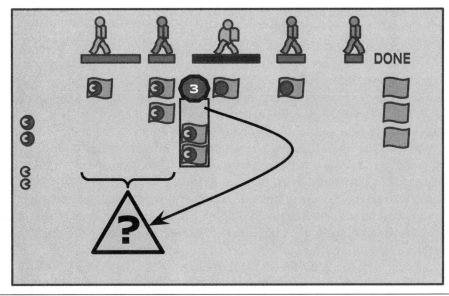

Figure 18.12   A "yellow" buffer indicates there is a potential problem upstream of the constraint. You must start to investigate where and what it could be, in order to be ready to intervene if it becomes worse.

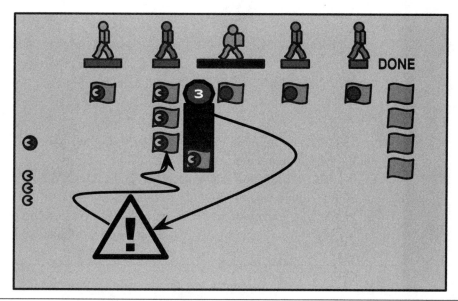

Figure 18.13 A "red" buffer indicates there is a problem upstream of the constraint; you must resolve it immediately before it impacts the constraint. Queues show where the problem is.

Replenishment Signals

The red buffer signals problems upstream of Herbie. However, things can also go wrong downstream of Herbie. Think of Greenie being left behind because he encountered some problem. How can we detect this *before* the line gets way too long and especially before we have to stop the line all together in order to allow Greenie to recover? Remember, stopping the line means stopping Herbie, and thus, certain loss of throughput. As long as Greenie is having recoverable problems (that is, Greenie has not become the new real constraint), we have to strive to manage the situation and put Greenie in the condition to recover without stopping Herbie.

This is where the replenishment tokens come into play as a signaling mechanism. While the Kanban token travels between Herbie and the end of the board, obviously there will be a corresponding free replenishment token at the beginning of the board. That was the replenishment token that got detached from the Kanban token while the corresponding card got pulled by Herbie. There will be as many free replenishment tokens in front of the board as there are Kanban tokens in transit between Herbie and the end of the board.

What becomes relevant is looking at the proportion of free replenishment tokens compared to Kanban tokens that are at the front of the board (and associated with replenishment tokens). The greater the disproportion is, the higher the work load or the chance of flow anomalies downstream of Herbie, as shown in Figure 18.14.

When there are only free replenishment tokens in front of the board and no Kanban tokens at all, it means that due to WIP limits it will be impossible to replenish the work flow, despite the fact of heavy evidence that Herbie is hungry. In this situation, illustrated in Figure 18.15, work will soon be blocked. There is a problem downstream of Herbie that needs to be handled immediately. As in the case of upstream problems, you will have had

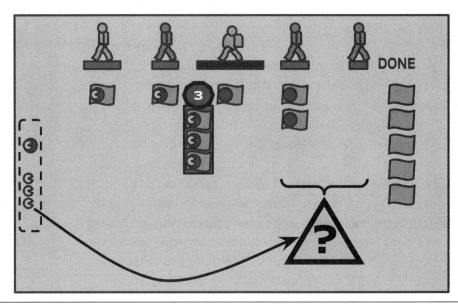

Figure 18.14 When there are more free replenishment tokens than *Kanban tokens* at the front of the board (and the buffer is green), it is a signal indicating that there are potential problems downstream of the constraint. You must start to investigate where and what they could be in order to be ready to intervene if they become worse.

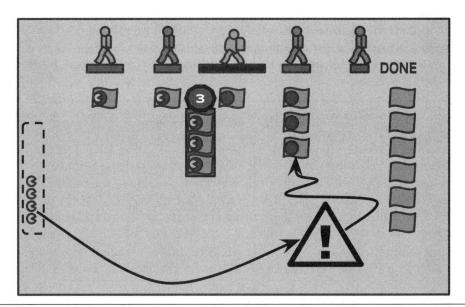

Figure 18.15 When there are no Kanban tokens at the front of the board, there is a problem downstream of the constraint, and you must resolve it immediately before it impacts the capacity to replenish the work flow. Queues show where the problem is.

the time to investigate the nature of the problem. You will be able to apply the Theory of Constraints' root cause analysis techniques to pinpoint exactly what you need to fix. These techniques will be described in greater detail later.

Another metaphor that may help to understand the visual signaling system is that of a seesaw. The constraint is the pivot of the seesaw. The objective is to try to keep the seesaw as flat as possible, with work flowing regularly, both upstream and downstream of the constraint. When there are buffer signals, there is too much WIP upstream of the constraint. Conversely when there are too many free replenishment token signals, there is too much WIP downstream of the constraint.

When Murphy Surrounds Herbie

In very rare but extreme situations, you can have buffer signals of trouble upstream of Herbie, as well as replenishment token signals of trouble downstream of Herbie. This is the case when the seesaw is broken in the middle, there is no balance, and the system is going into an unstable state. Naturally, resolute intervention is needed.

Even under such circumstances, one should not panic and believe that the constraint has moved. It is more likely a case of many *Murphies* hitting all around Herbie; there are multiple special cause variations showing up simultaneously in the work flow. It is unlikely that they represent the moving of the constraint because we are identifying the constraint with stable, long-running flow-time averages.

These flow times reflect structural limitations of the work process and not the temporary hiccups of the work flow. Temporary disruption does not necessarily mean that the constraint has moved. Even if the constraint has moved, it is better to assume that it is still in the same place until there is convincing evidence, such as flow-time trends indicating that things have really changed.

We will now examine another way to gain even better control over execution by giving more attention to time aspects by learning a few tricks from Critical Chain Project Management (the TOC way to manage projects); then we will see how to exercise continuous improvement while keeping the constraint under a managed condition. We will learn how to improve the work process all the while keeping the work flow in a stable condition.

Summary of TameFlow-Kanban

In this chapter we have introduced TameFlow-Kanban, a variation of the Kanban visual management method. TameFlow-Kanban is based on the merging of the following concepts, methods, and ideas:

- The Kanban board from the Kanban Method.
- The original Kanban system of the TPS, implemented with the *Kanban tokens*, used mainly to limit WIP, enable pull, and implement pull signaling.
- The DBR scheduling system to ensure optimal feeding of the constraint, to pace the release of work into the work flow, and especially to receive early signals of problems upstream of the constraint. This ensures that the constraint is exploited and that the system is subordinating to the constraint, as indicated by the 5FS.

- The introduction of the replenishment token, with the purpose of signaling need on the constraint and problems downstream of the constraint.

With respect to conventional Kanban, the difference lies in replacing the work-state (column) WIP limits with the system wide WIP limit of Kanban tokens (per class of service). Consequently, the functions played by work-state WIP limits have to be replaced by other mechanisms. The intent is the same—to have a policy-based change agent mechanism that fosters discussions between all individuals involved, though without disrupting flow, as is the case with work-state WIP limits.

19

UNDERSTANDING COMMON CAUSE VARIATION

In conventional Kanban, work-state work in process (WIP) limits are employed to get early detection of problems that might arise in a single work state. This is the essence of Kanban's *event-driven risk management* approach. By knowing in a timely manner where the work flow might encounter problems, intervention and remediation can be made. Intervention can take many forms, such as team swarming, changing of WIP limits, changing of policies, changing of the class of services, improvement initiatives (Kaizen and Katas), expediting, escalating, and so on. In all cases, it is a *reaction* to some *special* event that turns a work state into a bottleneck.

We can achieve the same result in TameFlow-Kanban. In TameFlow-Kanban we forgo the use of work-state WIP limits in favor of the TameFlow-Kanban approach described earlier. With this alternative we avoid all the negatives with work-state WIP limits (described in Chapter 17, *Challenges of Work-State Work in Process Limits*). By monitoring the buffer and the balance between Kanban tokens and replenishment tokens, we have visual signals of one or more oncoming problems. Just as in the case of the problems signaled by the busting of work-state WIP limits, these are problems due to special cause variation and are treated likewise. Later we will explain how problems due to common cause variation can be detected by other means. (Note: for an explanation of the terms *special* and *common* cause variation and others, see the section entitled Common, Special, Assignable, and Chance Causes later in this chapter.)

In either case, the operational idea is that when there is a signal of an oncoming problem, one has found a sign of special cause variation—something that disrupts the business-as-usual state and needs immediate attention. This is attuned to Deming's teaching of intervening only when special cause variation is identified, while one should not be concerned with common cause variation.

On the other hand, Reinertsen (2009) tells us that in product development settings, common cause variation should be taken into account; but this is more difficult, as Nolan (1990) states:

[...] identifying common causes usually requires more sophisticated methods and a higher level of understanding of the process than identifying special causes does.

The Theory of Constraints (TOC) will allow us to identify and to give due consideration to common cause variation for the purpose of improving our process. By using the techniques of the TOC we will learn to identify the constraints in the work process which are due to common cause variation, rather than the disruptions to the work flow which are due to special cause variation. With the focused approach of the TOC, we will deliberately not handle all sources of common cause variation indiscriminately. We will focus only on that one common cause (the weakest link) that is the most responsible for keeping the process from delivering at greater performance levels.

The most relevant practice that we can use to find common cause variation is *reason frequency analysis*. This is the key insight: identifying common causes needs reason frequency analysis. We can easily achieve this by extending how we work with buffer management, and what we do when we receive the signals thereof.

With this marriage between Kanban and the TOC, we have an excellent system that takes care of all emergencies (special cause variation) that happen in the project and that hinder stable work flow. At the same time, we have the power of the TOC to identify weaknesses (common cause variation) in the process and then improve it continuously, with the objective of increasing throughput.

The event-driven risk management of Kanban or TameFlow-Kanban will keep the project healthy; we can quickly extinguish any fire (special cause variation) that might develop. When a process is hit by special cause variation, it is easy to detect because flow gets disrupted. This is the very logic of having work-state WIP limits of Kanban (even though they exaggerate that effect by artificially inducing even more disruptions) or the mechanisms of TameFlow-Kanban. When flow gets disrupted (WIP work-state limits are exceeded in Kanban), or is about to get disrupted (leading buffer signals in Tame-Flow-Kanban), we can identify the causes and intervene. Such interventions typically happen outside the flow because the flow has been disrupted (or it will be shortly). We have to pull the *Andon* cord and fix the problem. (The *Andon* cord is what is used in Toyota's production lines to stop the line and fix production problems.) The improvement is outside the flow because the flow is typically stopped when this happens.

The systematic root cause analysis power of the TOC will allow us to realize its process of ongoing improvement (POOGI), and prevent fires from developing in the first place. Once we can improve our process systematically, the benefit will be harvested not only by the current project, but also by all projects that follow. The steady state throughput will increase and the average flow time will be shorter. In order to do this, we must be able to detect common cause variation. Notably, in this case, we will be able to improve the process while staying inside the flow. Problems can be detected and improvements can be done while the work is still flowing.

COMMON CAUSE VARIATION

We have observed several times (in the preceding section and in earlier chapters) how Kanban, with its event-driven risk management approach, excels at detecting and reacting to special cause variation. We also just stated that we should be more concerned about common cause variation too. We need to understand this well in order to appreciate what we are trying to achieve.

Let's first make sure we agree on the meaning of the terms. Shewhart (1986) and Deming (1982) identify *common cause variation* and *special cause variation*—common cause variation is *inherent* in the process itself, while special cause variation has *external* origins.

A brilliant example is given by Nolan (1990): when delivering a presentation to a number of people, their attentiveness can be influenced by many common causes. Such causes are *common* because they affect everybody—for instance, the environmental conditions, acoustics, topic matter, and so on. Such causes can be addressed by the organizers or the speaker. On the other hand, some attendees might have difficulty on their own accord, such as staying awake during the presentation after a hefty lunch. Those are *special* causes because they affect single individuals; they require action by the individuals themselves, and those actions will affect them alone, and not the other people in the audience.

We can make a parallel example, which will allow us to focus on the intent of this chapter. If we imagine the troop of the hiking scouts of Herbie and his peers (used in Part 1 to illustrate the *Five Focusing Steps*), any event that temporarily stops or slows down any individual can be considered as special cause variation. For instance, if Bluey stops for a moment to tie the laces of his shoe, that event is due to a special cause. It pertains to Bluey alone, even though it affects to various degrees the progress of the entire team. The same kind of event is still special cause variation if it affects Herbie and in this case the event will definitely slow down the entire team. (Remember, Herbie is the constraint. Unlike Bluey and the other scouts, he has no extra capacity to recover from his stops.) We might intervene by teaching Bluey (for instance) to tie his shoes better. The intervention is on a specific component (Bluey) of the system (the troop of scouts). This is equally valid for Herbie.

Now, in an effort to improve the walking performance of the entire team, we might intervene on elements that affect the team as a whole. For instance, we can change their equipment. Suppose that on the following hike we give out a new kind of high-tech, light-weight backpack; one that has a weight of less than one fourth of older backpacks. The intervention will affect the entire team. We have acted on a common cause (heavy backpacks) that was preventing the team from performing better. Naturally, the intervention affects Herbie too; so Herbie's performance will increase and consequently the whole team's performance will increase. The intervention was not on an individual level. The intervention was on the whole system, on some common cause that intrinsically determined the performance of the whole troop. Being an intervention on the whole, it also indirectly elevates the constraint.

THE SHORTCOMING OF KANBAN

The previous example illustrates what we mean when we talk about bottlenecks in the work flow compared to constraints in the work process. The case of Bluey stopping to tie his shoe creates a (temporary) bottleneck in the work flow. The case of a piece of heavy equipment (the backpacks), shared by all scouts, affects the entire system and exacerbates the performance ceiling due to the (enduring) constraint in the work process.

Kanban is excellent at detecting bottlenecks in the work flow (special cause variation) but gives no support to detecting the constraint in the work process (common cause variation). Note that this does not imply that Kanban practitioners are not aware of common cause variation; it is only that the ordinary Kanban practices they employ are not very good at finding and dealing with common cause variation.

Finding common cause variation is difficult. It is very easy to believe that the system is performing at its maximum and simply ignore that there might be common causes that always keep it from delivering more. This is especially so when the system is performing at a steady state, when there is no evidence of problems on the Kanban board. When the system is at its steady state, it is not affected by special cause variation, so there are no events that cause you to investigate queues or starvations.

The situation is even more subtle when some new common cause event appears and affects the entire team. There may be a slight slowdown of the whole team, but the effect is not disruptive on the work flow. There will be no queues or starvations giving away the birth of this new common cause, but its cumulative long-term effect can be very significant.

The buffer management techniques that will be introduced in the next chapter will give you signals as to when this is happening, even though you might not know directly *why* it is happening. To understand why, you will need the root-cause analysis techniques discussed in Chapter 21, *Root Cause Analysis the Theory Of Constraints Way*.

For the moment, the key questions are the following:

- How can you improve the process you are using while you are in a steady state and everything appears to be "flowing" in an optimal way?
- Are there any common causes that prevent you from flowing in an equally optimal way but at a higher level of performance?

We will find the answer to these questions in the present chapter and the following ones.

VARIATION ACROSS THE BOARD

Here we have to stress this important distinction on the Kanban board:

- Queue detection and event-driven risk management (with work-state WIP limits or without) will point out bottlenecks in the work flow due to special cause variation. Those are not constraints; they are (temporary) bottlenecks.
- Work-state average flow-time analysis will point out the (single) primary constraint in the work process due to common cause variation. (We will learn how to handle common cause variation shortly.)

On a Kanban board the formation of queues is a sign of special cause variation. (And, as we have seen, in the case when one is using work-state WIP limits, that special cause is often the artificial WIP limit on the work state.) Special cause variation gives rise to temporary bottlenecks in the work flow.

The formation of average flow times is more strongly influenced by common cause variation. That is why common cause variation will determine where long-term constraints are in the work process.

It is important to understand the above statements: they pertain to how we detect variation on a Kanban board.

In general, according to queuing theory, queues are simply a consequence of imbalance between demand and capacity. Both special cause variation as well as common cause variation can produce queues. Queues can build up when a single work state, or the entire system, encounters negative variation, and capacity decreases. Queues can also build up when there is a surge in demand.

On a Kanban board, however, common cause variation will mostly go unnoticed. Because of the *common* nature of common cause variation, any positive or negative fluctuation in capacity thereof will simply be handled by attempting to balance the workload. This is analogous to adapting to Herbie's average speed, rather than trying to eliminate those common and recurring causes that prevent Herbie from walking at his maximum sustainable speed, or increasing the average speed. In other words, a normal Kanban system will try to adapt to common cause variation.

As highlighted in Chapter 15, *Understanding the Impact of a Constraint*, once one recognizes the preeminent importance of a constraint on the overall performance of the system, this adaptation to common cause variation is not satisfactory.

From a constraints management perspective, we want to be able to detect the source of any negative variation whether it is due to special cause or common cause.

We need both. We need to be able to handle both developing emergencies given away by queues and bottlenecks (special cause variation), as well as those common and enduring limits that affect the primary constraint's throughput performance (common cause variation)—Kanban caters only to the former. In the following chapters we will see how to extend Kanban in order to handle the latter.

COMMON, SPECIAL, ASSIGNABLE, AND CHANCE CAUSES

In the literature about variation, the terms *common* and *special* are often replaced by the terms *chance* and *assignable*, and often used (respectively) as interchangeable synonyms. David Anderson (2012) shows a preference for the latter, and defines them as:

> **Assignable cause**: Something that has an assignable cause as identifiable; that is, you can point to it. As such, an assignable-cause problem that has the possibility of occurring is a risk, and should appear on a risk-management plan. An assignable-cause problem that has occurred should be recorded in an issue log.
>
> **Chance cause**: Variation that is endemic or systemic to a process and cannot generally be identified as having a root cause.

	Assignable	**Chance**
Special	**Special-Assignable:** This is what special-cause or assignable-cause ordinarily means. Something you *can* specifically point your finger at, which resides outside of your process.	**Special-Chance:** This would be exceptional variation outside of your process, which *cannot* be identified. It is like the ordinary special cause for which our investigative methods are insufficient to point out a root cause.
Common	**Common-Assignable:** This would be a common recurring variation, inside your process, for which you *can* point out a root cause.	**Common-Chance:** This is what common-cause or chance-cause ordinarily means. Something intrinsic to your process, which is always present, but *cannot* be pointed out because your investigative methods are insufficient.

Table 19.1　The orthogonal classification between special/common and assignable/chance causes.

When we start looking for a tool or a method that can assist us in identifying the sources of variation, we suggest it is more fruitful to look at the two pairs of terms in an orthogonal manner, as shown in Table 19.1.

Ordinarily, when talking about common cause (or chance cause) you do not expect to be able to find the root cause—this would be in the common-chance cause variation quadrant. The TOC, as we will see, provides tools for identifying common causes for which we arrive at their roots, hence we can reason about common-assignable causes.

With respect to what we are describing, we can see that Kanban (or TameFlow-Kanban) serves us well to detect special-assignable and special-chance variation. Such detection occurs through signals on the Kanban board (WIP limits, or drum-buffer-rope buffers). Hereafter, we will see how we can use the TOC to detect common-chance and common-assignable variation. Detection occurs through signals given by time buffers.

Detecting the variation is not the same as *identifying* the root cause of it; detecting simply means we have signals indicating the presence of variation. For proper identification we need to resort to root cause analysis. A successful root cause analysis will usually transform a special-chance or common-chance variation into, respectively, a special-assignable or common-assignable variation, because we will be able to pinpoint the root cause.

In the remainder of this chapter, we will stick with the customary terms of common cause and special cause variation, although the two pair classification previously described can help in better understanding what it is we are trying to achieve.

THE POWER OF IMPROVING WITH COMMON CAUSES

One of the most devastating errors in management is confusing the two kinds of variation. The TOC clearly distinguishes between them, and provides leading indicators that enable fast detection of either. It is this ability of getting signals for both common and special causes that sets the TOC apart and gives it an edge; even more so when it is successfully applied to, and combined with, other approaches like Kanban.

This is a significant insight, with far-reaching consequences. The TOC, unlike most other project management and general management methods, makes the distinction clear between common cause and special cause variation. Other approaches are concerned exclusively with special cause variation. In particular, with the event-driven risk management enabled by work-state WIP limits, Kanban is only capable of giving signals when we are in the presence of special cause variation; confirming that, even in Kanban, common cause variation is ignored.

The reason why common causes are conventionally ignored originates from the world of manufacturing, where techniques like Six Sigma are used to reduce variation. In manufacturing, statistical process control is used to discern if a process is affected by common or special cause variation. Such thinking, exemplified by the teachings of Deming (1993), sustains that one should intervene in such processes only in the presence of special cause variation or when there are exceptions to the state of business-as-usual. In other words, in manufacturing, the variations that are due to common causes are considered as acceptable—they do not affect the expected outcome of the work process.

Reinertsen (2009) goes into great detail about how to think about variability in knowledge work. In knowledge work, common causes have a greater impact than in manufacturing. Therefore common causes should be taken into consideration, especially for finding improvement opportunities.

Since common causes are, well, common (meaning that they are always present, or at least, they reoccur often), any improvement that comes from addressing them will have a much larger impact than an improvement addressing a special cause. Therefore it is well worth the effort to try to identify common causes. Identification of common causes is more demanding. Furthermore, because of their being common, it becomes important to have some criteria to understand if (once identified) they are worth addressing or not.

With the approach of the TOC, we have two levels of investigation for dealing with common cause and special cause variation:

- **Buffer Management for Detecting Both Common Cause Variation and Special Cause Variation.** We have already encountered the first level with the work item buffer used in TameFlow-Kanban. We will explore this further with the Minimum Marketable Releases time buffer technique (which we will introduce in Chapter 20, *Improving While in the Flow*). It is about how we may interpret buffer status. When we enter the yellow zone, we need to be alert and start investigating. When we enter the red zone, we know we have a problem. The buffer signals reveal the impact of special causes as well as the effects of common causes. Special causes will be revealed through further evidence given by the configuration of the Kanban board. Common causes need frequency analysis, which is the second level.
- **Reason Frequency Analysis for Detection of Common Cause Variation.** The second level is an approach to collecting information about the causes of buffer zone penetration and then employing risk classification and frequency analysis to clearly distinguish between common cause and special cause variation. This is what we will examine next.

WHAT IS NEXT?

How can we identify the constraint in the process while the work flows in a stable, sustainable, and steady state? It is obvious that there is always a constraint, even if we are confronting an immaterial process that, by virtue of being in the stable state, does not exhibit disruptions. How can the constraint be identified in the first place? This is the main question we will address in following chapter.

20

IMPROVING WHILE
IN THE FLOW

What we will examine in this chapter, and in the following one (*Root Cause Analysis the Theory of Constraints Way*), is applicable to either conventional Kanban (with work-state work in process [WIP] limits) *or* TameFlow-Kanban (as described earlier). The approach presented here changes nothing in the Kanban Method as it is introduced and taught by David Anderson (2010). This approach is an enhancement which provides a powerful tool for focused and ongoing process improvement to both Kanban and TameFlow-Kanban, by focusing on common cause variation rather than on special cause variation.

In this chapter we will see how we can improve our work process while the work flow is flowing regularly at a sustainable pace. This technique, which combines ideas from the Kanban Method, the Incremental Funding Method (IFM) and the Critical Chain Project Management (CCPM) of the Theory of Constraints (TOC), will also provide the foundation for doing deep root cause analysis.

MINIMUM MARKETABLE RELEASES

The IFM introduced the original concept of *Minimum Marketable Features* (MMFs), and was first described by Denne (2004). An MMF is a minimal set of features delivering market value.

In Kanban the MMF concept has been revived, and is known as a *Minimum Marketable Release* (MMR). David Anderson (2010) defines an MMR as "some atomic unit of value to the market or customer." For all practical means, the two concepts are equivalent and can be considered as synonyms, because as we will see, the important traits are in minimality and marketability. Kanban does not prescribe the use of MMRs, but suggests that they can be used. At times, since Kanban tries to emphasize continuous flow, the use of MMRs is discouraged because it is perceived as a disruption of flow. Also MMRs might be discouraged as they appear to imply early commitment to the features they include. However, with respect to the issue of early commitment, if one considers MMRs as atomic units of value, the commitment is about that value—about MMRs as wholes and not about the single work items that may go into an MMR.

Note: The Lean Startup movement has recently popularized the concept of the *Minimum Viable Product* (MVP) which is often equated with MMFs and MMRs. The two concepts, MVP on the one side, and MMF/MMR on the other side are entirely different:

- An MVP is used primarily to test a hypothesis about the marketability of a minimal product.
- An MMF/MMR takes marketability as a given condition that is assumed, and strives to define the minimal scope that delivers that marketability.

Use MVPs if you need to explore the preferences of new markets or the acceptance of new product ideas. Use MMFs/MMRs if you have an established product with an existing backlog of features that have been requested (and validated) by your existing markets, and that need to be implemented and delivered.

If the pool of work to be done is considered as a backlog (as in Scrum and other agile approaches), then MMRs are simply a partitioning of that pool into subsets, and then ordering of those subsets into a sequence which should maximize value, as illustrated in Figure 20.1. It is useful to think about MMRs in this way.

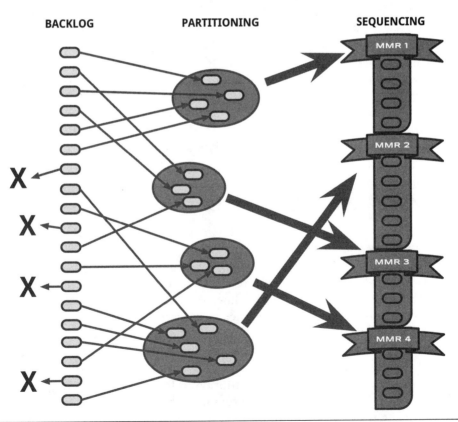

Figure 20.1   MMRs are an ordered sequence of subsets of a backlog. Each MMR is minimal and marketable. The sequence is such that it maximizes the business value of the project. Some backlog items may be discarded in the process.

The IFM teaches how to find the optimal sequence of implementation of such subsets in order to maximize the net present value of a project. While we might apply the techniques of the IFM, we consider such sequencing techniques as optional. In fact, in Kanban, pull selection is more appropriately handled with consideration to cost of delay and other risk factors, rather than maximization of the sequence adjusted net present value, as in the IFM.

The focus of the present discussion, however, is not about pull selection strategies, it is about the traits of MMRs that render them invaluable from a risk management and process improvement perspective, when combined with other elements of the TOC

MMRs AS A WIP-LIMITING UNIT OF WORK

An MMR is a unit of work, which is a collection—effectively a batch—of work items. The single work items can belong to different classes of service, if necessary. The key tenet is that all work items belonging to an MMR must be delivered together, as a single unit. We will advantageously consider an MMR primarily as a unit of work that is released into the work flow and secondarily as a unit of value that is released to the market once finished.

An MMR is a Small Target-Scope Project

An MMR represents the minimal amount of functionality that can successfully be offered to the market. "Minimality" and marketability together have a very important consequence: the scope of an MMR becomes very well defined, and can be thought of like a small target-scope project. In earlier writings I used to refer to this as a small "fixed-scope" project; however that terminology evoked images of a waterfall approach, which is certainly not the intent. The scope of an MMR can actually change, depending on what gets included and/or excluded with the requirements of minimality and marketability. Minimality and marketability change according to what we learn about market needs. Naturally, once work on an MMR is started, it is really beneficial to try to keep the scope of that MMR as fixed as possible. How to manage extra work and unplanned work will be explained towards the end of this chapter.

What does it mean to be a target-scope project? By definition, because of the requirement of marketability, we cannot take work items away from an MMR, or it would lose its marketability. Analogously, we cannot add items to an MMR, or it would no longer be minimal. Therefore, since we cannot take away nor add items, the MMR can be considered as a target-scope unit of work with marketable value, which must be delivered in its entirety—no more, no less.

We put a strong emphasis on target-scope—we should not change an MMR's scope, lest the very purpose of defining and identifying the MMR in the first place becomes vain. (Naturally, if there was an error in the initial definition of the MMR, then it has to be changed, but this is another issue altogether. Assume that the scope definition is appropriate and correct.) In a work/time diagram, an MMR can be thought of as a target amount of work that needs to be delivered, which is represented by a horizontal line. Figure 20.2 illustrates the delivery of three MMRs over time.

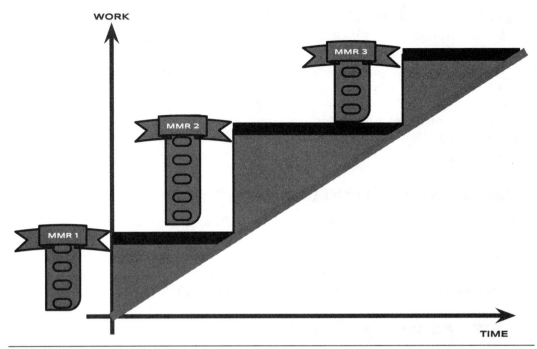

Figure 20.2 Each MMR is like a target-scope mini-project. Delivery of multiple MMRs is like Herbie walking the hike in stages. An MMR naturally limits WIP, so that demand (being limited to the target) is less than capacity. Flow time is proportional to WIP, and because WIP is limited there is an end in sight for the mini-project.

An MMR is a Unit of Commitment

In the quest of hyper-productivity, we have seen that the patterns of *Unity of Purpose* and *shared vision* are very important. On a smaller level, teams need to be able to aim at attainable, intermediary objectives; and they need to get serious about achieving them. For instance, in Scrum it is customary to have sprint goals, and it is expected that teams commit to deliver such goals. The sprint goal is a statement about the purpose of a sprint, and one of the behaviors expected of a Scrum team is that the team commits to deliver the sprint goal.

An MMR has an analogous function, as it defines a target in terms of scope. Naturally, such a precisely defined target should be further extended with a clear statement of what business problem the MMR is trying to address. Typically, such a statement will refer to the marketability aspect of the MMR. An MMR thus becomes a unit of commitment. It is expected that a team undertaking to work on an MMR will commit to delivering the target-scope in order to pass the stated marketability criteria by doing the least amount of work possible (applying the Agile principle of *maximizing the amount of work not done*).

An MMR Limits Work in Process

On a cumulative work-flow diagram, the MMR appears as a demand line that is horizontal. In other words, WIP is limited from the outset. The delivery line grows progressively until it intercepts the demand line. At that point, all work has been performed and can be delivered as a unit.

In virtue of Little's Law, we can assume that there is a finite flow time for the delivery of the MMR. In other words, because the MMR interrupts an (ideal) continuous flow of work, we have a future time point when the MMR will be delivered. (We will see shortly how to arrive at that time point.)

Notwithstanding that an MMR interrupts continuous flow of work, it brings the significant advantage of limiting WIP; and limiting WIP is a fundamental control mechanism that favors better flow.

MANAGE RISK BY VARYING TIME, NOT SCOPE

Kanban does not require explicit risk management because there is a lot of risk handling capabilities that are built-in and come for free, even with the shallowest adoption of Kanban. The event-driven risk management that is enabled by work-state WIP limits of Kanban (notwithstanding their many disadvantages mentioned several times in this book) or the signals of TameFlow-Kanban will adequately take care of most special cause variation risks.

While not prescribing risk management, Kanban strongly suggests that explicit risk management should be performed, nonetheless. On the other hand, the IMF, where MMFs were first conceptualized, mandates explicit risk management precisely because of the nature (target-scope) of MMFs.

It follows to reason that if we use Kanban with MMRs, which are target-scope, too, then explicit risk management becomes mandatory. Furthermore, the IFM mandates explicit risk management, but does not prescribe or define how to realize it. Hence, it becomes interesting to see how risk can be managed.

Cutting the Backlog Does Not Cut It

The most common and popular agile risk management approach of cutting the backlog— or *descoping*—cannot be applied. Cutting the backlog does not work with a target-scope MMR because of the properties of minimality and marketability, as previously explained. Risk must be controlled in some other way.

Lessons from Critical Chain Project Management

If we cannot vary the scope because of the nature of the MMR, we have to get better at managing time. In fact, it is possible to deal with risk by managing time. This is where we can be inspired by the CCPM approach of the TOC so let's get familiar with it.

CCPM is characterized by a network of project activities, just like the traditional and well-known, *Critical Path Method* (CPM). The CPM is basically the method that is supported by the majority of project management software packages, such as Microsoft Project.

Unlike the CPM, CCPM gives explicit attention to resource dependencies in addition to task dependencies. (Without resource contention, CCPM and the CPM would essentially be the same as far as the project network is concerned.)

CCPM derives its name from the *Critical Chain*. The Critical Chain is defined by Sullivan (2012) as:

> The longest sequence of dependent events through a project network considering both task and resource dependencies in completing the project. The critical chain is the constraint of a project.

One key insight here is that no matter what kind of process or methodology is employed, at the end of the project all work must have traversed a network of tasks executed by resources. An undeniable fact remains—to get to the final delivery, the project network must be traversed. Inside that project network, the critical chain is still the constraint that is limiting the project's capacity to deliver, no matter what methodology or approach is used.

In CCPM, the project network is used for planning the project, just as in the CPM; but the logic used to schedule the activities is different. For our purposes, the project network of CCPM is uninteresting. We simply assume that the activities involved in delivering an MMR (and managed via Kanban or TameFlow-Kanban) are equivalent to the activities represented inside such a project network.

The other major distinguishing difference between CCPM and the CPM is that in CCPM, a single project buffer is placed at the end of the project network. In the CPM, padding typically occurs at the task level.

This project buffer is a time buffer. In Kanban we are much more concerned about time aspects. Ordinarily we use flow time metrics for many purposes, and, in particular, for establishing the service level agreements associated with classes of service. Shortly, we will see how we will make use of this observation.

The TOC teaches us to identify, protect, and elevate the constraint. In the project network the constraint (i.e., the critical chain), is protected and managed by constantly monitoring the project buffer. A superficial explanation of why the project buffer is needed is that it is there in order to absorb any variability that might adversely affect project delivery. That would be true if the buffer were used only for the purpose of padding. As we will see, that is not the case because we will use the buffer for another purpose. We will continuously monitor the buffer, in order to get leading and operational signals about oncoming trouble that might affect the health of the project.

The essential part that we preserve from CCPM is the project buffer at the end of the project network; we do not care about the scheduling aspects of CCPM and the actual building of the project network. Unlike the network that is used during planning, the project buffer is used during the execution of the project. We will execute all planning activities as suggested by Kanban. What we will transfer over from CCPM to Kanban is the interpretation and use of the project buffer. We will use the project buffer exactly in the same way as it is done in CCPM and, thus, getting the well-documented advantages typical of CCPM project execution.

Such advantages include:

- Leading indicators of imminent risk materialization
- Just-in-time risk registry compilation
- Frequency analysis to identify sources of common cause variation

- Root cause analysis identifying the source of those problems that are most expensive or frequent
- Process of ongoing improvement driven by focusing and leveraging solutions to those expensive or frequent problems

The most significant outcome of this approach is that it will allow improvement of the process being employed, resulting in shorter flow times and increased throughput. We will be able to increase the capacity of the team and/or process, with improvements that will be beneficial, not only for the project we are working on at the moment, but also for all future projects. This is because we will be able to address common cause variation, so that the improvements are systemic.

The Best of Two Worlds

The improvements induced by this approach are not replacing those that we achieve with Kanban or TameFlow-Kanban, because the two are complementary. One completes the other in a significant way—more specifically, we achieve the benefits of both:

- The event-driven risk management typical of Kanban or TameFlow-Kanban allows us to react very quickly to special cause variation (either through work-state WIP limits or through TameFlow-Kanban signals).
- The buffer-monitoring risk management technique typical of CCPM allows us not only to identify sources of common cause variation, but also to discern and select those which are adversely affecting the team's and/or the process's capabilities, and start improvement initiatives around those.

The Theory of Constraints Perspective

This management technique can be seen from the TOC perspective. Software development has seen a proliferation of Agile methods in the last 15–20 years, which are now being adopted more generally by all sorts of knowledge workers. CCPM is in many ways anchored to approaches which cannot benefit from the advances seen with Agile methods or other modern management methods. Therefore, this approach can be seen as an enhancement that introduces Kanban or TameFlow-Kanban within the Theory of Constraints' operational practices for project execution (buffer management).

The TOC practitioners will gain the complementary advantages offered by Kanban or TameFlow-Kanban which are most significant for their event-driven risk management capabilities. Moreover, the TOC practitioners will recognize and appreciate that the principles, practices, and values of Kanban are surprisingly aligned with what Eliyahu Goldratt defined as the *Viable Vision* and the *Ever Flourishing Company*.

THE MMR BUFFER

As CCPM protects the activities on the critical chain with a project (time) buffer, we will, likewise, protect the implementation of an MMR by (conceptually) adding a buffer to its end, and constantly monitoring it.

When partitioning a project into MMRs, we can consider each MMR as a target-scope project. For any single one of those MMRs, we know in advance how much work we have to perform. By adding up the average flow times of the work items that belong to an MMR, we get an expected average flow time for the corresponding MMR.

Naturally, because MMRs vary in size, each one will have a buffer of a different size, as illustrated in Figure 20.3. This also means that we are actually expecting the start time of work on subsequent MMRs to vary, depending on whether we finish an MMR sooner or later, as shown in Figure 20.4.

This extra buffer is *not* a kind of padding that we add just in case something goes wrong. Reinertsen (2009) refers to this as:

> [Principle] V11: The Buffer Principle: buffers trade money for variability reduction.

This is typical of the CPM, where padding (deliberate or not) is used to buy safety.

In CCPM (and in our approach), the buffer is not there for this purpose, although it is often presented like this and can even be (mis)used in that way. The primary purpose of

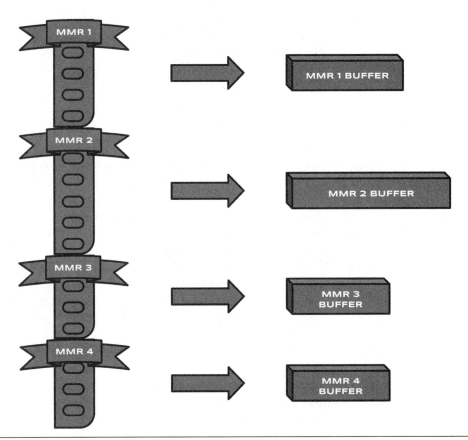

Figure 20.3   A time buffer is associated with each MMR

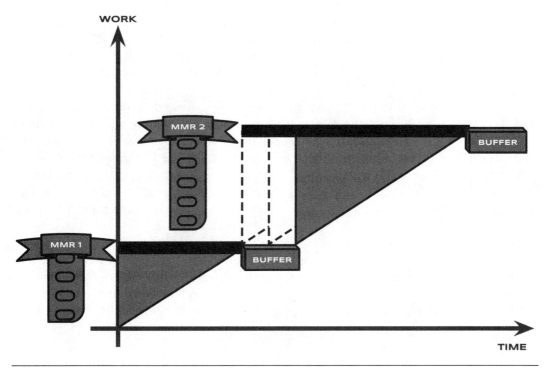

Figure 20.4   The buffer safeguards the delivery date and absorbs variability

the MMR buffer is to provide an operational monitoring tool that gives significant lead-ing signals of oncoming risk materialization. The critical chain is the constraint, and the constraint has to be exploited to the fullest. The objective in a CCPM project, or in our approach, is to deliver any work item as soon as possible. The buffer is not used to reduce variability, as in the case of padding, but to detect unfavorable variability early enough to be able to take any necessary countermeasure in time—before it affects the whole project adversely. The buffer is sized in a deliberate manner; and, more importantly, it is actively used to steer the execution of the project and raise signals of oncoming trouble.

In order to size the buffer, we take the simple procedure of dividing the expected flow time in half. The reason this makes sense is explained by CCPM, and we will look into the rationale of it in the following section.

This buffer is important from a hyper-productivity perspective too—it is not only about absorbing uncertainty or managing risk, but also about building a *Community of Trust*, by making project delivery more reliable.

BUFFER SIZING

We must choose the size of the buffer carefully. To start, consider the expected average flow time from historical flow metrics. Conceptually, sizing the MMR buffer is like going in the opposite direction of what happens in CCPM. In CCPM, we halve the critical path time, to get a 50% due-date probability; then we add the project buffer to the end of that.

In the case of the MMR buffer, we start with the historical data of average flow times. Let's consider one single work item that might be included in the MMR. The work item will belong to a predetermined class of service and, consequently, it has an expected average flow time (the average flow time associated with that class of service), as shown in Figure 20.5.

The probability distribution of flow times is invariably skewed, as illustrated in Figure 20.6. The average time is not the most likely time. In most cases, we will need less than the average flow time to deliver any work item. We then have a few work items that take much longer than the average time. That's why we get the skewed distribution.

Another consequence of the fact that the distribution is skewed is that we will have a higher probability of due-date performance the more we progress along the time axis. The idea is to add a buffer to the average flow time in order to reach a time point where we have very high due-date performance, as illustrated in Figure 20.7.

As a first approximation, we can size the buffer to half of that average expected flow time. By adding half the average flow time, it is very likely that we are already reaching into the areas of very high probability of on-time delivery, in the order of 80% due-date performance or more. We will see how this buffer (like the buffer in TameFlow-Kanban) will be used to give significant steering signals. It can be worthwhile to experiment with

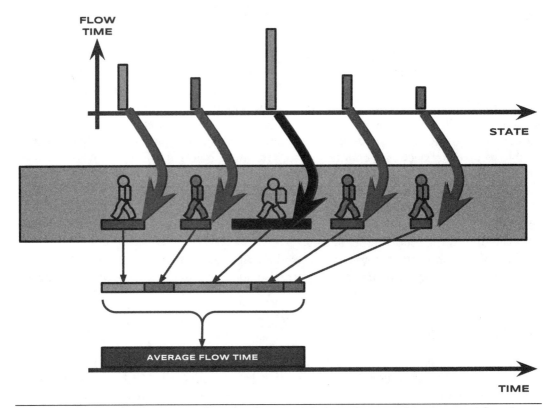

Figure 20.5   Consider the average flow time for a work item as the sum of the (average) flow times of each work state (and do this for each distinct class of service)

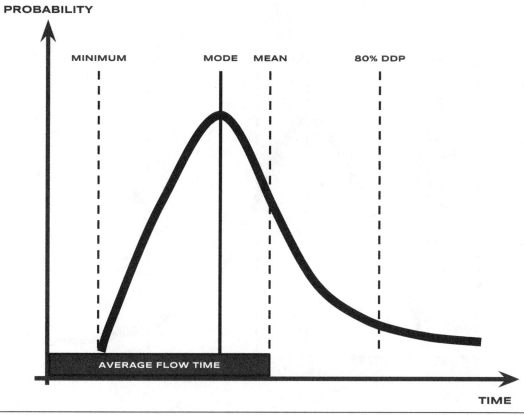

Figure 20.6 Flow time probability distribution—the curve is skewed to the right. The bar at the bottom represents average flow time.

different sizing techniques for the MMR buffer because the size of the buffer is critical for the effectiveness of the signals.

If the buffer is too big, signals come too late. If the buffer is too small, signals come too frequently, with many false positives. Eventually, one can use the advanced dynamic buffer sizing technique of the TOC to get the optimal buffer size with respect to any project's unique characteristics. Determining the size of the buffer is of critical importance; and it can be sized in many ways.

For example: Geekie (2006) reviews seven common methods. Fallah (2010) uses uncertainty for sizing the buffer. Cox (2010) describes *dynamic buffer sizing*, where the size of the buffer is changed dynamically during the due course of the project.

While knowing about advanced buffer sizing techniques can be very useful, it is also out of the scope of (and inconsequential to) the presentation of the concept here. What really matters is the approach that the buffer enables in terms of risk management. In other words, how the buffer is used in practice.

In more practical terms, the buffer must be appropriately sized. The slashing in half mentioned before is just a gross simplification, used primarily as a simplifying procedure, that works surprisingly well in most cases.

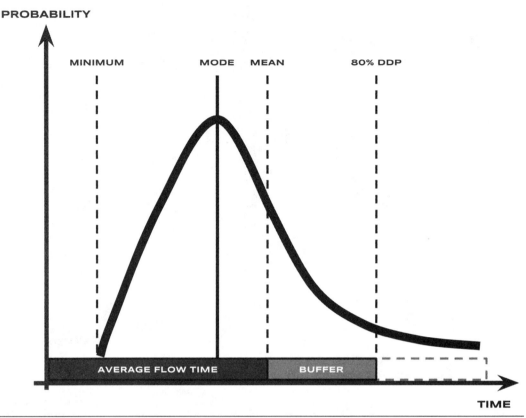

Figure 20.7　The buffer is placed after the average flow time, and it is sized to 50% of the average flow time. The end of the buffer falls in a zone of very high due-date performance (80% or more).

Aggressive Buffer Sizing with TameFlow-Kanban. When using TameFlow-Kanban, we are already tracking the average flow times of all work-states because we use them to find *Herbie* (the constraint) in the work flow. In this case, instead of considering the average flow time of the work flow, we consider the average flow time on the constraint. This will be a much smaller buffer; it might be too small to be workable. However, it gives us a good heuristic. We can take the halves of both flow times and consider them as extreme points for determining our buffer sizing—we might find a good buffer size somewhere in between.

Once the average flow times and buffers of all work items in the MMR have been determined, they are aggregated to find the corresponding flow time and buffer for the whole MMR, as shown in Figure 20.8.

Remember that work items can be of different sizes and belong to different classes of service; all of which might be associated with their own average flow time. We must take this into account when sizing the buffer. (For the sake of simple illustration, Figure 20.8 shows work items belonging to just a single class of service and, therefore, they are all showing the same flow times.)

Figure 20.8 The average flow time of the MMR and its buffer are the aggregation of all work item average flow times and buffers

Again, it is important to stress that this buffer is not created for the purpose of padding the delivery time—it is an operational tool that will be used during execution. Next, we will see how to use and interpret the buffer for this purpose.

BUFFER MANAGEMENT, USAGE, AND INTERPRETATION

The buffer management techniques that we are going to explore now are an integral part of the TOC in general and of CCPM in particular (in the context of project management). The project buffer is a safety instrument. It protects the project (i.e., the implementation of an MMR in our case) from disruptions that might happen when the work activities (on the critical chain/in the MMR) are performed. The buffer is constantly monitored to detect unfavorable variability.

An appropriately sized buffer will give good leading indicators of oncoming trouble. Just like the drum-buffer-rope (DBR) buffer on the Kanban board gives signals about problems that are happening upstream of Herbie before they affect Herbie's own work, the signals from the MMR time buffer are reliable clues that problems are happening before they negatively impact reliable delivery. The buffer gives a signal while there is still time to recover. Of course, one must also act and take the opportunity to do so.

Buffer Burn Rate

Buffer management plays a critical role, and the key is the concept of *buffer burn rate* (also known as *buffer consumption*). The buffer burn rate is defined by Sullivan (2012) as follows:

> The rate at which the project buffer is being consumed [...]. The rate is calculated as the ratio of the percent of penetration into the project buffer and percent of completion of the critical chain.

For our purpose, the completion of the critical chain corresponds to the amount of work items in the MMR that have been completed. The percentage of buffer consumption can be computed in virtue of Little's Law. We can determine when the MMR will be delivered by using the current throughput and comparing that time point to the start and end points of the buffer. (An example of this will be given later.) High buffer consumption, relative to completion, is a sure sign that something is wrong.

Figure 20.9 illustrates the elements (relating to one MMR) which are needed to compute the buffer burn rate. The calculations will be shown with real numbers in the section later on in this chapter called *How to Build and Monitor an MMR Buffer*.

In CCPM the buffer is used to coordinate resources on the critical chain (and have them ready when needed) and to prioritize work. Monitoring the buffer is the reason the buffer is created. It is the premier activity indicating whether or not the project is healthy. Woeppel (2005) describes the role of the buffer very clearly:

> Project execution is THE most important part of achieving success [...]. Monitoring and responding to the condition of the buffers is the key to that. Rather than responding to individual tasks, the project team responds to the condition of the buffers.

The buffer is a focusing mechanism, too. When the buffer burn rate shows that on-time project delivery is at risk, any task that consumes the buffer is given the highest priority. In our case, since we are not dealing with tasks but with work items in an MMR, when the buffer gives signals, we will look at the configuration of the Kanban board to know where to intervene and identify the work items that might be having a problem. If the Kanban

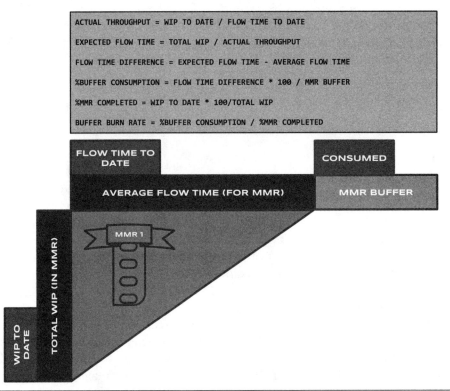

ACTUAL THROUGHPUT = WIP TO DATE / FLOW TIME TO DATE

EXPECTED FLOW TIME = TOTAL WIP / ACTUAL THROUGHPUT

FLOW TIME DIFFERENCE = EXPECTED FLOW TIME - AVERAGE FLOW TIME

%BUFFER CONSUMPTION = FLOW TIME DIFFERENCE * 100 / MMR BUFFER

%MMR COMPLETED = WIP TO DATE * 100/TOTAL WIP

BUFFER BURN RATE = %BUFFER CONSUMPTION / %MMR COMPLETED

FLOW TIME TO DATE

CONSUMED

AVERAGE FLOW TIME (FOR MMR)

MMR BUFFER

MMR 1

TOTAL WIP (IN MMR)

WIP TO DATE

Figure 20.9   The buffer burn rate is the ratio between the percentage of buffer penetration and the percentage of completion of the MMR

board is not giving any special signals (that is, everything is still in the flow), then we will use the techniques explained later to find ways to counteract common cause variation.

Monitoring the buffer is an operational activity performed during the project's execution. The critical chain is used for planning the project, but the buffer is used for managing execution of the project. This is why we forgo the Critical Chain's planning methods (we use Kanban or TameFlow-Kanban instead) and take advantage of the buffer for what it gives in terms of managing execution.

The ability to have a leading indicator given by the buffer consumption ratio is the strongest contribution of CCPM. This indicator does not report the amount of work done. This is very different from most other project management methods, which tend to report project status in terms of work done ("We are 90% done!" "Yeah! Right!"). This indicator represents work done in relation to how much time has been set aside (the buffer) to absorb unforeseen problems. The extent to which this margin is consumed is an indication of the project's health. Consequently, there are many operational advantages, which all enable improved risk management. For example, one such advantage relates to frequency of reporting. Leach (2004) suggests that monitoring time should be as frequent as the shortest task duration. We can equate the shortest task duration to the shortest average flow time of any class of service present in the MMR. If we monitor the buffer that often, the reporting frequency can be much higher. If the shortest planned task is measured in hours, then reporting can be made on an hourly basis rather than weekly, as is typical in most project environments, thus giving even earlier signals about problems.

Buffer Zones

The project buffer is divided into three zones. The zones are often represented in Green, Yellow, and Red as shown in Figure 20.10. Typically these zones are sized to one third of

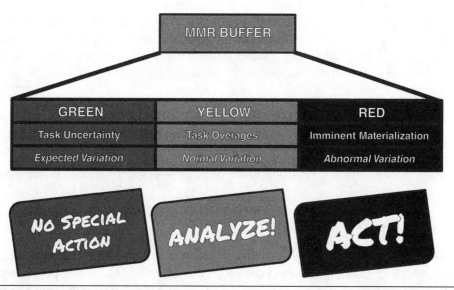

Figure 20.10   The three buffer zones

the buffer; though relative sizes may be changed dynamically in the more advanced applications (this relates to how to appropriately size a buffer).

The three zones give a finer control about knowing when to act. C. Spoede Budd and J. Cerveny (Cox, 2010) offer a crucial insight; the three zones are representative, respectively, of expected variation, normal variation, and abnormal variation.

Monitoring buffer consumption with respect to the three zones gives visible and actionable signals:

- **Expected Variation** ("Green Zone"): Everything is working according to plan. The green zone absorbs inherent task uncertainty. No special action is required. In fact, any interference in this zone is most likely counterproductive, as it would produce what Deming (1993) referred to as tampering—a waste of productive time that causes loss of focus.
- **Normal Variation** ("Yellow Zone"): Everything is under control; but we must investigate and prepare for action. The yellow zone absorbs the inherent uncertainty in task duration prediction. Time is consumed to cover task overages—prepare plans to recover lost time, but take no action yet (avoid tampering). Focus on understanding what is causing time consumption and what can be done.
- **Abnormal Variation** ("Red Zone"): When the red zone is reached, *we must act*. Implement the plans prepared while buffer consumption was in the yellow zone. Most likely, unique events outside the normal course of the project's operations have caused the problem.

A note on the terminology: The TOC terminology can be mapped to the customary common cause and special cause variation. The normal variation and abnormal variation can be thought of, respectively, as common cause variation and special cause variation. The distinction will be made clearer later. Since buffer zones do not always represent this faithfully, we will be using other tools for distinguishing between common and special causes. What matters most is the operational valence of the three buffer zones.

Dividing the project buffer into three zones provides a powerful tool for anticipating and acting on risks. Other project management practices don't detect the problems until later. Leach (2004) concludes that: "buffer management provides a unique anticipatory project-management tool with clear decision criteria."

BUFFER CHARTS

Anytime we have quantitative data, it is natural to use diagrams to gain insight into what the numbers really mean. The burn rate and the buffer consumption percentage can be used as the basis for plotting two significant diagrams—respectively the *buffer fever chart* and the *buffer control chart*.

Buffer Fever Charts

To visualize the status of a buffer, we typically use a fever chart, where we plot the buffer consumption (as a percentage) toward the project completion (again, as a percentage). For instance, we could have a diagram that looks like the one illustrated in Figure 20.11.

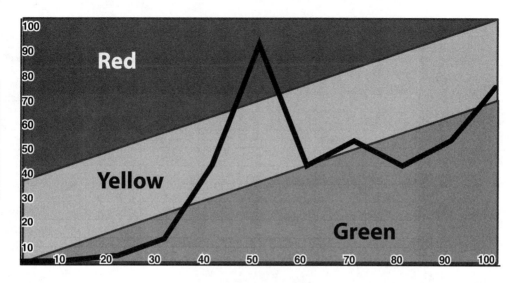

% MMR Complete

Figure 20.11   A fever chart shows the buffer consumption (as a percentage) toward MMR completion (also as a percentage)

In Figure 20.11, the line represents the progress of the project's execution. We can see that it started off in the green (gray) zone, progressed into the yellow (light) zone, and then ran into problems when it penetrated into the red (black) zone. Problems were addressed, execution went back into the green zone, and remained there until nearly the end of the project, meaning that due-date performance was overall acceptable ("green"). This figure is only illustrative. The actual placement and slope of the two threshold lines depend on how we have sized the buffer and, especially, how we have sized the three zones. In this case, the zones are one-third of the overall buffer. The buffer fever chart is great for reporting the project health to stakeholders. It can also be used in multi-project environments, where the status of all projects can be represented on a single chart, as will be shown later.

Buffer Control Charts

We can realize further refinements via *control charts* as shown in Figure 20.12. In fact, Leach (2004) suggests to plot trends of buffer consumption. That representation is very similar to a control chart, and can be used in similar ways. Even more interestingly, the chart gives a time history of buffer consumption with respect to the project's timeline.

This kind of chart certainly helps to improve control (of work versus time). A control chart gives a very clear indication about the project's health with respect to (real) calendar time, rather than with respect to the (percentage of) buffer consumption. It can be used to get an idea if the project is healthy day-by-day and can be used as the basis for insight and reflection during the daily meetings (such as stand-up meetings), and also when retrospections or *katas* are performed.

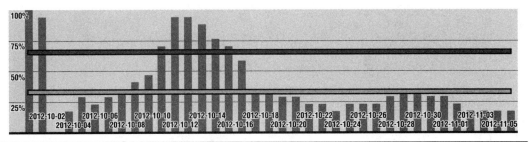

Figure 20.12   A buffer control chart

As we shall see shortly, a powerful visualization is the combination of a buffer control chart with a cumulative flow diagram. This is possible because both diagrams can share the same timeline.

Thresholds and Signals

The buffer control chart is used like any control chart, with two control limits at the thresholds between the zones, which are separated, respectively, by a yellow (investigate) and a red (act) line, as illustrated in Figure 20.13.

The transition across the first threshold (entering the yellow zone) signals that we need to start investigating potential problems. We should not act at this point, but simply start thinking about what might be a problem. The root cause analysis techniques that will be presented in the next chapter will be very helpful, as they not only uncover sources of special cause variation, but they will also uncover sources of common cause variation.

The transition across the second threshold (entering the red zone) signals that there is a real problem and that action must be taken immediately. There is still time to recover

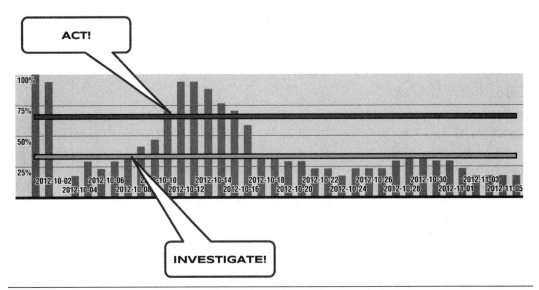

Figure 20.13   Signal threshold lines and signals on the buffer control chart

when this threshold is passed, but there is no time to waste. Action should be quick and decisive. The nature of the action should already have been decided while the project was going through the yellow zone.

Trends

We can refine the use of the control chart by means of *trend analysis*. For instance, four points in a row, trending toward a threshold, as shown in Figure 20.14, might be enough to take action resulting in the detection of the oncoming trouble even earlier. Use judgment when deciding whether to act upon such signals or not. At least we now have the possibility of considering such early signals. As noted by Shewhart (1986), if our process is *not* under statistical control, the use of trending data is even more important.

Empirical processes are seldom under statistical control, and as we have seen in Part 1, software development and knowledge work can be considered as dynamic complex adaptive systems that can only be controlled through empirical processes. Spotting trends in diagrams might be hard and might require experience, but they are a powerful tool that can provide additional, early and leading signals and insights.

Cumulative Flow Diagrams

It is not coincidental that Scrum uses *burn-down charts* and that Kanban employs *cumulative flow diagrams*, such as the one illustrated in Figure 20.15. Both of these kinds of charts reveal trends in an empirical process. All such charts can be used to reveal emerging trends and help in taking decisions based on such trends.

With the buffer management techniques of the TOC (and the further techniques we will explore in the next chapter), such decisions can be taken with better insight about the nature of the problems that we might be facing, especially with respect to common cause variation or special cause variation.

Cumulative flow diagrams are very commonly used in Kanban. (For an excellent introduction to them, see Pawel Brodzinski's blog post, http://brodzinski .com/2013/07/cumulative-flow-diagram.html). Such diagrams contain a lot of information and provide visual cues about the load of WIP through each work-state. The formation of queues and starvation are easy to spot. The problem, though, is such signals usually come late; they are an indication that risk has already materialized.

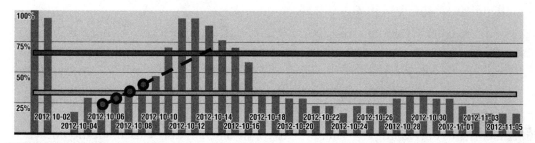

Figure 20.14   Four points in a row reveal a trend

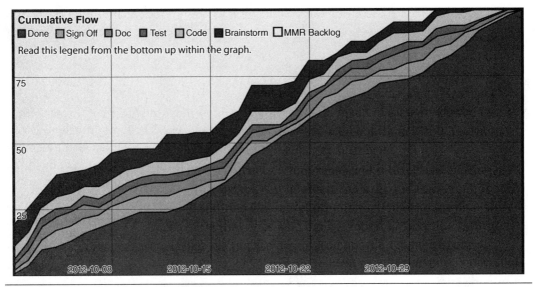

Figure 20.15   A cumulative flow diagram

Buffer signals, instead, are leading indicators, and their signaling can be reinforced if there is a trend developing in the cumulative flow diagram as well. Therefore, the best results can be achieved when the cumulative flow diagram is combined with a buffer control chart so that both trends can be detected, as we will see shortly.

Burn-up Chart with Buffer Zones

Scrum practitioners are used to using burn-down charts, which can be turned upside-down and become a burn-up chart that shows how much work is being added as time passes. The burn-up chart is essentially the last line in the cumulative flow diagram, so it bears less information than the cumulative flow diagram. However, the burn-up chart becomes particularly appealing when we represent the buffer zones superimposed over it. As you can see in Figure 20.16, the line representing the burn up stands out against the three buffer zones, giving an immediate visual clue about the project's health. The top horizontal line represents the target-scope of the MMR.

Combining Diagrams and Charts

The combination of a cumulative flow diagram with a buffer control chart, as shown in Figure 20.17, gives a particularly powerful representation of the project's progress. Both the diagram and the chart share the same horizontal axis—the timeline.

With this combination the leading nature of the signals provided by the buffers become very apparent. In Figure 20.18 we can see this combination, with the most important features highlighted. The diagram and the chart represent the same situation, on the same timeline. Trends developing on the cumulative flow diagram can be used to pinpoint where problems are and to confirm the early signals of the buffer control chart—yet, the buffer signals were evident much earlier.

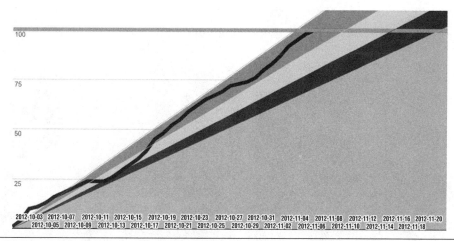

Figure 20.16   A burn-up chart with the MMR's target scope and the three buffer zones

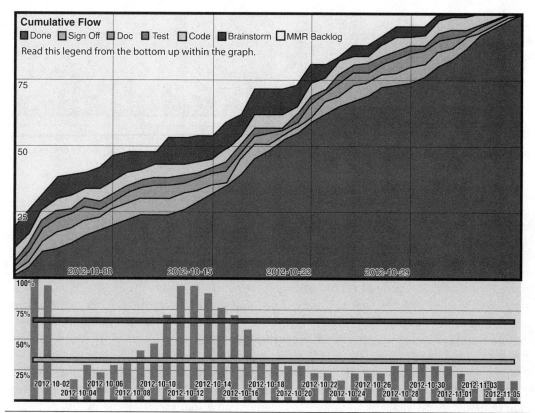

Figure 20.17   Cumulative flow diagram combined with a buffer control chart. They share the same timeline (the X-axis).

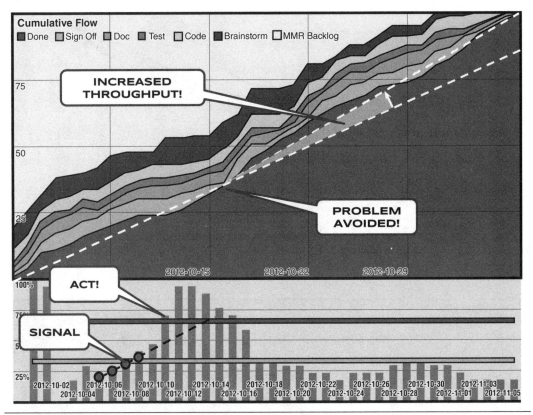

Figure 20.18   Evidence of leading signals. The signals to investigate with the trend line and the signal to act anticipate problems that will become visible on the cumulative flow diagram much later.

For instance, in Figure 20.18 we can see that when the control chart signals that buffer consumption has entered into the red zone, the WIP of the *Sign Off* state is progressively getting lower and lower—it is trending toward starvation. Without the leading signal of the buffer control chart, this trend in the cumulative flow diagram would go undetected until much later. It is evident how the cumulative flow diagram reveals a problem that is solved more or less in the middle of the timeline. However, if we observe the corresponding buffer chart (bottom of Figure 20.18), we can see that a yellow signal (lower horizontal line) was raised seven days earlier, and the red (Act!) signal (higher horizontal line) four days earlier. Six days earlier the buffer chart exhibited four points in a row revealing a trend toward the red zone.

In other words, compared to a situation without the buffer chart, in this case, we have between four and six days advance notice of oncoming trouble. The effect of the intervention that was made in virtue of these early signals can also be read off the cumulative flow diagram, where a noticeable increase of throughput is evident after that mid-point hiccup. A general rule of thumb is that we don't need to look at the cumulative flow diagram unless we are receiving signals from the buffer control chart. As soon as such signals appear, watch out for any trend that we see developing both on the buffer control chart as well as on the cumulative flow diagram to understand which work-state(s) might hide some problem.

Another combination you can try is to use the burn-up chart with buffer zones together with the buffer control chart, though that gives you the buffer consumption information twice. Usually combining the cumulative flow chart with the buffer control chart, and then using the buffer fever chart separately is preferred. The buffer fever chart becomes particularly significant when dealing with a portfolio of projects, as we will see later in this chapter.

Signal Reaction Handled by Normal Kanban Policies

Whenever the MMR buffer raises a signal, we must identify the root cause that is the source of the problem (in the next chapter we will learn how to do this). If the resolution requires action by the team, we create a corresponding issue/impediment card. Since we are managing work flow with Kanban, we must assign a class of service to the impediment card. Hence the impediment card will be handled through normal Kanban class-of-service policies.

HOW TO BUILD AND MONITOR AN MMR BUFFER

We have already seen that sizing a buffer for an MMR is simple. We add up the average flow times of all work items and take half of it. (If statistical data is available for different work item sizes and/or different classes of services, then the process is repeated for each one of those, and the results aggregated.) What might not be so clear, at this point, is how to use the buffer *in practice*.

For the sake of illustration, let's assume that we have 100 work items in an MMR and that the average flow times add up to 34 days. In other words, we are expecting to deliver the 100 work items in 34 days with a confidence level of 50% (because that is the average).

We divide 34 in two, and we get a buffer of 17 days. So, for instance, if the project starts on October 1, the expected end date would be 34 days later, on November 4. (In this illustration we do not consider weekends or holidays; though, naturally, in a real case all dates might need to be adjusted accordingly depending on your company's policies.) The buffer would extend for another 17 days from November 5 to November 21.

Let's examine the situation on October 7. Suppose that 18 work items have been delivered. The amount of work done is 18% (we had 100 work items to start with). To understand whether we are in a healthy or unhealthy state, we need to figure out the buffer status. This is where we will invoke Little's Law. We know that the time elapsed is 7 days, so, actual throughput up to this date is the delivered WIP of 18 divided by the flow time of 7, resulting in 2.57 work items per day.

We now assume that this is the sustainable throughput performance of the team, and that it will be kept until full delivery. Let's look at how much time we would need, with that actual throughput, to deliver all 100 work items in the MMR. Again, we invoke Little's Law. The time needed is the original WIP of 100 divided by the actual throughput of 2.57, which gives us 39 days (rounding up to whole days.)

The expected 39 days are 5 days more than the 34 days established through our historical flow time. If the actual throughput remains unchanged we would consume 5 days of our 17 day buffer. Our buffer penetration is 5/17 or 29%. This is less than 33% so we are in the *green zone* of the buffer. There is nothing to worry about.

Let's now suppose that on the following day, October 8, two more work items are delivered for a total of 20. Elapsed time is 8 days. Actual throughput is 20 work items divided by 8 days, or 2.5 work items per day. The estimated time to complete the 100 work items in the MMR is the original WIP of 100 work items divided by the latest actual throughput of 2.5, or 40 days. Now 40 days are 6 days more than the 34 days from our historical average flow time. Buffer penetration is 6/17 or 35%. This is above the 33% threshold. We have just passed into the yellow zone of the buffer. We need to investigate what might be adversely affecting throughput performance.

We have just illustrated this basic calculation twice. Take advantage of Little's Law and calculate the expected delivery date based on the original WIP and the measured actual throughput. Look where that date falls with respect to the buffer and if it is later than the starting day of the buffer, calculate the percentage of penetration. Once we have a spreadsheet set up with the calculations, it is no harder than inputting the total amount of WIP delivered up to date.

The numbers used in this example are those that can be seen in the figures with the cumulative flow diagram and the buffer control chart presented previously.

Little's Law and the Assumption of Steady/Ideal State of Flow

Naturally, what we are doing is relying heavily on Little's Law to make the sizing of the buffer and the subsequent calculations meaningful. Little's Law is significant only when the system is in a steady state, and this means that the (average) input is balanced to the (average) output.

We have seen how we can achieve dynamic balancing through the DBR, Kanban tokens, and replenishment tokens used in TameFlow-Kanban. The TameFlow-Kanban approach is more stable than the original approach used in Kanban, with work-state WIP limits. This can literally be seen when comparing cumulative flow diagrams of Kanban projects with those of TameFlow-Kanban projects. Kanban projects present a cumulative flow diagram that is much more jagged, with many stop-and-goes, and flats-and-spikes; these are all consequences of the nature of work-state WIP limits. A cumulative flow diagram of a TameFlow-Kanban project (like the one shown earlier) is much smoother with slower accelerations/decelerations of the flows that are detected and acted upon earlier, both, because of the DBR mechanism, and even more so, because of the MMR buffer management techniques presented here.

As we have mentioned many times, work-state WIP limits introduce artificial disruptions to the flow of work. Artificial disruption of flow makes the application of Little's Law less reliable. The implication is that, even though the MMR buffer technique works very well with Kanban (in fact, it was first devised for Kanban before TameFlow-Kanban came about), it works much better with TameFlow-Kanban because TameFlow-Kanban strives to interfere with Little's Law as little (pardon the pun) as possible.

Little's Law and the Conditions of Maximum Sustainable Pace

The method works even when the team is working at its *maximum sustainable* pace. A steady state (that is, when Little's Law is applicable) might be achieved even at a level of throughput that is *less* than the maximum sustainable one. This happens, typically, when flow is balanced to average throughput exhibited by Herbie, rather than to Herbie's real capacity, as was shown in the section *The Mirage of Balancing the Flow* in Chapter 14. It is very easy to fall into this trap when one seeks to *balance the flow*. And it is a situation that the DBR mechanism will avoid.

Even if we are most likely not getting anywhere close to the team's maximum sustainable pace with Kanban (though we would with TameFlow-Kanban), the peculiarity to notice is that when the team is at its *maximum* sustainable pace, one would not be able to apply the normal Kanban strategy to increase the WIP limits in order to gain more throughput. That would effectively introduce a special cause variation disruption into the work flow. Herbie will trip and fall—so to say—and halt the whole troop's progress.

Because we do not want to lose *sustainability*, the only way to improve throughput is to decrease flow time and, as we have learned in the earlier chapters, such a flow time reduction must involve Herbie, the constraint.

This is an important point—we cannot increase throughput indefinitely by increasing WIP. There comes a point when, by increasing WIP limits, the team's ability to cope with the additional workload will become unsustainable. It is at this point that any further attempt of increasing throughput by increasing WIP limits will fail. Such attempts will be tampering with the WIP limits and thrashing the system.

The failure will certainly show up on the Kanban Board, but the application of the *Five Focusing Steps* will only reveal the special cause reason why the greater pace could not be sustained (additional WIP). It will not reveal the inherent reason why the troop cannot walk any faster, notwithstanding that Herbie still remains the overall constraint (the reason why capacity is limited). Finding out that we are going slower *because* we have increased the load does not give us any more information. We added that extra load ourselves. Instead, finding out why capacity is limited can bear much greater fruits. If we can increase capacity, then we will be able to increase the load too.

It is like an athlete practicing endurance sports. An increase in the WIP limit will just result in a sprint (may the readers who are into Scrum pardon the pun here), that will make everybody run out of breath after a short while. But we want to run marathons, not sprints. We want to keep a sustainable pace for as long as possible and increase that pace without falling to the ground breathless.

When we are at the maximum sustainable and steady state, WIP limits should be kept untouched in order to maintain that level of sustainable performance. It is in this situation that we will use buffer management to reveal what is preventing the team from being even more productive. The improvement that will result will affect the entire process. The improvement will not just remove one temporary (and maybe artificial) impediment from the current project or work flow. The improvement will be of benefit to all future projects, too, because it will be a lasting improvement to the process, and not just the removal of an impediment in the flow.

The focus of any improvement attempt has to shift from the individual resources, to the entirety of the team, seen as a system. We want to find what prevents the team from increasing their maximum sustainable pace—all the while we keep the process in the ideal/steady state. This is what is meant by improving *while in the flow*, but to achieve this, we must start hunting for sources of common cause variation. Reacting to special cause variation alone will not allow us to make such breakthrough improvements. The nature of these improvements are truly breaking systemic constraints, and they are Archimedean levers that will increase performance to much higher levels.

ADVANCED BUFFER MANAGEMENT

After the delivery of a few MMRs, the benefits of the approach become more and more evident and tangible. In addition to the obvious benefit of having leading signals of oncoming problems, and the ability to plan and act on such signals, there are other benefits, too.

One of the major benefits is the reduction in meeting times. The daily inspection of the buffer status, and the ensuing reflection on it, will allow us to reduce the duration of retrospectives. Retrospectives should be had at the end of the delivery of any MMR. However, if the daily standups develop the discipline to record the reasons why the buffer status changes (a technique that will be explained in more detail in the next chapter), the retrospectives will be much more focused and can refer to effective data.

Similarly, using probabilistic forecasting techniques to determine the average flow time (and the sizing of the buffer) allows a significant reduction of the duration of any planning meetings. The time savings in the meetings translate into better team morale, better quality work, and more time available for additional effective work.

Further benefits can be realized by reasoning about the implications of buffer management in the broader context of any single project. We will look at four situations where buffer management is beneficial when looking beyond the single MMR:

- Management of extra work, other work, and failure demand
- Cross-team collaboration
- Slack management and improvement capacity
- Portfolio management

Management of Extra Work

At the beginning of this chapter, when introducing the concept of the MMR, we stressed that it is all about treating the MMR as a target-scope mini project, and we insisted on the importance of getting the scope right, as an act of balancing minimality (to ensure time and money are not wasted) and marketability (to ensure there will be a customer willing to pay for the effort). If the needs and available resources are assessed correctly, such a balance is relatively easy to reach; often it is just a matter of all stakeholders actually agreeing. Therefore, once again, the importance of the noble patterns of Unity of Purpose and Community of Trust is prominent.

The intent to not change the scope of an MMR is also dictated by another important need—that of keeping the team focused on the work at hand. One of the original precepts of Scrum is that a sprint cannot be interrupted by management in order to change the sprint backlog. The reason is precisely to allow the team to focus on a work package, and work on its delivery undisturbed. The same principle applies to MMRs—if possible, you do not want to disrupt the work on an MMR.

However, the real world is a place full of variation and surprises. At times, the change of reality or the change of our understanding of reality (because new information becomes available, or new insights are gained) really requires changing what is being worked on.

While an MMR is a target-scope project in principle, in practice it is possible to change what goes into it during due course. The only caveat is that one needs to recalculate the average flow times and then resize and reposition the buffer, as illustrated in Figure 20.19.

The figure shows the increase in scope as a stair step in the horizontal line that represents the target scope to be delivered. The recalculation can be done with reference to the original throughput used when the MMR was first defined (as shown in the figure); or more accurately by using the actual throughput measured on that MMR up to the point when the new scope is added. Naturally, just as scope can be added, it can also be removed and again the buffer needs to be resized and repositioned.

Things become tricky if the due date of the MMR is fixed, too. This is where the quality of the decisions become important; in particular, if the MMR was started soon enough and planned with an initial throughput reliable enough to make the buffer sizing good enough to protect the fixed due date.

Even when there is a fixed due date, it is possible to accept additional work. However, in this instance, the buffer cannot be resized or moved, because otherwise its protective function with respect to the due date would be compromised.

So how can you accept additional work when there is a fixed due date. You let the buffer status decide. If the buffer status is green, there is capacity to handle extra work. If it is yellow, it becomes a balancing act and a judgment call—you might be able to take on the extra work, but the risk is higher. If the buffer status is red, no extra work should be accepted, and it should be postponed for inclusion into the scope of the subsequent MMR. If, as in this last instance, reality is harsh and dictates that the extra work must be done no matter what, then you can use more sophisticated economic approaches to decide what should have priority. (For instance, cost of delay, sequence adjusted net present value, and throughput octane are all valid approaches.)

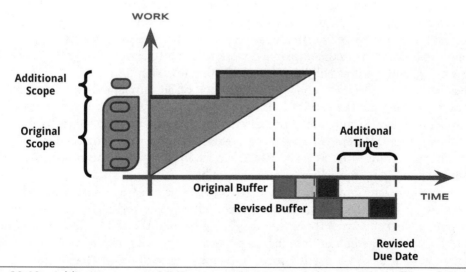

Figure 20.19 Adding scope to an MMR means repositioning and resizing the buffer, and then managing according to the new buffer

Management of Unplanned Work

Work that needs to be done can be classified in various ways. For instance:

- Business work: this is work that you would typically include in an MMR on the basis of the marketability criteria—work that is needed to make paying customers happy.
- Internal work: this is work for which you need to have a functional infrastructure in place—for instance, paying off technical debt falls into this category.
- Change work: this is work you do in order to improve the processes and optimize the whole system. This is the *sharpen-the-saw* kind of work.

All these kinds of work can be envisioned and planned for. If they have to be performed by the team working on an MMR, then they should become work items that are included into the scope of the MMR. The progress on such work should always be reflected by the buffer status of their corresponding MMR.

There is yet another category of work, which creates problems:

- Unplanned work: this is work that is of a compulsory and immediate nature that you could not possibly foresee. This is *Murphy*'s work. The typical example is failure demand, that is, problems that arise from a live system encountering critical bugs that need to be addressed immediately, no matter what.

While it might be tempting to add this unplanned work to the scope of the MMR, it is better not to do so. All such work should be managed by a separate distinct backlog, with distinct metrics and charts. In sophisticated applications, you can use buffer management on that set of work, too, though it is not strictly necessary, precisely because of the urgent nature of the work (it has to be done ASAP—no matter what).

Naturally, taking attention and effort away from the MMR to work on unplanned work will affect the MMR's odds of successful delivery. This will be progressively reflected by the buffer status. If in the daily standups the buffer status keeps on worsening, the reason will be evident—it is the extra, unplanned work that is hitting you. (You can record this in the reason log, and use it as will be suggested in the next chapter.)

What is more important is that you keep track of all unplanned work that has been encountered during the delivery of an MMR. At the end of the MMR, the ratio between the number of delivered unplanned work items and the number of delivered planned work items (those in the MMR), will give you a precise idea of how the unplanned work loads your team. You can use that as a key metric; you want to see that ratio decreasing all the time, and hopefully get it as close to zero as possible.

Let us examine an example. In Figure 20.20 you see a burn-up chart with buffer zones of a challenged MMR (green at the top, then yellow, then red). The burn-up line (the darker line) is almost constantly in the "gray" area beyond the red buffer zone. While the scope of the MMR (the lighter line) increased somewhat, that scope increase alone did not explain why the project was having such problems. The burn up was flat at the beginning. Because the team was being hit by external events that deflected all resources to investigating, debugging, and fixing live issues, work on the MMR was not progressing while the team was busy taking care of this unplanned work. In fact, during the course of the MMR you can count five or six periods when the team had such problems (you can see it clearly any time the burn-up line stays horizontal for more than a couple of days).

The unplanned work was managed with a separate backlog, as suggested previously. The additional information provided by such a backlog can be visualized by adding three more lines to the chart. In Figure 20.21 you can see the three new lines. The new line at the very bottom represents the burn up of all unplanned work performed. The new dotted line in the middle represents the burn up of the total work performed by the team (that is the planned work plus the unplanned work). The new line at the very top represents the unplanned work backlog on top of the target-scope of the MMR. As you can see, notwithstanding the few times when the backlog of unplanned work was reduced, the sheer

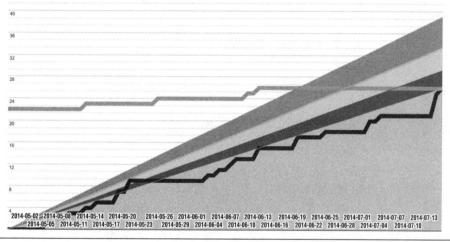

Figure 20.20   The burn-up chart of a challenged project. Apparently the team is underperforming, as the delivery is almost constantly past the buffer zone. But is it?

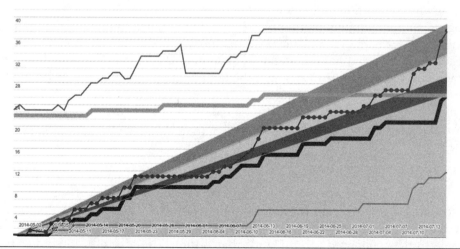

Figure 20.21   By visualizing the impact of all unplanned work, it is clear that the team was working at the expected capacity. The team was not underperforming, but was being hit by a disproportionate amount of unplanned work.

amount of unplanned work was still killing the project, as the burn up kept on staying in the gray area beyond the buffer zones.

However, through this visualization, at the end of the MMR one can conclude two things. First, the team was still working at the expected capacity (the dotted line in the middle was practically always within the buffer zones). Second, the volume of the unplanned work, which can be read as the height between the top two lines in Figure 20.21, was considerable: at the end of the MMR it amounted to almost 1/3 of all work delivered. In fact, the team not only hit the delivery of the MMR at the last day of the buffer, but did so by doing an extra 50% of the original target-scope which came in the form of unplanned work. Well done, team!

With such data, the team was able to negotiate management's attention and get approval to spend more effort to produce quality work (for instance, by paying back technical debt) in order to avoid or reduce future live issues; and possibly get more resources to cater to the growing need to maintain the existing product in a live setting, in addition to developing new functionality.

Slack Management and Improvement Capacity

By now it should be clear that when there are interdependent processes, like the line of scouts walking in the woods that we recall in the story about Herbie, there will always be some resource that is *slower* than all others (Herbie). If all other resources subordinate and help the constraint (carry Herbie's gear), then the system should be working at the maximum sustainable pace that is possible. It is this maximum sustainable pace that should be used to perform all the business-as-usual work.

Yet, the other resources (Bluey and Greenie) still have more capacity than the constraint. Rather than using this slack to create more WIP, the additional capacity should be considered as improvement capacity, and it should be used to realize the process of ongoing improvement.

A useful tool is using the concept of *staff liquidity*. After mapping up which team members have what skills and at what levels, whenever the buffer status is green, work should be assigned to the members that have the least skill at performing the task at hand. This will push them to learn. At the same time, the most skilled members should be in standby and ready to step in and help the learners as soon as they need. The skilled members, in other words, act as the Roman Veterans—the last ones to go into battle. The less skilled will be learning while doing the job.

On the other hand, if the buffer status is red, then tasks should be given to those who are most skilled at doing them. The lesser skilled people will assist with ancillary tasks.

Cross-team Collaboration

Strictly related to slack management is cross-team collaboration. If an organization has two or more teams that all employ MMRs and buffer management, whenever one team has a critical buffer status, any other team with a green buffer status can afford to lend some of its people to the challenged team. Notice that if the above idea of using buffer management to guide the usage of staff liquidity is in place, then the most skilled people in the green team will be those going over to the red team to help.

Cross-team collaboration is always an issue in traditional project management settings, especially if there are cost-allocation processes in place. Then it is often a matter of fierce battles between project owners about the ownership of resources; these issues are pathetically addressed by matrix-organizations trying to give some semblance of rationality to the impossibility of anybody being able to satisfy two bosses at once.

This is where the noble pattern of Unity of Purpose becomes even more meaningful. If two projects need to be delivered, there certainly will be one that is more business critical than another, at any given time. Metrics, such as cost of delay, sequence adjusted net present value, and throughput octane can all help in identifying which project has the highest business value or criticality. Once that has been established, does it really matter who owns the resources? This is especially true if you have buffer management in place that can tell you which resources are available, at any given time, to work on the more critical parts. This is where it becomes important to have an overview of what is happening across all projects. In other words—this is where portfolio management becomes relevant.

Portfolio Management

It is easy to fall into the trap of thinking that portfolio management is just about managing and synchronizing a multitude of projects, which might even share resources. Even in this instance a system's thinking approach is necessary—it is not only about managing many projects, but it is about managing them prominently so that each of them maximizes their contribution to the overall success of the company. Notice that it is not about maximizing the result of every single project in isolation; it is about maximizing the result of the set of project's outcomes as a whole for the company.

When there are a number of projects to examine, it becomes very important to know how they are doing with respect to one another. The previous section about using slack capacity to manage cross-team collaboration gives the general idea of how to proceed. It is beneficial to know what the buffer status is and how it is trending for all projects at the same time. How can this be achieved without information overload? It can be accomplished very simply with a variation of the buffer fever chart. The same diagram is drawn, but instead of plotting a line representing a single project, each different project is represented by a set of decreasingly smaller bubbles, as shown in Figure 20.22.

Every set of bubbles represents a point for that project in an earlier reporting period. In Figure 20.22, the status is reported about three projects: A, B, and C. The figure represents three reporting periods (weeks, months, etc.), represented by the smaller sizes of the bubbles—the biggest bubble is the current period, and the smallest is the most remote in time. The figure highlights how Project A is going very slowly: the bubbles seem to pile up into each other. Also Project A is going from yellow to red, so some action needs to be taken. Project B is progressing faster than Project A—the bubbles are more spread out and leaving a longer trail. Project B is also recovering, going from red to yellow. Project C is going very well. It is the fastest, the bubble trail is very long, and it is progressing toward early delivery.

By looking at this chart, the portfolio manager should take the decision to use the extra capacity of Project C to help Project A recover, naturally assuming the necessary skills and knowledge are available in Project C. If the skills and knowledge are not available, then people from Project C should still try to learn the skills and acquire the knowledge needed

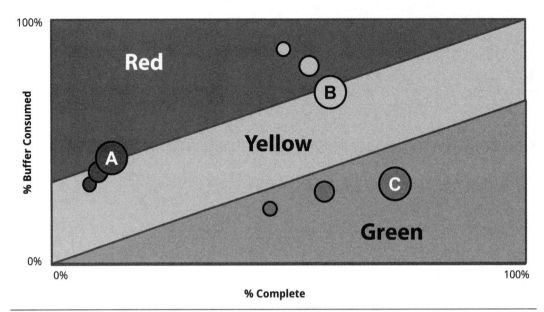

Figure 20.22   Buffer fever chart with project bubbles. Shows the status of a multitude of projects, and how the status is trending.

to support Project *A*. Keep in mind that the people who will do this on Project *C* are those who are the *veterans*, the most skilled and experienced ones on that project, precisely because of how slack is managed with respect to staff liquidity.

The representation of the fever bubble chart is vivid, and its interpretation is immediate. The purpose is to move the bubbles from left to right as soon as possible; and whenever there might be conflicting priorities, only economic considerations that benefit the portfolio as a whole should be used to decide where action should be focused. The project owners will trust each other (Community of Trust) because they will be helping each other, and they will see the common goal (Unity of Purpose). Portfolio management with a system's thinking approach is, thus, entirely consistent and supportive of the noble patterns.

21

ROOT CAUSE ANALYSIS THE THEORY OF CONSTRAINTS WAY

The technique presented in Chapter 20 can be used as described just for the purpose of getting even more signals about the state of a project. The combination of the work-state work in process (WIP) limits of Kanban or the mechanisms of TameFlow-Kanban with the techniques of minimum marketable releases (MMRs), MMR time buffers, and buffer management provide excellent tools for managing the execution of projects.

However, the use of the MMR buffer is much more powerful than this. We can take advantage of the signals raised by buffer penetration episodes to undertake investigation that will allow us to uncover common cause variation. As we saw at the beginning of Chapter 19, if we can identify common cause variation, we may be able to introduce improvements that affect the whole system, and not only remediation that resolves an incident in the current project. Doing this is a key aspect in the quest to reach a state of hyper-productivity.

RISK DETECTION AND CLASSIFICATION

It is easier to understand how the Theory of Constraints (TOC) suggests to proceed by examining a concrete case. For this purpose, throughout this chapter we will work through a fictitious example that will illustrate the steps involved.

Let's assume that we have been monitoring several projects conducted by a team, and that we have followed the recommendation about how to manage the MMR buffers.

What happens when trends penetrate through the various zones of the buffer? We need to start thinking about why this is happening while in the yellow zone, and then act in time as soon as the red zone is penetrated. Whenever the buffer penetration or trending lines raise a red signal, then is the time to act, before problems become critical. This is possible due to the leading nature of these signals. These signals indicate that a risk is about to materialize; or, at least, the materialization effects are about to impact the overall project schedule negatively.

Reason Tracking

When we encounter such a signal, we should strive to identify the triggering reason. We should do this systematically, every single time this happens, and keep track of such reasons by means of a reason log, and by attributing reason codes. Make the first log entry as soon as the first yellow zone penetration is detected. Make and keep the record even if there is no ensuing red zone penetration.

By deliberately finding a reason, we are actually identifying a risk that is about to become a problem. The signals announce risk materialization impact. Any time we discover a new reason, we have effectively uncovered a new unmanaged risk. In this way we are compiling a risk registry. Unlike other approaches that do up-front speculation about potential risks, this gives us a just-in-time compilation of actual risks when we have a real clue that it might be there (the yellow zone penetration). We need to analyze our situation to uncover the root cause of the penetration episode. (We will cover root cause analysis soon hereafter.)

If there is red zone penetration, we also document the kind of action taken. Whenever we decide to take action (because we go into the red zone), we annotate the corresponding reason code; we also document the trigger condition and the kind of action taken (preventive, mitigation, avoidance, etc.), and the specifics of the action.

We will find one of the following two situations:

- A onetime occurrence of a buffer penetration reason is likely due to special cause variation—use common risk analysis techniques to establish if that is the case, and if exceptional action is required. If a reason is not due to exceptional circumstances, then it is likely due to common cause variation, but we have to resort to occurrence counting and frequency analysis to decide if action is required.
- A recurring reason might indicate a systematic process problem. The repetitive nature is the clue—the problem is due to common cause variation. It gives us the opportunity to initiate profound process improvement.

Nonrecurring reason codes indicate potential special cause variation; one that would need urgent action once confirmed. This is the case when a reason is recorded for the first time and added to the risk registry. As soon as a new reason is identified, we have to give attention to the state of the Kanban board. Queues and starvation with work-state WIP limits in Kanban, or with drum-buffer-rope (DBR) buffer signals in TameFlow-Kanban, will show us where to investigate in order to find the sources of the special causes.

If the Kanban board gives no evidence of special cause variation, this new reason is probably due to common cause variation. We need to keep on monitoring the buffers and take notice if it repeats again. If it repeats, it is even more likely due to a common cause.

The Example

In the fictitious example that we will use throughout this chapter, we suppose that work has been managed with MMR buffers over a period of time and that we have experienced a number of buffer penetration episodes, both in the yellow and in the red. (This example might appear somewhat hilarious and unreal—this is done on purpose so that you can focus on *how* the situation is confronted, rather than on what it is about.)

We have recorded the triggering reasons as: *Chet Pulled the Plug, Cat Shredded the Printout, Dog Ate the Floppy, Power Outage, Fire,* and *Team Got Drunk.* We also recorded the actions taken, respectively as: *Educate Chet, Bring Toys for the Cat, Feed the Dog, Bring Candles, Call the Fire Brigade,* and *Cold Shower.* The situation is depicted in Figure 21.1.

Already it is evident just by the nature of the problems that some of these are due to special cause variation—such as, there was a power outage, so candles were brought in, and an accident happened and the candles ignited a fire, so the fire department had to be called. But, what about the other problems? This is where recording the number of occurrences becomes significant because it will allow us to perform frequency analysis.

Frequency Analysis and Pareto Analysis

The objective of performing a frequency analysis is to find out which events happen most often. What is striking is that if we represent this information with a bar chart, plotting the occurrences underneath each triggering reason, we have the same kind of visual clue for finding the *Herbie* of all these events, as illustrated in Figure 21.2. The event that happens most frequently is probably a constraint due to common cause variation; or at least it is a symptom of this being such a case.

It is clear that some problems are occurring more frequently than others. They may *not* be of such magnitude as to disrupt the flow of work, but they do slow down the flow to the point that the slowdown is caught and signaled by the buffer penetration episodes.

Reason	Action	# of Occurrences
Chet Pulled the Plug	Educate Chet	2
Cat Shredded the Printout	Bring Toys for the Cat	4
Dog Ate the Floppy	Feed the Dog	8
Power Outage	Bring Candles	1
Fire	Call Fire Brigade	1
Team Got Drunk	Cold Shower	2

THINK ABOUT POSSIBLE REASONS WHILE IN THE **YELLOW ZONE.**	ACT WHEN YOU REACH THE **RED ZONE.**	REPEAT SYSTEMATICALLY AND **COUNT ALL OCCURRENCES.**
ANY NEW REASON UNCOVERS A NEW **UNMANAGED RISK.**	NOTE THE ACTION YOU REALLY DID FOR: **PREVENTION, MITIGATION, AVOIDANCE,** ETC.	**SINGLE OCCURRENCES** ARE LIKELY DUE TO **SPECIAL CAUSE VARIATION.**
JUST-IN-TIME RISK REGISTER WHEN THERE IS A CLUE ABOUT THE RISK.	(EVEN IF THERE IS NO RED ZONE PENETRATION, **DOCUMENT ALL REASON ANYWAY**)	**MULTIPLE OCCURRENCES** ARE DUE TO **COMMON CAUSE VARIATION.**

Figure 21.1   Reasons, actions, and occurrence counts

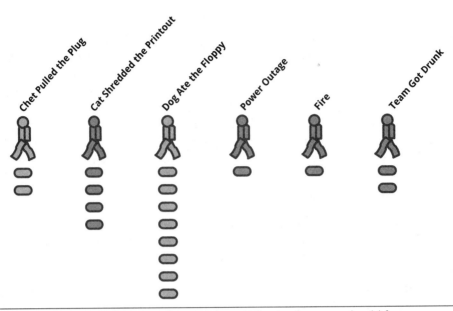

Figure 21.2 Frequency analysis: a Herbie stands out! That is where you should focus process improvement actions. The TOC philosophy is clear: not everything is worth improving; only the most common or most expensive problems are worth addressing.

Timely intervention will promptly restore the normal conditions of flow. Obviously, in the long term, the problems that occur more frequently have a combined and aggregate negative effect that can determine a decrease in the overall long-term throughput, even in the absence of disruption of flow. In fact, these effects might be so subtle that they normally go undetected, but because they inevitably affect the constraint of the process, their resolution can have a dramatic effect on performance improvement.

This is what is significant—we have found a systematic way of identifying where we can improve the process by acting on common cause variation. Naturally, the nature and the impact of the risk materialization episodes must be considered as well. We can then perform a Pareto analysis in order to find the most common or expensive problems. This is how we find the constraint in the process due to common cause variation in the work process rather than the bottleneck in the work flow due to special cause variation. This is the greater constraint that prevents us from systematically improving performance.

By doing this systematically and repeatedly, many sources of common cause variation (inherent and systematic problems in our process) can be eliminated or reduced. Since these interventions affect common causes, the whole work process will improve and not only the work flow of the current project.

Naturally, a reason code by itself is not sufficient to trigger an action. While all the reasons producing a yellow zone penetration should be recorded, they should not induce us to take action. We must record all the reasons producing red zone penetration, and record the corresponding action too. They might not be the real cause of the incident; there might be concomitant causes, cumulative effects, and so on. In essence, apply common risk management wisdom.

In any case, as soon as there is a yellow zone penetration, we have to resort to root cause analysis in order to identify the ultimate reason (or reasons) and ensure that the process improvement effort can be focused and effective. In the next section we will see what tools the TOC has to offer to allow us to perform root cause analysis.

A Note on Classical Process Improvement Initiatives

It is enlightening to compare this approach to classical (and pharaonic) process improvement initiatives, such as Capability Maturity Model Integration (CMMI) and similar ones, where all and everything is improved all the time; yet they consistently fail to deliver, despite all such improvements. This is an instance where we can see the TOC in action, giving us focus and leveraging power. The TOC philosophy is clear: not everything is worth improving; only the most common or expensive problems are worth dealing with. Focus efforts where they can have the most effect.

A Note on Agile Retrospectives

When the suggested approach is adopted in teams practicing agile retrospectives, like sprint retrospectives in Scrum or operations reviews in Kanban, the natures of such events change. While it is still suggested that retrospectives be naturally held between the finishing of one MMR and the start of the next one, their natures change substantially.

Teams using buffer management will typically notice a buffer zone penetration during their daily standup. And that is the moment when the reflective introspection/retrospection happens. In other words, the retrospective action happens on the spot, ad hoc, as soon as there is a signal that there is something that needs attention.

There are several benefits to this approach:

- The reasons why things are slowing down are very fresh in the minds of the team members. Unlike periodic retrospectives, where negative aspects tend to be forgotten or diminished, this approach keeps the focus vivid and spot-on the problem when it happens.
- The periodic retrospective starts off with a well-defined reason log and focuses discussions about improvements suggested by analyzing the reason log. The reason log shows both the negatives (the reasons) and the positives (the actions taken) that can give plenty of inspiration about what can be improved and how.
- The periodic retrospectives are much shorter in duration, as all the material work has already been performed during the daily standups.
- Retrospectives are *not* called for when things are going well (green buffers), which contributes even more to a decrease of the time teams spend in meetings, and an increase in productive time instead.
- Team morale improves as the team feels much more in control of what is happening, even if things are challenging.

Since buffer management produces a much sharper focus on improvement opportunities, the effect is akin to having continuous retrospectives rather than periodic ones. The retrospective elaborations and actions are always triggered by real events, and not by post-fact recollections.

ROOT CAUSE ANALYSIS

As mentioned earlier, whenever the buffer signals a new problem, we must record the reason that triggered the event. The reason might be symptomatic, it might not be the real cause of the problem. That is why we must perform root cause analysis, to find out where and how we need to intervene. However, root cause analysis might not be easy to do if we only have one or a few clues. This is also why a *recurring* problem can be easier to investigate—there is more information available every time it repeats. Therefore, it is easier to go to the root of things if we deal with a repeating problem.

When we attribute reason codes and plan to act, we must identify what triggered the problem in the first place and find the root cause(s). It is at this point that the *Thinking Processes* of the TOC really come into the game. We will see how the underlying reasons and the counteractions taken are related to undesirable effects (UDEs) and root causes. The reasons are *not* necessarily giving away the root cause of the problem directly. More likely they are UDEs, and the root cause might be several layers away in a complex network of effect-cause-effect events. We can go full circle and relate the identification of risks to the performing of root cause analysis and then resolve the problems.

Relevant Problem and Current Reality Tree

By focusing on the most frequently occurring reason codes, or those causing the most disruption, we can identify good candidate UDEs from where we start the root cause analysis. If we look at the earlier fictitious example, let's illustrate what usually happens when common cause variation is repeatedly hitting the process. We noticed that the *Dog Ate the Floppy* was the most common reason, with eight occurrences as highlighted in Figure 21.3. (Note that here "floppy" refers to a "floppy disk"—we assume that this example happened during the early years of the personal computer when floppy disks were common storage media.) At first we noted that there was one action taken. However the event was far more common-place; consequently a number of different actions were taken at different times.

Let's suppose that out of those eight occurrences with obvious yellow zone penetration, four also had red zone penetration which caused four actions to be taken, such as, *Feed the Dog, Give a Bone to the Dog, Let the Dog Chase the Cat,* and *Work in the Park* (meaning we went out to take the dog to the park, and work with a brick heavy laptop from the last millennium).

Obviously, we are trying to solve the same problem, which occurs over and over again, in different ways. Most likely, each one of those solutions would be successful, to some extent for the time being—yet, the problem keeps on recurring, again and again.

Each recurrence suggested a different action, but none really resolved the problem (otherwise the recurrences would have stopped).

This is a case of *resolution thrashing*. Many things are tried, but none hits the nail on the head. This is because we probably are not focusing on the right problem. The reasons are just signs about some deeper cause. We need to work backward from the effects that we see, going through a chain of causes and effects, to find the root cause.

Reason	Action	# of Occurrences
Chet Pulled the Plug	Educate Chet	2
Cat Shredded the Printout	Bring Toys for the Cat	4
Dog Ate the Floppy	**Feed the Dog** **Give a Bone to the Dog** **Let the Dog Chase the Cat** **Work in the Park**	**8**
Power Outage	Bring Candles	1
Fire	Call Fire Brigade	1
Team Got Drunk	Cold Shower	2

Figure 21.3 Each action was successful for some occurrence, yet the problem keeps repeating. Is this an instance of tampering with resolutions? Are we focusing on the right problem? Is this a sign that there is a common cause that is escaping us?

We must address the relevant problem and build the so-called current reality tree (CRT).

From Reason Codes to Undesirable Effects

We must start by identifying one or more UDEs. Remember that we call these UDEs rather than problems because we want to highlight that there might be causes that bring them into existence in a cause-effect relationship. Our mission is hence to uncover those causes.

In the fictitious example, the reason identified for the buffer penetration episodes was the *Dog Ate the Floppy*. Because the floppy disk stored all work, the overall UDE was that work had to be restored from backups. So we can write *"Restore Backups"* in a box at the top of our CRT diagram, as we set out to build it. At the bottom of the diagram we list the reason and the four actions that were taken, leaving space in between (as shown in Figure 21.4) that we will fill up as we add to the diagram.

We want to keep our focus and attention on that most frequent reason and on the actions that were taken. In this case, the reason can be considered as a UDE, too. So we write it, with appropriate wording, in a box by itself underneath the box with the first UDE, and we connect them with an arrow, as shown in Figure 21.5. We can read the diagram as: *If the Dog Eats the Floppy then we must Restore Backups.*

We still keep the four actions listed at the bottom of the diagram because now we need to think about what assumptions we made when we decided to take those actions.

Assumptions for Actions May Be Undesirable Effects

For each action we try to identify what assumption prompted us to take the action. We might ask ourselves: *"Why did we feed the dog?"* and reply *"Because we thought the dog was hungry."* So we write *"Dog is Hungry"* in a box further down and connect it to the box above.

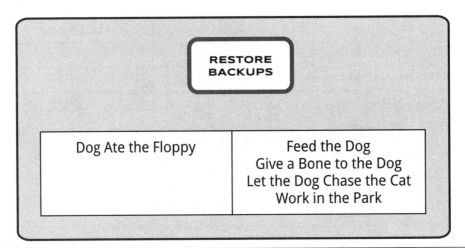

Figure 21.4   The undesirable effect (*Restore Backups*), caused by the observed reason (*Dog Ate the Floppy*), and the attempted actions

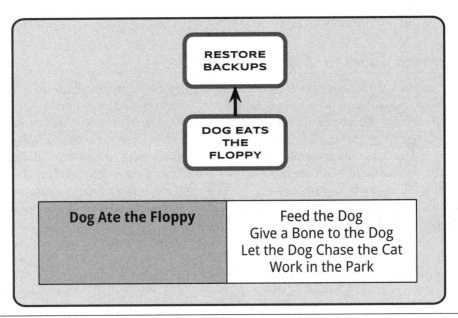

Figure 21.5   The observed reason (*Dog Eats the Floppy*) causes the undesirable effect, and it is an undesirable effect, too

We start to see the chain of causes and effects, like this: "*If the Dog is Hungry, then the Dog Eats the Floppy. If the Dog Eats the Floppy, then we must Restore Backups.*"

Likewise, for the other three actions, we can write boxes with "*Dog Enjoys Chewing,*" "*Dog is Bored,*" and "*Dog is Inside*" (meaning inside the office or building) and read the corresponding cause and effect relationships off the diagram, which we can see in Figure 21.6.

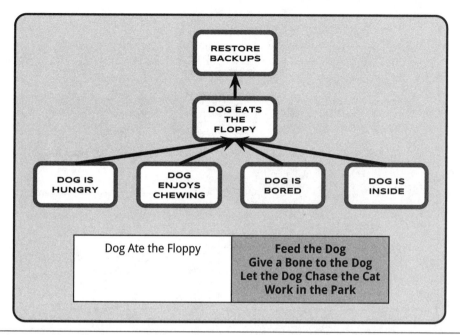

Figure 21.6 Each action is sustained by an assumption; we believed each assumption caused the observed reason. The assumptions are UDEs too.

VALIDATING THE ASSUMPTIONS

The assumptions we have identified need to be *validated*. We need to analyze what we know about our current reality and draw conclusions from what we observed after applying our actions. We might conclude that *Dog is Hungry* is not a valid assumption because we always make sure that the dog is well fed.

Likewise, we might conclude that *Dog Enjoys Chewing* is not a sufficient cause explaining why the dog would still prefer to eat the floppy—we observed, for instance, in subsequent recurrences that the dog was still eating the floppies, despite having a bone to chew.

With these observations we can *eliminate* two boxes from the CRT, as illustrated in Figure 21.7. This is a common process in building a CRT. We identify what we think might be good UDEs, but then we remove them upon deeper analysis.

VALIDATING THE CAUSE-EFFECT RELATIONSHIPS

We should question any cause-effect relationship that we identify; see if it really holds, and ask ourselves if it is really convincing. At times we might need to remove UDEs from the diagram. At other times we might reckon that the cause-effect chain is different from what we are representing in the diagram, and maybe we need to rearrange the boxes and the relationships between them.

For instance we may recognize that *Dog is Inside* is not a real cause for *Dog Eats the Floppy*. However, it can explain why the *Dog is Bored*. We modify the diagram accordingly, as shown in Figure 21.8, and can then read the whole chain of cause-effects as: *If the Dog is Inside, then the Dog is Bored. If the Dog is Bored, then the Dog Eats the Floppy. If the Dog Eats the Floppy, then we must Restore Backups.*

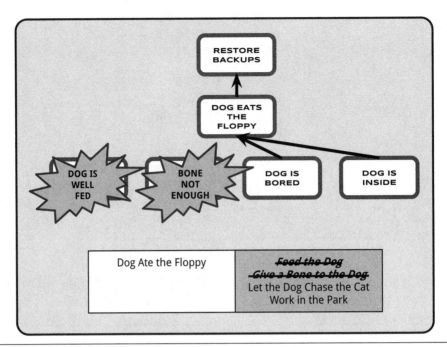

Figure 21.7   Prune the tree of unlikely UDEs

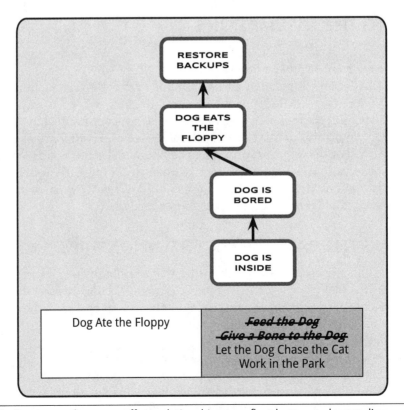

Figure 21.8   Rearrange the cause-effect relationships to reflect better understanding

Searching Deeper

For any UDE that we might draw in the diagram, we must continue to ask if it is caused by some other entity. The easiest way to do this is to ask "Why?"

For instance, after the last step, we might ask ourselves why the dog is inside, in an office environment. We might find out that it is because the office practices a dog friendly policy and any employee with dogs is allowed to bring them to work. So we extend the tree diagram accordingly, as shown in Figure 21.9. (Notice that we ignore the remaining actions from the previous figure for the sake of illustration, though in a real setting they should be subject to the complete analysis too.)

Now the cause-effect chain will read as: *If we have a Dog Friendly Policy, then the Dog is Inside. If the Dog is Inside, then the Dog is Bored, etc.* As we will see shortly, when digging deeper, we should take care to stop once we reach the limit of our Sphere of Influence.

Searching Wider: Multiple Causes and Additional Causes

The search for causes must not only go down the tree, but also look at concomitant causes, which contribute to the effects we observe in reality. In other words, we may need to search for additional causes needed to explain the effects found so far.

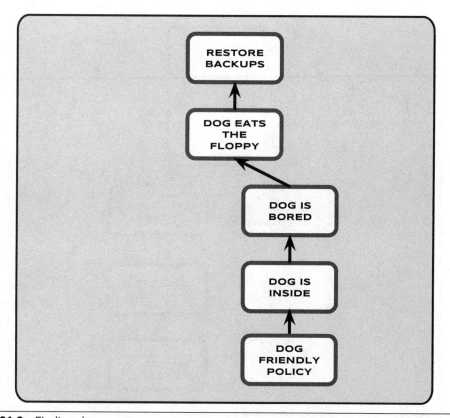

Figure 21.9   Finding deeper causes

For instance, *Dog is Bored* may not be a sufficient cause explaining why the *Dog Eats the Floppy*. The dog might exhibit that behavior when it is bored *and* wants attention. We can express this condition by drawing the new cause entity for *Dog Wants Attention* on the diagram and drawing an ellipse around the arrows that point to the common effect, as shown in Figure 21.10.

The ellipse represents the fact that both causes are needed to explain the effect; they are sufficient to explain the effect when considered together, but not alone. We can interpret this as an "AND" operator. In this case that part of the diagram will read as follows: *If the Dog wants Attention AND the Dog is Bored, then the Dog eats the Floppy.*

Additional causes may also be independent if they can explain the effect alone. In such a case they are drawn without the ellipse surrounding the arrows pointing to the effect. We would interpret this as an "OR" operator, although we are not illustrating this case in the figure.

Do Not Ignore *Obvious* Causes

In a similar vein, we might arrive at the conclusion that the top-most UDE is caused not only by the fact that the *Dog Eats the Floppy*, but is also caused by the apparently *obvious*

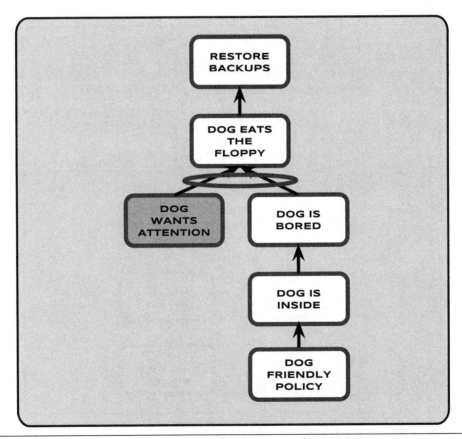

Figure 21.10   Multiple and additional causes; the ellipses signifies "AND"

fact that the work is actually stored on the floppy disk to begin with. So we add another entity, *Source Code on Floppy* and make sure that the arrow (that points to the top most effect) is connected to the other arrow by an ellipse, as shown in Figure 21.11.

The top of the diagram will read as: *If we have Source Code on Floppy AND Dog Eats the Floppy, then we must Restore Backups.*

Multiple Root Causes

When we are satisfied by our investigation, we can look for root causes in the diagram. Normally, root causes are found as leaves that are at the extremes of the branches of the tree. Since we are representing cause-effect relationships in a tree, one important observation is that we might easily arrive at a situation where the top-most UDE is explained by cause-effect chains that go out in different branches. This means that there can be multiple root causes and not just one root cause.

In the example we can see that we have three root causes: *Source Code on Floppy*, *Dog Wants Attention* and *Dog Friendly Policy* (as illustrated in Figure 21.12). However, not all root causes are created equal. Some may contribute more, or less, to explain the reality you are describing. For instance, *Dog Wants Attention* might be less important than the other two root causes identified. Often it is effective to focus on and address the root causes that have more weight.

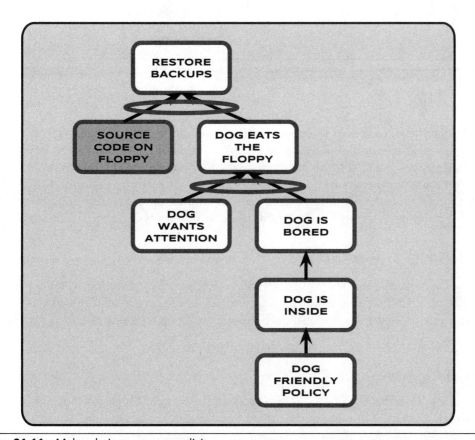

Figure 21.11   Make obvious causes explicit

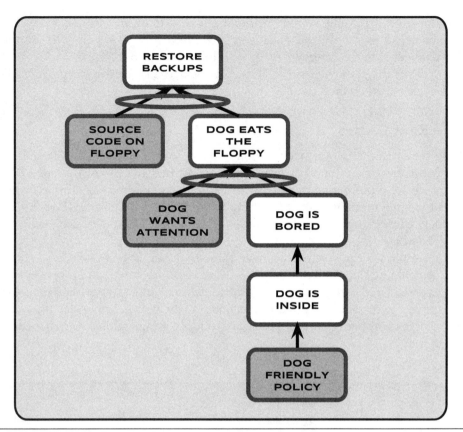

Figure 21.12   There can be more than one root cause

Although the tree is easier to handle if there is only one single root cause, it is comforting to know that we can deal with more complex situations, in which several concomitant root causes might exist. Note, however, that when we have multiple root causes we will be tempted to analyze the situation even deeper, to try to identify one common cause. Many times, though, this search will run out of options because of reality; this happens when we reach the boundaries of our Sphere of Influence, which we will examine hereafter.

CHANGING THE REALITY

Once we have identified root causes, we will be ready to do something about them. However, this raises the question if we *can* do anything about them at all. This is where we can see the value of clearly distinguishing between our Span of Control and our Sphere of Influence.

Span of Control

As we saw in Chapter 10, *The Thinking Processes*, the *Span of Control* is that part of reality over which we have complete authority and power to change anything we want. Ideally, we can visualize our span of control in our diagram by drawing a border enclosing those entities that are directly under our control, as shown in Figure 21.13.

Sphere of Influence

Likewise, we can draw a second border that encloses all those entities which we cannot change directly because they fall under the authority of other people, as shown in Figure 21.14. This border represents our *Sphere of Influence.*

It is important to realize that the Sphere of Influence is determined by the kind of relationship we have with these other people. If we have a relation of such nature that we are able to communicate and influence the decision making of these people, the entities under consideration fall inside our Sphere of Influence.

Many Whys

The *Lean* school of thinking has popularized the root cause analysis technique known as the *Five Whys*, which is an integral part of the Toyota Production System as described by Taiichi Ōhno (1988). The Five Whys originated from the factory floor, with the habit of observing how things were done and questioning "Why?" five times. The way we build

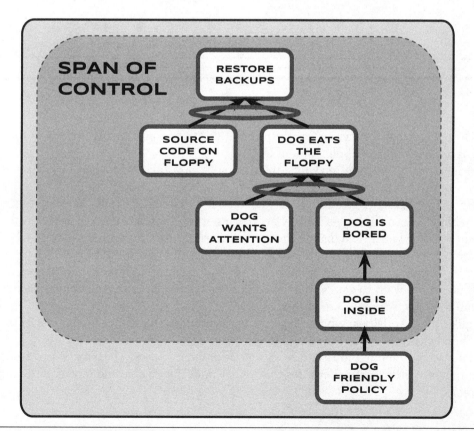

Figure 21.13   Span of Control: where you have complete authority to take any decision alone

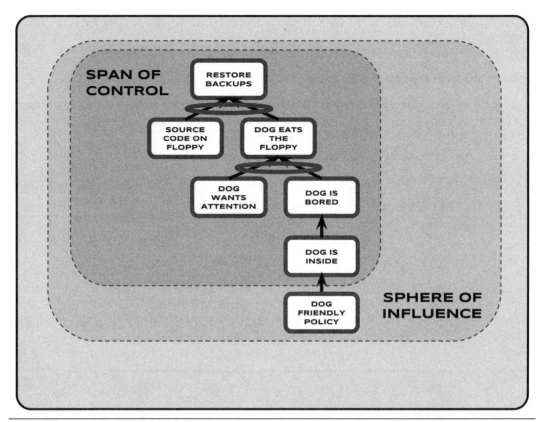

Figure 21.14   Sphere of Influence: where someone else has the authority to make decisions, but you have the ability to influence them

a CRT is somewhat similar, at least in principle, with the Five Whys though in the TOC there is a more rigorous application of logic.

For instance, we have to recognize that it is not *worth* following a chain of cause-effects as soon as this leads us outside of our Sphere of Influence. If the fifth entity is outside of our Sphere of Influence, we just have to accept it as a state of reality, as shown in Figure 21.15. Nothing can be done about what we cannot even influence, let alone control.

On the other hand, if a chain of cause-effects extends for a number of levels which are all within our Span of Control or Sphere of Influence, then we should follow that chain for as deep as it goes, as illustrated in Figure 21.16. As long as we still remain inside our Sphere of Influence, we want to gain as detailed an understanding as possible about all causes that explain the effects that we are observing.

Unlike the Five Whys, which give rise to very linear sequences of cause-effects, with the Thinking Processes our investigation is often broader as we have already seen in the previous section about multiple causes and additional causes. The Five Whys technique often misses such additional entities that might radically change the interpretation of the diagram.

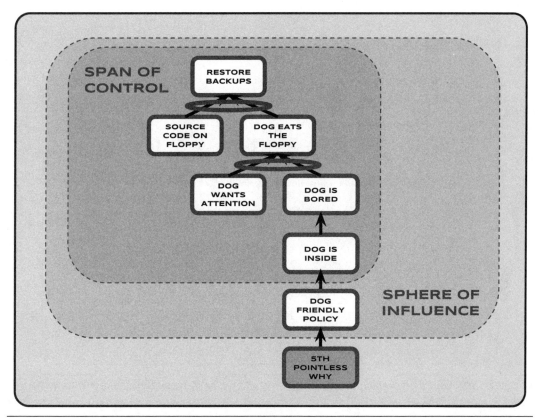

Figure 21.15   It is vain to go beyond your Sphere of Influence. At times the Five Whys techniques can be misleading because it goes too far.

Injections

Once we are satisfied and believe that the CRT we built truly depicts our situation, we can start thinking about how to change the reality to solve our problems. This is done first at a conceptual level by changing, removing, or adding entities to our diagram.

For instance, if we fast forward our example scenario from the mid-'80s to 2014, one injection that would certainly solve the problem is to store our work in the *cloud* rather than on floppy disks, as illustrated in Figure 21.17. With such a solution, there would be no critical floppy disks for our dog to chew, and the problem would have been solved at its root.

In the mid-'80s, a solution such as storing data in the *cloud* would have been seen as pure science fiction. In fact, it would have been called, in the TOC jargon, a "flying pig injection"—something impossibly difficult to achieve or even to imagine. Though you should always strive to ensure that all injections are feasible, flying pigs are often an inspiration for innovation so don't ignore them either.

Influence and Change

When there are no possibilities within our Span of Control, we still have the option to leverage our influence. For instance, one of the root causes was the *Dog Friendly Policy* so

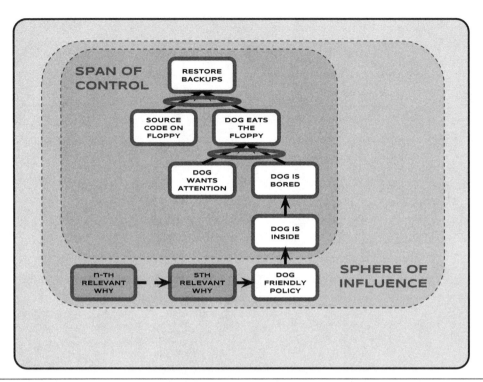

Figure 21.16   Follow any chain of causes and effects to the limit of your Sphere of Influence. At times the Five Whys technique can be insufficient.

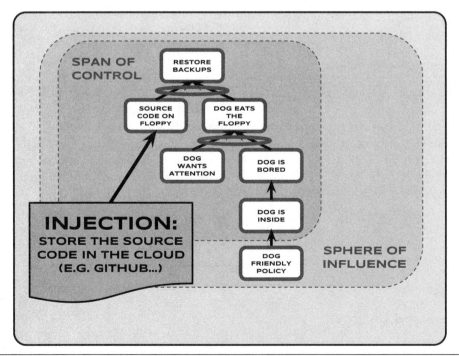

Figure 21.17   An injection into your Span of Control can change your current reality and avoid all undesirable effects. We must ensure that the injection is feasible.

one course of action could be to try to influence the policy makers to change that policy, as shown in Figure 21.18.

Layers of Resistance and Persuasion Techniques

The CRT is just a supporting tool in the process of overcoming the layers of resistance through the persuasions techniques that we briefly introduced in Chapter 10. As mentioned there, the creating of a CRT is an exercise in logic; and the investigation can bring us to look outside of our normal domain, and into our Sphere of Influence. The CRT will give us the confidence to direct our investigation toward the correct or relevant problem.

When we need to persuade other people about the benefits of the improvements we are proposing, it is useful to use the CRT to support our motives. What is more important, though, is that we gain the buy in of those whom we try to influence.

Improving means changing, and changing can be effective only if all people involved are truly convinced. Gaining consensus is not enough. Unanimous decisions are what are needed to get to a hyper-productive state. The tools offered by the TOC (Constraints Management, Throughput Accounting, Buffer Management, Thinking Processes, and so

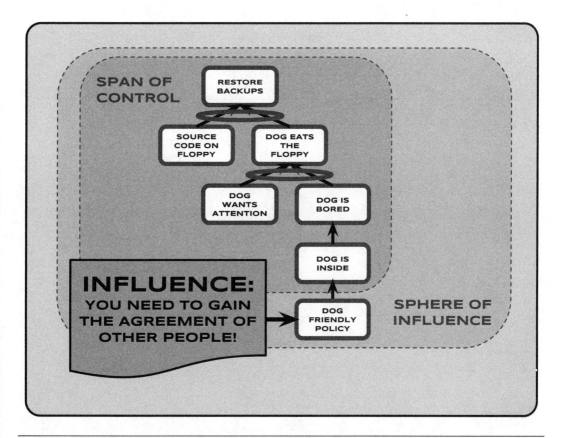

Figure 21.18   We can also change our current reality by exercising influence in our Sphere of Influence

on) have this incredible power—if used correctly, they will lead the organization to make unanimous decisions about any change that needs to be implemented.

Unanimous decision making is the hallmark of an organization wherein the noble patterns of Unity of Purpose and Community of Trust are truly at work. And that is the secret of reaching a state of hyper-productive flow throughout our organization.

22

IN PRACTICE WITH SCRUM

This chapter, similar to the previous one, is of a Theory of Constraints (TOC) practical nature and shows how significant improvements in productivity can also be achieved by starting with Scrum rather than with Kanban. Here again, the TOC is used as the catalyst that enables continuous performance improvement. Organizational change is considered from the point of view of the TOC, and especially how it relates to the flow of work throughout a knowledge-based organization. The nature of constraints is explained, as well as where and how to start an improvement initiative, going from major releases to backlogs. Execution of control becomes paramount when it comes to balancing resources against demand and achieving due-date performance—ultimately reinforcing the *Community of Trust* that is grown within the organization. Specific tools of the TOC—such as, drum-buffer-rope scheduling and critical chain buffer management—are described in a way that further enhances Scrum.

ONE WAY TO HYPER-PRODUCTIVITY

There are many ways to achieve hyper-productivity—this chapter will elaborate on one of them. To achieve hyper-productivity you have to pick a starting point, and then proceed step by step. In this part of the book you'll get some ideas that will help you to find your own way. You are free, of course, to use them exactly as described here as well.

In fact, I (Wolfram Müller) have seen hyper-productivity realized in many projects—by myself and by others. Together with my team of around 40 project managers, we have done more than 500 projects. Many of these project teams reached hyper-productivity. What does hyper-productivity mean? Hyper-productivity is achieved when all the involved people and stakeholders can honestly say, "We have no idea what we could have done better. The project was pure creative and productive flow!"

To reach this goal, being *good* is not enough—you have to be the *best* in all disciplines. It's like a decathlon; it's not just using one method, finding the right people, or having a suitable vision—you must have it all: leadership with vision, passion, and discipline (yes, discipline, too). Even more important, you will continually have to make decisions quickly and correctly; decisions with huge impacts. But that is not all, the underlying processes have to be innovative, lightweight, and highly efficient (with minimal waste).

Some may think it's easy—just set up a big Kaizen, a continuous improvement program, or even a change program—run some workshops, generate improvement ideas (the more the better), get some commitments from staff, and start changing. Make sure that the one who had the original idea is the driver for implementation. The next day, everything is done, and we are magically hyper-productive. Okay—being realistic, everyone knows that is not how it works.

So how does it work? Which steps have to be undertaken, and in what order? How can we ensure that hyper-productivity is achieved—and not just reached, but reached at the optimum speed?

ORGANIZATIONAL CHANGE IS HARD AND TAKES A LONG TIME

Perhaps you know about J-curves in change processes.[1] Many consultants and managers think that when you change something, unavoidably, the performance of the system will initially go down. They say, "It has to get worse before it gets better"—and, very often, things work out exactly as they predicted. But is that necessary?

It could be even worse because they may say, "It takes too long to change the habits and values of the people." If you think it is going to work out like this, it often does. But is that a law of physics?

No, and no again. All around us, people are frequently changing things, with immediate success. Just think about the smartphone or tablet computer revolution—it wasn't hard to get people on board. The new devices were much easier to use. Did it take long to change? No! The change was almost immediate. After a few minutes of using these devices, no one wanted to go back. Thus, it's all about designing a good change. The criteria are easy to state:

- Everybody has to have a profit
- The profit has to show up immediately
- After the change, the world must be easier for everyone

There is just one question left: "How does one design such a change?"

HOW TO DESIGN EASY AND FAST ORGANIZATIONAL CHANGE!

All systems that produce something are somehow limited in their performance. If they were not, they would grow with infinite speed, and dissolve in a flash of energy. Thus, being somewhat constrained is a good idea.

If you look even one step closer, all systems are built up of subsystems. One of these subsystems must be the constraint mentioned previously, and it is precisely the one that defines the productivity of the whole. If you try to improve the whole system by optimizing all the subsystems, you will gain nothing important. In the best case you'll get a proportional gain. This is often called the magic triangle of project management (schedule, resources, and scope), and many project managers believe that it is true—but the managers seldom know about constraints.

For example, suppose you have a development department with four teams, as shown in Figure 22.1. Three of them have a capacity of 100, and one has 50 person-days per time frame. The projects have an equal footprint of 50 person-days per team so you have a throughput of about 1 project per time frame.

What happens if you increase the capacity of all teams by a factor of two, as in Figure 22.2? Nothing interesting—you'll get (hopefully) twice (+100%) the output with double the costs (+100%). In reality, you'll get less than twice the output because of nonlinear negative effects.

But what happens if you increase just the capacity of the constrained team by a factor of two, as in Figure 22.3? You'll still get the doubled output, but with only 14% increased resources. The overall effectiveness increases dramatically—by 100%.

Thus, the key for drastic improvements is focusing all your activity on the constraint. And, by the way, it makes no sense to load all stages at 100%—this would be a system with many constraints and it would be hopelessly unstable. The rule of thumb from production—*never load the constraint more than 80% and all the rest even less*—applies here, too.

Little's Law, or *why it is not a good idea to have too many customers in a store*, says that, under steady state conditions, the average number of items in a queuing system equals the average rate at which items arrive, multiplied by the average time that an item spends in

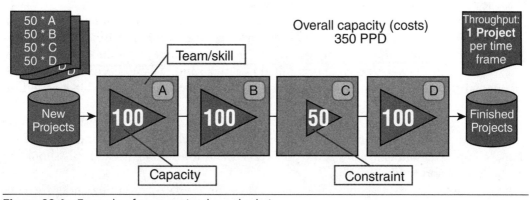

Figure 22.1   Example of a constrained supply chain

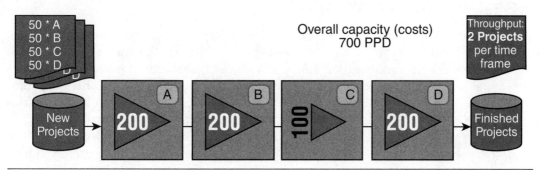

Figure 22.2   The constrained supply chain with doubled capacity

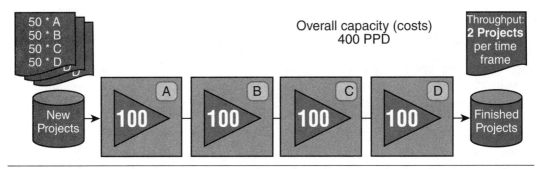

Figure 22.3   The constrained supply chain with doubled constraint capacity

the system.[2] Letting L = average number of items in the queuing system, W = average lead time in the system for an item, and λ = average number of items arriving per unit time, the law is:

$$L = \lambda * W$$

For example, consider the scenario of people entering and leaving a retail store. If the same number of customers went into and came out of the shop, the *waiting* time (better to say *lead* time) is proportional to the people who are inside (see Figure 22.4). In fact, the roots of Little's Law are actually in the sales business.

So what is the lesson learned from this law? *It makes no sense to overload a constraint.* The only thing you'll get is longer lead times among other troubles. After all, we are humans rather than machines, and if we are overloaded, we lose motivation, make errors, and start to shift between tasks. This is called negative multitasking. Each shift consumes energy and time, so it becomes even worse—the more you overload, the longer the lead times will be, as shown in Figure 22.5.

On the other hand, you will always have a constraint. Having a constraint is good because it stabilizes the system and reduces the visible complexity. Whenever someone thinks complexity and chaos are good, don't take them too seriously. The focus should be on stable flow and stable growth.

If you don't overload the constraint, and start to subordinate everything under the constraint, you'll get a huge gain in performance and, better yet, you'll gain happy people.

WHERE IS THIS CONSTRAINT?

Be aware that the constraint will not always be a team—it could be more. It could be a special skill, or an ability to solve problems or generate ideas (in the integration or concept phase). It could be communication bandwidth or the availability of management. There are several layers of constraints: resources, virtual resources, management attention, communication, policies, and ability to change. In practice, you will find them in exactly this order.

In Agile organizations, the low-level resource constraint is typically addressed. You have dedicated teams, and they can pull as much work as they can manage. Very often you hear the statement, "It will be done when it's done." The combination of dedicated teams and

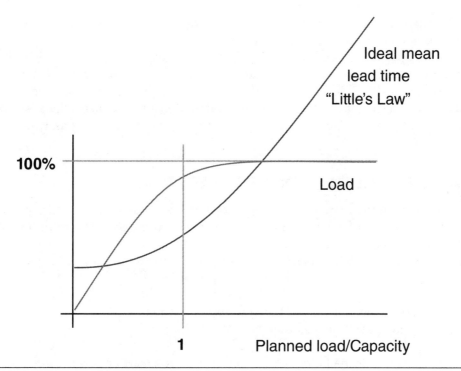

Figure 22.4   Little's Law idealistic

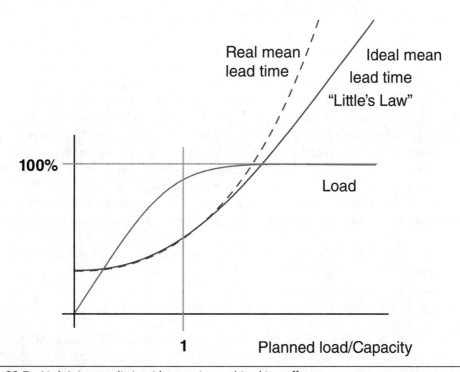

Figure 22.5   Little's Law realistic with negative multitasking effects

the lack of target scope ensure that the constraint (the developer) is not overloaded, and therefore is not a bottleneck anymore.

When it comes to change (and that's what we are talking about), we have an interesting situation—a different constraint. Change is driven by the managers, but the managers are also deeply involved in operations. If productivity is low, the managers are busy with operational management and may not have time to prepare for a change. That's why management attention is the most common constraint in current organizations, which leads us to another important question.

WHAT IS THE RIGHT ORDER TO START?

If you are aware of the aforementioned points, and if you have accepted that you have to subordinate yourself to the constraint, the next issue arises; you have to decide in what order you are going to proceed.

It's easy to find the right order. For example, you want to travel by car to a city nearby, but the gas tank is empty. Which sequence do you prefer?

A. Drive onto the highway, and then to the gas station
B. Go to the gas station, and then onto the highway

Okay, the answer is clear—filling the gas tank before you start driving is a good idea. But, how should you proceed in the following situation?

A. Empower the people, then think about reducing the load in the constraint
B. Reduce the load in the constraint, then empower the people

In the past I've seen situations like this: without a real vision and leadership skills, the management started with Scrum or Kanban. They invested a lot of trust in the methodology and the teams. They sent the teams, Product Owners, and Scrum masters to training. The teams came back highly motivated and ready to rumble. But what happened? The team tried hard, but the management processes didn't support the new methods. In this case, what you may end up with is a highly frustrated team in a very short time—they may even leave the company. As you see, the sequence of measures is very relevant.

In an organizational change process, you have to undertake at least 20, and maybe even up to 100, steps of measures. So, the question is still, where to start?

If you know about constraints, Little's Law, and how important it is to set up a productive environment before empowering the people, then a good start proceeds like this:

• Find or define the constraint—as a first step it's good to take the developer as the constraint
• Ensure that the constraint is not overloaded
• Ensure that the load in the constraint stays under control

These steps will result in immediate improvement in the constraint (in this case the developer's performance). They should now be more focused and concentrated on their work, and able to deliver as promised. As a result, there will be more trust in the new idea. The trust of the team toward itself grows steadily, and the trust toward the team from an outside perspective grows, too. Trust is the key to reduce the amount of control (e.g., disturbances and communication), which leads to even more capacity in the constraint. That is what is called a *positive enforcement loop*.

Now the next steps can be started:

- Reduce the amount of work in the system even more—until the first developer actually runs out of work. Solve the occurring impediments.

Now you have a pure flow system, with no impediments. Soon the system becomes efficient and motivating, too.

- Now is a good time to do the rest—work with the people. Empower them and give them more and more responsibilities.

Normally, it is much better to get the organizational processes straight first, and afterward invest in people. When energized people face unproductive organizations, it leads to frustration and poor results. Well-managed organizations with energized people are real rockets.

Ideally you will choose a measure that addresses the constraint first and will gain success quickly. This will help stakeholders and directly affected people to gain trust in change processes, and will free additional resources and energy to reach the next levels much faster.

Let's start. One way to go is typical of current organizations; they usually have some kind of Agile method working. Often they are not well integrated in organizations—there are only local teams. Therefore, there are many problems resulting from this situation:

- To secure the throughput, they put a hard limit on the work in process (WIP) of a team, but they cannot deal with uncertainties, and therefore, they cannot commit to a specific scope in a specific time. There is no WIP control over the entire *project* or release.
- Without an explicit buffer and committed due date there is no relevant operational monitoring.
- There are still negative social group dynamics due to the lack of a project due date and lack of buffers. The only steering possibilities are the small work packages (the so-called stories). Especially in Scrum, the team has to commit to an amount of stories to deliver in a short time. If something goes wrong (as it often does), the team is punished (in sometimes very subtle ways). As a result, they put more and more buffer into their stories and velocity.

The solution should be to find a way to make Agile methods compatible to the organization so that they can easily be used, if applicable. Additionally, one has to find a way to define a buffer and to monitor the progress relative to buffer consumption. Furthermore, it will be important to improve Agile methods to the theoretical optimal throughput and minimize flow time by reducing inventory (open stories and tasks) to a minimum level and get rid of unnatural batch sizes.

Get your work organization right—rules are easy to change.

Step 1: Reliable Scrum or Reliable Kanban

Select Scrum or Kanban, calculate a reasonable due date and add some buffer at the end. Then measure progress to buffer consumption to get effective operational steering. The result is both agility and reliability.

The team knows what the goal is and has no pressure on the sprints—the velocity rises. The stakeholders know what they get and see a transparent status—micromanagement evaporates and velocity rises again. Motivation and quality get better, and throughput is improving.

Step 2: TameFlow-Scrum or Drum-Buffer-Rope

Ideally, you would want to get rid of the sprints in Scrum and come to continuous flow. Get rid of the stages and their buffers in Kanban. Use a two-stage process—first, break stories into tasks, and second, generate deliveries out of tasks. Focus on minimum inventory of open tasks and you'll get flow at the theoretical optimum.

The team focuses on getting rid of any impediment—throughput increases. The inventory drops to a minimum—flow time drops to the theoretical minimum. They get even faster feedback from the Product Owner. There will be no discussions about the process any more—the focus moves toward the next steps—reducing waste and developing developers.

But that's not the end. Now the development process is streamlined to the maximum and you don't have to think about that anymore. You now have the time and the capacity to focus on the supporting and surrounding processes. What about quality, continuous integration, deployment, requirement engineering, prototyping, test stages, and production releases? Everything can be improved, step-by-step.

And finally, the way is free to work with the staff itself. They can develop real craftsmanship, leadership, or even train themselves in creativity methods. Thinking outside the box starts within the team, helping them to improve the company even more. In short, do all you can to reach hyper-productivity.

REFERENCES

1. J-curve, on Wikipedia http://en.wikipedia.org/wiki/J-Curve_Effect
2. Little's Law, on Wikipedia http://en.wikipedia.org/wiki/Little%27s_law

23

RELIABLE SCRUM AND
RELIABLE KANBAN

Scrum has found its way into many development departments, within many enterprises. The consequent control of work in process (WIP) within the sprint or WIP limits, the strict building of teams out of the best available experts, the iterative way of working, and the continuous integration were major breakthroughs, and have shown favorable results most of the time.

But, normally, we work in *big* enterprises and we want to solve *big* problems—usually in the form of *big* projects. That is where the problems occur. Scrum and Kanban are now confronted with the needs of a surrounding organizational structure, such as:

- *The need for reliability.* For example, if you want to sell a new product in a campaign, many things have to be planned and executed. If the product is not available on the target date, a lot of damage will happen to the company. Therefore, the company needs a reliable due date as to when the product will be available, without a reduction of the project or product scope.
- *The need for transparency.* There are always persons who are accountable for the success of a project. They delegate the responsibility of establishing results within a time frame with given resources. But they stay accountable, and therefore, they need to be sure whether the project is going well or whether they have to take some measures to bring it back on track. Consequently, the accountable person needs objective transparency about the status of the project at all times.

Of course, the Scrum gurus will say: "We are more reliable than the classic project managers" and "We are absolutely transparent." And, on the other hand, they say, "It's done when it's done" and "We have this product burn-down chart. It shows, after every sprint, the current estimated time of finishing. I can tell you after every sprint whether the due date fits, or not."

Scrum is good, but at the end of the day, the need for reliability and transparency is not fulfilled. In bigger organizations, this results in a reduced acceptance of Scrum. So, let's do something about it and make Scrum (and also Kanban) more reliable.

From the project management community we know of an approach called Critical Chain (Goldratt, 1997). This is a holistic, systemic methodology with many success stories all over the world—the internet is full of good testimonials. Out of this methodology, two parts are especially interesting for Scrum:

- Dealing with uncertainties by aggregating the buffers in the estimations at the end of the project; as a result the due dates become much more reliable
- Showing an operational and objective project status by monitoring the progress according to the buffer consumption as an easy-to-read fever chart

The Scrum framework, as it is, is actually good; it doesn't have to be changed at all to get Reliable Scrum working. One important thing to remember is that Reliable Scrum makes sense in a project environment only. If you have already built the product, and if you are in this incremental improvement mode, when you deliver after finishing a story to the customer, then you won't get anything out of project management, and therefore, Reliable Scrum brings you no benefit. You are, in fact, in production mode and you won't get anything out of project management. But if you are in a mode where you are building a new product, or if you're working toward a big, important release, you can definitely benefit from Reliable Scrum. But, what has to be done to start Reliable Scrum?

1. Define that which is part of the release or product. In the case where you keep the sprints, this should be more than five sprints, but not more than six months worth of work.
2. Find an appropriate due date for this release or product where the amount of work in the backlog and the velocity fits together. This due date has to be calculated in a way that there is enough buffer to ensure a realistic chance of success.
3. After each sprint, or if you have finished a story, or even in between, plot the new status in the form of a fever chart to get transparency.

If you have a portfolio of Scrum work streams, you can do this for all of them. Just put the results together in one diagram and you'll get a perfect overview about all work streams.
    The following effects will be visible soon:

- The focus changes from a sprint-to-sprint basis to a bigger release that delivers real and recognizable value to the customer.
- The backlog will be clarified in many ways. First, stakeholders (there are typically more than one) are identified. The backlog will be completed (as much as possible) and the backlog items are qualified whether they are part of the release or not. Based on this backlog, the stakeholders can give their sign-off. All stories are estimated (in story points), and big stories are broken down into smaller ones. The result is a clear set of qualified stories, adjusted with the stakeholders. Attention: this backlog is not fixed; it can change according to the Scrum process. But, there is a baseline and therefore the possibility to discuss changes.
- The team, including Scrum Master and Product Owner, are able to estimate the expected variations in the backlog and velocity. They collaborate together about the risks and chances and will make them transparent.

- A realistic due date, or a realistic amount of backlog for a release, can be established. It helps to identify the correct amount of resources needed to fulfill the expectations of the stakeholders. As a result, the team gets an accurate probability of success.
- The fever chart will become an excellent tool for the Product Owner to assess how many stories he can pull into the release or must leave out. He can adjust the backlog to always be in the yellow zone. In this case, there will always be a realistic chance of success. For this reason, Product Owners will love Reliable Scrum.
- The team gets a buffer at the end of the release and qualified feedback about their performance. The focus is not as strong on each sprint. They don't have to protect the sprint results. As long as they stay in the green zone they are safe, so they can pull stories as much as possible with an optimistic velocity. The *Student Syndrome* (if you know that you have buffer, then you consume it in the beginning and you start late) and *Parkinson's Law* (work will always expand to fill the time available for completion) will disappear, and as a result, the velocity will improve (more than you expect).
- The stakeholders get an objective, easy-to-read status report and feel very confident about the reliability of the team. Consequently, they leave the team undisturbed. The team can work self-managed and as concentrated as possible.
- In big projects, with a lot of Scrum teams, the stakeholders will get an overview about all the streams at once. They can concentrate on the red ones. They can focus on just the most important issues.

It's the same with Kanban. Kanban is more flow oriented, but it cannot guarantee a due date, either. That's why the same ideas can be used in Kanban, and the discussion in the following paragraphs apply equally to both Scrum and Kanban. Being reliable is independent of the control method you use. In the following chapter you'll find a step-by-step guideline on how to implement Reliable Scrum or Reliable Kanban.

DEFINE A *Major Release*

Reliable Scrum doesn't make sense for Scrum teams or products that are in an incremental or maintenance mode. If you can release after each finished story, and the customers (and the stakeholders) are happy with this, just leave it like that.

From my experience of more than 530 projects, there are reasons why there will always be *major releases* (formerly known as projects). First, to come into this incremental mode, you must have a product to start with. You must have this minimum saleable feature set and this is typically not done in the first sprint—you need several sprints to get there.

Second, after having this minimal product, you have to decide how to make money with it. Small increments are not saleable without annoying the customer. To really get the focus of a customer, you have to have a release with some extraordinary new features. And, to build them, you need more than one sprint; you need a major release.

How to start? Sit down together with the Product Owner and the stakeholders and define this major release. Define the name, write down the story for the customer, identify the use value, and list the features. The result is a named release with a feature list, adjusted with the stakeholders. If you have difficulties doing this, you have a real problem—one that can't be solved with Scrum, Kanban, classic project management or even Reliable

Scrum. In this case, you're missing a business strategy or a creative idea, and you should focus on that first.

Complete THE BACKLOG

You now have the feature list of this major release and, typically, you have some kind of a backlog, too. In your current backlog there might be stories which don't belong to this release. So the best procedure is to tag only the stories that belong to this release, and leave the other stories as they are.

If there are stories which are partly needed for the release, break them apart. If there are stories missing that are needed to build the features, add them. Also add conceptual, research, or refactoring stories as needed. The result is a more or less complete list of stories necessary for this release. The meaning of *complete* means *best effort*. This should not be a way back to Waterfall; it's not finally defining all requirements in detail. However, it's important to reduce the risk in the backlog. If just a few stories are missing, not estimated, or estimated with more than 100 story points, that's okay, as long as it's not *too* many. A good indicator is that approximately 90% of the stories are estimated below, or equal to, twice the mean size of all stories.

The result is a workable backlog with an effort estimated in story points. Normally, you can't reach this clarity before the first sprint. Therefore, all the steps need to be done in parallel with the normal set up of a Scrum team. But after two or three sprints, it should be possible to define a complete backlog, otherwise, as suggested in Step 1, you have bigger problems that need to be addressed first.

Maybe you've seen that there is no usage of the MoSCoW[1] scheme anymore in Reliable Scrum. In practice, this scheme has proved futile because everybody understands the meaning a little differently, even if it is defined clearly. For Reliable Scrum it is not necessary any more. Stories are part of a release or not—in or out.

The common way in Scrum to protect (*buffer*) the due date with optional stories in practice is very problematic. The stakeholders just hear, "I'll get feature X, Y, and at the due date Z". They understand optional stories as, "I'll probably get it!"—and if not, they are definitely disappointed. This ambiguity leads to disappointment on both sides. This can be avoided with Reliable Scrum and buffering over time—not by descoping should-haves and could-haves.

BALANCE RESOURCES, BACKLOG, AND DUE DATE

The most important part and essential precondition for reliability is the realistic due date, the realistic amount of backlog, and the correct amount of resources. In the end, all three factors must be balanced to have a realistic chance of success, to fulfill the expectations, and deliver the release on time, within scope, and on budget.

But how can you establish reliability? Of course there are a lot of problems associated with this. We don't know the correct amount of work to be done, the estimations are often wrong, and the number of stories in the backlog are not fixed (remember, it's Agile). And on the other hand, we have deviations in the velocity. Sometimes everything goes well, but sometimes people leave or join the team and suddenly group dynamics affect the team's velocity. There are vacations and sometimes illnesses, too. That's life. That's normal. We have to take this all in stride.

The solution is just around the corner. There are a few tricks that help us to achieve the goal. (Note: there is never absolute certainty—even with Reliable Scrum you won't reach 100%.) One trick is already done—aggregating a few sprints together into one release. If something goes wrong in one sprint, it can be repaired in the next. If you aggregate uncertainty, you get more certainty. If you have more than four sprints in the release, it should work pretty well, in practice.

The second trick is to make the probability of success transparent, and (in collaboration with the stakeholders) improve this probability to a realistic value. To do so, all we need are some estimations and mathematics. First, we need an estimate of the amount of work to be done. This is simply the backlog of the release with its story point estimates. This is a base from which to start. But estimations are never one point value—they are probability curves with best-case, realistic-case, and pessimistic-case estimates (see Figure 23.1).

For the amount of work to be done, it should go as follows: The current estimated story points in the release backlog are the best-case estimations (I've never seen a project that needed less than estimated in the first round—it's called Parkinson's Law). The other two values we get by team estimation. The team gets together with the Product Owner and estimates how many more story points they expect in a realistic and in a pessimistic case. This is a mutual-agreement deal and, therefore, the Product Owner, as representative of the stakeholders, has to participate, understand, and agree upon these estimations.

The other factor in the game is the velocity. Typically, the team has done some sprints and therefore knows a little bit about their velocity. The average of the real velocity is a good value for the realistic case. The best and the pessimistic cases are again estimated by the team (see Figure 23.2)—this time, done together with the Scrum Master. They are responsible for their velocity; no Product Owner can argue about this. The only thing the Product Owner can do is to invest more money to add more resources, or even more Scrum teams. The deviation out of the last sprints can be a good indicator for this estimation, but the team has to keep in mind the whole release with all the fluctuations, holidays, illnesses, and ups and downs. The past is not a valid way to predict the future.

The rest is easy. On these two probability functions, the convolution operator can be applied and, as a result, you get the relative probability of success over time. Now you just

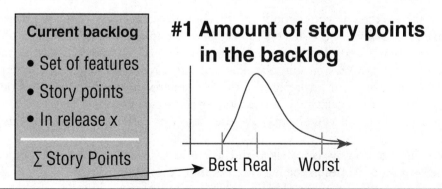

Figure 23.1   Typical relative probability distribution for a backlog

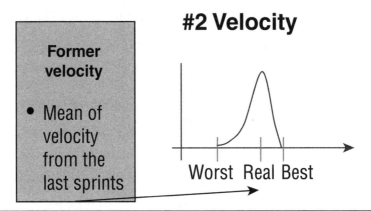

Figure 23.2   Typical relative probability distribution for the velocity

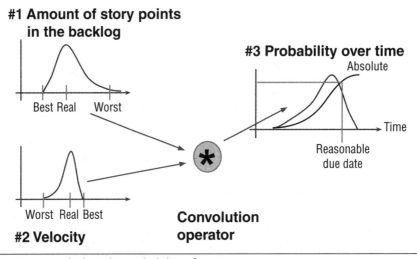

Figure 23.3   How to calculate the probability of success

have to integrate the curve and you'll get the absolute probability of success over time, or a reasonable idea of what the success can be, as shown in Figure 23.3.

From experience and many projects, we know that 100% probability is far too much and too expensive; 80% is absolutely okay and has a realistic chance of success. By the way, 80% is the upper turnover point of the S-curve in Figure 23.4. After this point, you won't get much more certainty, but far longer release durations. Longer durations lead to too much buffer, and you always have the danger of Parkinson's Law and the Student Syndrome.

All you have to do now is to talk with the Product Owner and the stakeholders to re-duce the amount of stories in the backlog, get more resources (hopefully higher velocity), or adjust the due date (number of sprints). That's the real work, but very healthy.

Another tip—when it comes to how to talk with stakeholders about probability of suc-cess—it's not possible, just forget it!

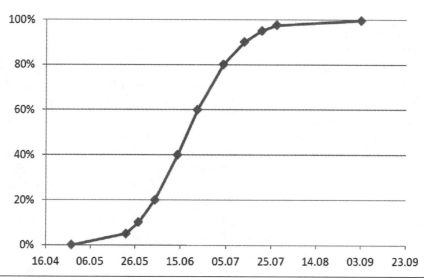

Figure 23.4   Example of a probability of success

The easiest way to avoid this issue is to reduce the stories in the backlog for the release until you reach the 80% absolute probability of success. Then go to the stakeholders and state, "That's it. That is what you'll get within the given time and given resources." Of course, on the other hand, you have an Excel spreadsheet in which you can add more features (stories) and calculate new due dates. If the stakeholders ask for more, you can tell them the correct due dates immediately. You're not blocking; you're just telling them the truth. Thus, it's easy to negotiate with them for a valid backlog, due date, and velocity combination.

The result is a balanced backlog, velocity, and due date, and a realistic probability of success for the team and the release. While it might seem overwhelming, all these calculations can easily be handled with a spreadsheet.[2]

EXECUTION CONTROL

The hard work is already done. Now it's time to harvest the results. Project management, and even Scrum, are all about trust. In the end, the stakeholders stay accountable for the results. They delegate some responsibility to (a) the Product Owner—he has to define the correct stories to build a good product, (b) the Scrum Master—he has to make sure that the team performs, and (c) the team—they have to deliver.

Responsibility always comes with some reporting; those responsible have to be able to respond (I love this definition), and if they can't give a correct, clear, and objective status, their trust is diminished. As a result, micromanagement may occur and the team is disrupted in their work, with corresponding negative side effects.

The Scrum proponents will now say, "We are absolutely transparent. We have the product burn-down chart." Yes, that's right—the product burn-down chart is a useful status report. But what is the message? The stakeholders will get an overview after each sprint whether the burn down follows an ideal linear curve or not.

But, if the customer has a due date in his mind (and she always does, otherwise the product would be of no interest to the customer), there are just two messages: (a) the burn down is higher than expected—perfect, (b) the burn down is lower than expected—the project is lost. There is simply a success or a failure; nothing in between. And the customer always has in the back of his mind that the backlog can change every time, and a project can fail in any sprint. This creates no confidence and you lose trust.

Sometimes you'll see a corridor of three ideal burn-down lines; that does not help either. What's the meaning of +/−10%? Is 10% right? No one knows, thus there is no gain in trust. What is the alternative? If we do the exercise of finding the correct amount of work or a realistic due date, we find something very important—we get some buffer at the end of the release. We estimate some buffer in the backlog and some in the velocity.

If we change the burn-down chart a little, and add the now-fixed due date in the product burn-down chart (see Figure 23.5), we will see the remaining buffer. If you look closely, you'll see that the burn-down chart changed dramatically. There is no ideal linear burn-down line any more. Now it's a real forecast. You just take the last known size of the burn down, use an estimated velocity for the rest of the release, and forecast an estimated time of completion.

Sometimes you'll find a diagram called an *enhanced burn-down chart* with two forecasts—one for the burn down and one for the increase of the backlog (burn up). This can be used perfectly in the same way. You just have to enhance it by the due date, progress, and buffer. And if you want to enhance it one more time, you have to use estimated burndown and burn-up lines, and do not use the calculated ones. But it works perfectly fine with the classical burn-down or, nowadays, burn-up charts.

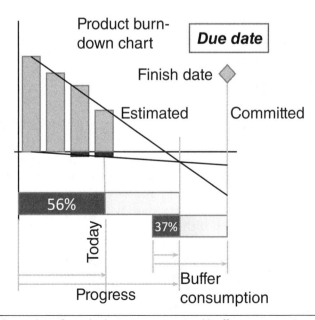

Figure 23.5 Burn-down chart for calculating progress and buffer consumption

Just take a look at this example. After two sprints we have some real burn down and an estimated time of finishing (where the estimated burn-down line and the x-axis cross). That is what is left from the buffer. Why is this not the whole buffer anymore? To explain this you have to think about different situations. The goal is to get an objective, really good project status to gain the trust of the stakeholders. Therefore, you have to answer the question as to whether the project is green (on track), red (critical), or yellow (getting in danger). With the buffer you have an extremely good indicator.

What do you think? If the progress in the release is less than the buffer consumption, is it good or bad? Bad, of course—it's red. If there is some buffer left, it is possible to reach the due date, but it is critical. If you have no buffer at all, it's really bad—because you have no chance to win anymore—the color is black (a new, but meaningful color in status reporting).

If the progress in the release is more than the buffer consumption, is this good or bad? Yes, of course it's good—the color is green. So the best case would be if the progress is something near the buffer consumption. Each release starts with a progress and buffer consumption of 0% and ends, hopefully, with progress of 100%. At the end, buffer consumption can be 100%, which would be okay. It is better to have some days left to deal with surprises at the very end of a project, so 90% is normally a good choice. With this in mind, you understand that after two sprints and the shown burn down, the progress is something around 30% and, thus, the buffer consumption should be nearly the same.

But how big should the buffer be in the beginning? There is no absolute number, just some rules of thumb. If you set the buffer to 0% of the lead time (duration between start and due date), then this monitoring doesn't work—that's clear. If you set the buffer to a very high value (e.g. 50%), then everybody knows there is a lot of buffer, so the Student Syndrome and Parkinson's Law will kick in. Because of such a big buffer, it will take a long time, and lots of problems will occur until the red flag is raised. So the solution should be something in between. In practice, (out of thousands of Critical Chain projects) the value of 30% was found very suitable. Thirty percent is enough buffer to cope with *Murphy's Law* and agility, so you can react quickly if something goes wrong. For agile releases, I prefer something near 20% because, if the teams have already been working together for some time, a lot of the negative effects have already been removed and the big buffer is not needed any more. Putting all these ideas together, you'll get the following diagram, called a fever chart, as shown in Figure 23.6.

On the x-axis you'll see the progress, and on the y-axis, the buffer consumption. Each release starts in the lower left corner and ends in the upper right. The perfect release will always stay at the border between yellow and green. Each point is the end of a sprint (or any reporting time in between), which is pretty easy to follow (even for stakeholders). The result is an objective, easy-to-understand release status.

Progress and buffer consumption are calculated as shown in the product burn-down chart, and charted over time in the fever chart. With just a little more input data (such as the start date for the release, start date for the buffer, and, of course, the due date of the release), you can easily program a spreadsheet to draw the fever chart.[3]

In the excel file, you will find a line for each measurement point to enter the burn-down data. It starts with Sprint 1—this is the amount of initial story points in the release backlog. After each sprint, one new line is added. In this example, the team had previously worked

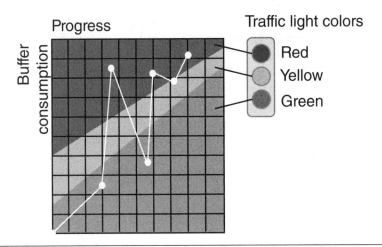

Figure 23.6   Example of a fever chart

a long time with Scrum when they applied Reliable Scrum. The result was that the velocity information stayed very stable.

After each sprint the remaining amount of story points are entered in the column backlog. Out of this information the sheet calculates a velocity (linear regression), but it's just a hint. More important is the estimated velocity for the rest of the release. This is provided by the team and the Scrum Master. In this case, the calculated and the estimated velocity are equal—an unusual case.

Now the sheet calculates the estimated time of completion, the progress, and the buffer consumption, and shows this as a fever chart. In this case, because of the small buffer, the release is in the red zone, but with a clear tendency to the yellow and green. The team recovers buffer. That's it—that's Reliable Scrum.

RELIABLE SCRUM, THE HERO FOR PRODUCT OWNERS

In the first project steered with Reliable Scrum, I expected that the teams would appreciate the fever chart most. But for them it wasn't the *most important feature*; instead, they concentrated on the flow—and that's all. But the Product Owners are the ones who really loved it. It's the first time they had a working tool in their hands to fulfill their responsibilities and accountabilities.

In a healthy, innovative, and growing company there are always more opportunities around than resources available. The stakeholders are the ones who see those opportunities. Those chances are valuable for the company. So the Product Owner faces many stakeholders with many ideas all the time—demanding more and more features. Actually, that's great for the company, but how can a Product Owner handle this? If he says, "No chance, the backlog is full!" then he is called a blocker or against innovation. If he says, "Yes, no problem, we will manage to deliver this feature additionally!" then he knows that he and the team may not succeed. He is trapped in this situation.

With the fever chart, it is a lot easier for him. If the release is in the red zone, the team is currently in the buffer recovery mode. In this case, it's absolutely clear for all stakeholders that each additional feature will make the situation worse. They will immediately know that a new feature can only be done when another feature is removed from the backlog. If there is a group of stakeholders, it's even easier. The one who wants the new feature has to deal with the other stakeholders about the trade-offs. This situation has some good attributes—with each trade-off decision, the remaining features will be more valuable. That means, automatically, that the value of the release increases, too. As long as the release doesn't go deeper into red, everything is fine for the team.

On the other hand, if the development of the release continues for a long time within the green status, the Product Owner is allowed to pull in the due date or pull in some more stories (features). Everything is allowed while the fever chart stays in the green. He can simulate the effect of pulling in the due date or features with the fever chart. This can be ideally done in collaboration with the stakeholders. As long as they stay in the green, the chance of success remains good. The Product Owner now has a tool that can be used to negotiate with the stakeholders without disturbing the team, so it's a win-win situation:

- The stakeholders get immediate feedback on what is possible. They gain trust in the team and the Product Owner. They understand and will take part in protecting the team and the release.
- The team's work is undisturbed. As long as the curve on the fever chart stays green, they can continue working while negotiations continue in parallel to their work.
- The Product Owners get an easy-to-use tool to fulfill their responsibilities and accountabilities—they will love it.

And as a result, the probability of success is preserved and the WIP stays under control.

THE PORTFOLIO OVERVIEW

With a hyper-productive team of four to seven developers you can achieve a lot, but if you want to do larger projects, you need more developers—you simply can't do it with just one team.

By the way, Reliable Scrum has an interesting side effect. Due to clarification of the project goal and the well-defined backlog, you can enlarge the team. My experience shows that it is possible to go up to 15 people at two locations without any problems. I really believe that it is possible to extend that even further.

But even then, there will be some point at which you'll have more than one team working on a project. At that time, you will need an information radiator or dashboard status of some sort about all streams at once. Have you ever looked at a wall of burn-down charts? Without some type of information radiator, it's very difficult to identify which stream is okay, or which stream needs your focus.

If you have a set of fever charts, it's already much better, and it can be improved even more. If you put the last status of each stream as a dot with the name of the stream in the same diagram as shown in Figure 23.7, you'll get a perfect overview in a single glance. If you want, you can even show the status before, with an arrow to show the tendency—then it's perfect. If possible, you can write below the chart the reason for the changes. You'll get the most effective status overview for the stakeholders, and again, this will lead to an enormous gain of trust.

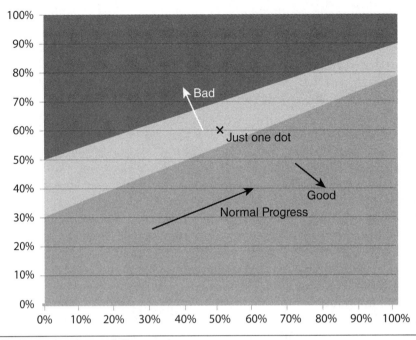

Figure 23.7 Example of a portfolio overview

REFERENCES

1. The MoSCoW scheme to prioritize requirements (see http://en.wikipedia.org/wiki/
   MoSCoW_method).
2. An example of such a spreadsheet can be found in the Web Added Value (WAV)™ section of J. Ross Publishing's website at http://www.jrosspub.com/wav. The spreadsheet is
   continuously being used and improved by the authors, and you can find the latest version at http://www.reliable-scrum.info/downloads.html. The spreadsheet provides the
   functionality to balance the workload and due date. All you have to do is to fill in a few
   input cells, and you will see the result in other cells. The result is given as either a probability of success or a reasonable due date. The amount of work in process is adjusted to
   the given velocity and due date. Doing this is always difficult, but it is absolutely necessary for success, and helps the team in many ways.
3. The spreadsheet is available in the Web Added Value (WAV)™ section of J. Ross Publishing's website at http://www.jrosspub.com/wav and at http://www.reliable-scrum
   .info/downloads.html.

24

FROM RELIABLE TO
TAMEFLOW-SCRUM

After implementing Reliable Scrum, the situation should be much better. The work in process (WIP) is under control, the scope is much clearer, the team has a realistic probability for success and the Product Owner has a tool to talk to the stakeholders. Everything is fine.

Really? Or might there be one more step to go? No problem. Self-organization will find the optimum. But if the team doesn't know where the optimum is, there will be no need to improve. The team doesn't know whether they are heading toward the optimum, or how fast they are improving. Self-organization is the most powerful tool we have, but it needs a clear direction. TameFlow-Scrum is all about the optimum, and how to reach it as fast as possible. Thus, sometimes you'll find it under the label *Ultimate Scrum*.

THE OPTIMUM

One interesting side effect of an optimum is that it must be easy to describe. If you reach the optimum, all the complicated side terms of the equation are set to zero. One sentence is enough to describe the optimum in hyper-productivity: *You have reached the optimum when there are less tasks open than the number of developers on the teams!*

It's so simple and easy to explain. In software development, the following example is typical. One software developer starts programming (working on a task). After finishing, he asks another developer for a review. While reviewing, both the developer and the reviewer are working on the same task. If the review takes approximately 20% of the time, and you have ten developers, the equivalent is that eight are programming and two are reviewing. So the optimal number of open tasks is eight, which obviously, is less than ten.

But is that the optimum? If you are doing pair programming, it should be even less—the number of open tasks should only be half of the number of developers. And it makes no sense to go even further—no one can imagine three developers at one computer to develop.

Thus, it's easy to define the optimum. If you've chosen to use pair programming, the optimum for open tasks is 50% of the number of developers. If you just do pair reviewing with 20% review time, then it is 80% of the number of developers, but never more. How many open tasks compared to the number of developers do you have? Perhaps you'll say that doesn't matter because the throughput of the team is independent of the amount of open tasks. Yes, you are right, but to concentrate on as few open tasks as possible has some advantages.

According to Little's Law (see Figure 24.1), the lead time of tasks in the system is proportional to the inventory of open tasks. The more open tasks you have, the longer the lead time, and the longer it will take to get customer feedback. If you really think agile, it's absolutely necessary to have prompt feedback.

But that's not the main argument. If you reduce the inventory of open tasks, something really interesting will happen. Taiichi Ōhno (the inventor of Lean Management) gave us one very enlightening metaphor. He said, "If you really want to reach smooth flow in a river, you have to reduce the amount of water to see all the rocks that hinder the flow and remove them."

It's the same with development teams. If you reduce the open tasks one by one, at some point you will encounter the first developer with a blocked task—an impediment occurred. It is very valuable to remove this impediment exactly at the moment it occurs. That is the best way to improve the flow of all future tasks and, thereby, gain throughput.

But who removes this impediment? Fortunately, one of your developers has some capacity left over—he's the one with the impediment. If you reduce the number of open tasks, you'll be in the comfortable situation whereby every time an impediment occurs, a developer will be free to fix that issue. And, better yet, they learn to do it right away

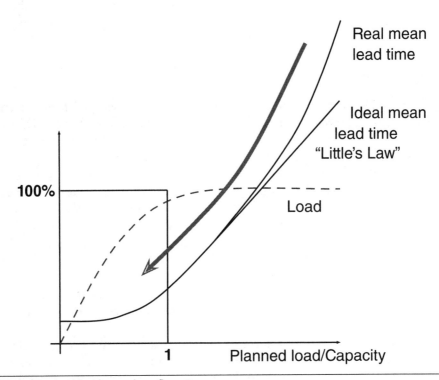

Figure 24.1 Optimal load to reduce flow time

without asking you—they start fixing the impediments as soon as possible, all by themselves. That is real self-organization.

HOW TO BRING TAMEFLOW-SCRUM TO LIFE?

The goal is clear: less open tasks than developers. The first step is to get rid of the unnatural breaks at the end of the sprints. Sprints are like batch sizes that elongate flow times and blow up inventory (remember that ideally you want to lose sprints altogether). Many things from Scrum will survive (most of it is very useful)—only the steering needs adjusted. It's good to have retrospectives—you have to have planning first, but that is already done in *Reliable Scrum*. Reviews make sense, too, but not in a defined repetition. Each time a story is finished, and after five to ten finished stories, it makes sense to show something to the stakeholders. There should be no discussion about half-finished stories anymore, but standups and definitions of *done* and *start* remain the same—they should happen as per standard Scrum.

So what has changed? There are no sprints anymore. It's all a continuous flow, with the goal to have as few stories and tasks open as possible. If you start with Kanban, the situation is a bit different. The open tasks are not piled up in sprints; instead they are piled up in the buffers before each stage of the process and in some of the blocked tasks. It's much easier to start because the only things you have to get rid of are the piled-up tasks. That can be done by changing the steering mechanism to TameFlow-Scrum (or TameFlow-Kanban as shown in Chapter 18). It's not entirely simple, and there is a bit more to it. You have to work on the upstream and downstream stages, too, so they won't be a problem in the future—but that's already part of the game.

DRUM-BUFFER-ROPE AS THE STEERING MECHANISM

In Scrum, the WIP is kept under control by the *time boxing mechanism*, in combination with the pull of the team. In Kanban, it is done explicitly by the WIP limits at each work-state. Both steering mechanisms have more tasks open simultaneously than absolutely necessary.

Assuming you remember the story of Herbie from Chapter 12 (shown in Figure 24.2), putting Herbie in front of the queue is the easy solution. But sometimes you can't change the order so you would have to do it in a more advanced way—this is called drum-buffer-rope (DBR) (Goldratt, 1992).

The Herbie metaphor can be transferred into a work flow shown in Figure 24.3. The DBR consists of three parts, as the name implies. There is a drum—this is the constrained resource—(in Figure 24.2, Herbie) in our case, the developers. The drum is like the heartbeat of the production chain. You need some buffer, normally in front of the drum, but if you have just one constrained stage, the inventory (amount of open tasks) can be considered as the buffer. And you need the rope, which is the mechanism that signals you to start a new task. This signal is triggered by the buffer. In this case, it's very easy; if one task has been finished a new task can be started.

In software development you often have to deal with two different levels of work: the stories and the tasks. In the end, the developers are focused on tasks—that is what they are working on. The developers are the constraint, and you need a buffer before them, which should always be filled. The process is divided into two independent parts. Part A consists

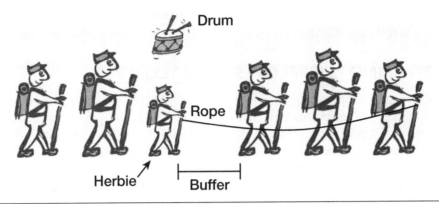

Figure 24.2   Another way to paint the Herbie metaphor

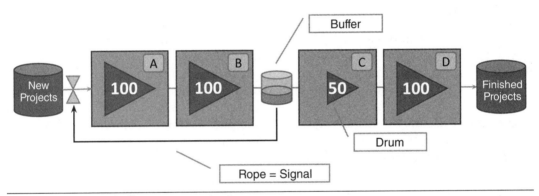

Figure 24.3   Drum-buffer-rope in production

of breaking down stories into tasks on the left side of the task buffer, and Part B consists of processing tasks to deliveries on the right side, as shown in Figure 24.4.

The steering on the left (story) side is easy. It usually takes less than ten minutes, and it should definitely not take longer than four hours for one person to break a story into tasks. This can also be done by the team, but it works just as well if one developer does this task, then presents the results to the team for a review.

So everything is steered by the amount of task in the tasks buffer (sometimes called planned tasks). If there are only two tasks left, one of the developers has to take the next story from the backlog and break it into tasks. It may be the case that waiting until the last two tasks is too risky—you can see that if a buffer hole occurs (no tasks left in the task buffer). If you see that phenomenon, increase the alarm threshold by one, until no buffer hole occurs. The alarm threshold should not exceed the number of developers divided by two.

Normally, it is not necessary to deal with alarm thresholds at all. In reality, finding the first task of a story is easy—it's most likely preparing something before development. For continuous flow in development, it's necessary to have one task left over. This task can be found within minutes. As a result, it is often okay to set the threshold to zero. In the moment no task is left, you can open the next story.

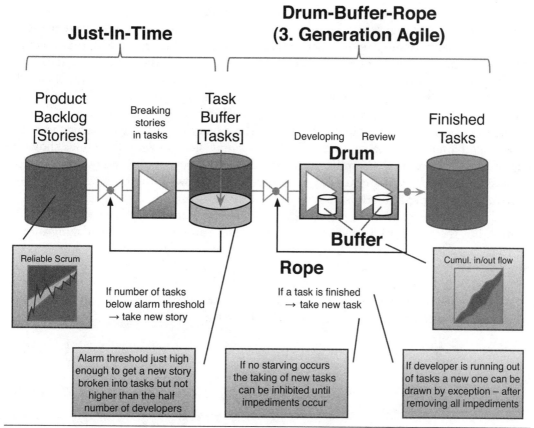

Figure 24.4   Drum-buffer-rope in Agile development

Management of a queue like this is often called *Vendor Managed Inventory* or *Just-In-Time Replenishment*. The vendor (backlog) looks at the stock before the production starts, and refills this autonomously. The golden rule about tasks applies here, too; as few as possible open stories—one or two are enough.

The best ways to monitor story burn down is by using the product burn-down chart and the fever chart (as shown in Reliable Scrum). These diagrams should be updated after a story is finished. This way you get real-time monitoring of the burn down (not just after each sprint). That's the reason why there are more data points in the fever chart.

And now to the right side—the management of the task flow. This is a second DBR steering. Well, this is not a classical DBR either. In a classical DBR you have, as in Kanban, more than one workstation. But if you have just one type of resource (e.g., flexible developers that can work at any workstation), then the situation is comparable to one stage. Of course there are additional people with different skills, up and downstream, involved in the work flow. If you accept that there is just one constraint (e.g., the developer), then all of the up and downstream stages must have protective capacity. This protective capacity enables the up and downstream stages to manage themselves in a way that subordinates perfectly to the constraint. In this moment they are not relevant for the work flow control any more.

Even if you have two stages for processing a task, such as development and review, it looks like one stage because it's the same constrained resource. Sometimes, developers are assisted by Quality Assurance members who write the tests, but in the end, the constraint is the developer. One constraint equals one stage. The drum is the constrained developer. The buffer is the inventory of open tasks in progress (development or review), and the rope is the signal from the buffer to release new tasks. In this case, every time a task is finished, a team member is allowed to open (start development of) a new task.

The right (task) side is monitored by an *aggregated input/output diagram* which is sometimes called a *flow diagram* or, better yet, a *cumulative flow diagram (CFD)*, as shown in Figure 24.5. The goal is to keep the inventory (difference between in and out lines) as low as possible. If you look at the CFD, you can see Little's Law in the marked area 2. There were more tasks open, thus, it is no wonder that the flow time doubled.

With the rule *one task finished, one new task opened*, you already keep the WIP under control. But the goal is to decrease it even more. This can be achieved by making sure no new tasks can be started until the first buffer hole occurs. If the first developer runs out of work, you have to increase the buffer by one. But this should be an exception, and has to be analyzed. Buffer holes are full of information about impediments or process problems. Finally, if everything has been done, and buffer holes still occur, you have to increase (slightly) the buffer/inventory to secure the throughput.

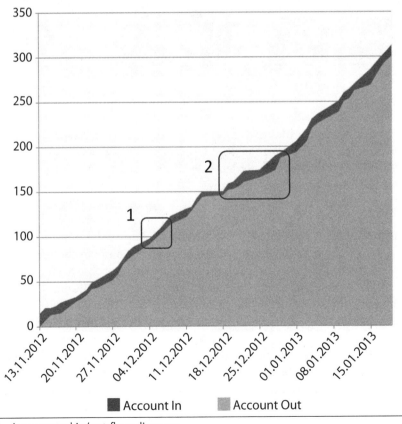

Figure 24.5　Aggregated in/out flow diagram

TameFlow-Scrum, in its deep core, is a DBR production steering method. DBR is often called a third generation production steering method. Henry Ford defined the first generation method where the WIP was controlled by the marked space on the floor before the production line (which has many similarities to time boxes). That was efficient, but inflexible. The second generation method was introduced by Taiichi Ōhno, and is called Kanban. Here, the WIP is limited explicitly by the WIP limits at each stage. This is much more flexible, but requires a lot of inventory and a steady flow. The third generation method was introduced by Eliyahu Goldratt. The WIP is controlled by the constraint, and the start of new work is signaled over the upstream flow time—the DBR method.

DBR is known for the lowest possible inventory (open tasks), therefore the best possible flow time and, on top of that, the maximum throughput. That's why it is considered as the new way of controlling the WIP in Agile environments, and earned the prefix *ultimate*. In the end, all production control systems have the same systemic foundation, and if you optimize them, they all have to convert to the same DBR—the optimum.

So that's it. Now you have:

- Continuous flow,
- With the least possible open tasks,
- And the shortest possible flow time and lead time,
- And the best possible throughput.

That's the basis for empowering people.

25

FROM PRODUCTION
TO PROJECTS

Throughout this book we have been talking about working in small teams, but sometimes that is not enough. If you want to achieve something really great, while having to work with many external partners, then you are in the project world, or even in the multi-project world. Here you have to play according to other rules. You have to deal with dependencies and deviations in your estimations. This is much more complex than working with *just* a team.

But there is hope. It is possible to use all the ideas of hyper-productivity. You just have to do a little bit more when it comes to managing projects.

CRITICAL CHAIN

Critical Chain is the same as Reliable/TameFlow-Scrum, but for projects. Projects are more complex, they have lots of dependencies, the flow time is near the lead time, and deviations in the durations are far more critical. You have to actively manage these by inserting buffers at appropriate places—before the integration point and at the end of feeding chains. These buffers do not prolong the project, they come out of the estimations of the story estimates themselves.

Critical Chain is not just single project management, it's also portfolio or multi-project management. The approach is the same: identify the constraint team (or virtual skill), stagger all projects according to the constraint, and calculate the start and due dates. This ensures that the whole development system is optimally loaded (but not overloaded)—nothing else than work in process is under control. By the way, this is also a drum-buffer-rope steering.

The core element of Critical Chain is, once again, the fever chart. It is calculated similarly to Reliable Scrum. It's the progress over time on the critical chain (the longest chain of depending work packages, under consideration of the available resources) and, of course, the buffer consumption. To get this data, you normally estimate the remaining duration for each open work package every day, calculate the position in the fever chart, and you'll get the traffic light status automatically.

What makes Critical Chain so powerful is that the resources are focused according to the traffic light status over the whole portfolio of projects. The project with the least progress on the critical chain and most buffer consumption gets all the focus and all the resources because it needs to get back into the yellow zone and, eventually, into the green zone.

The objective of the overall closed loop corrective action of Critical Chain is to keep the amount of red projects below 10%. If you achieve this, then you did the work in process control (the staggering) correctly. If you additionally use the operational priority to distribute the resources according to the traffic light, you can be sure that the due dates will be met with approximately 90% assurance. Both corrective actions lead to high reliability.

Because you control the system focusing on the red projects (around 10%), there is always a driver toward shortening the lead time. To get resources, the project manager would be interested in having projects in the yellow, or sometimes in the red zone. Therefore, he has an intrinsic interest in reducing the lead times of his project. As an additional benefit, you'll obtain information about which team uses more than the typical consumed buffer. This team is seldom the root cause of the delays, but is still a good starting point when looking for problems, and when starting a continuous improvement process.

AGILE ENTERPRISE

If you put all these things together you'll get a blueprint of a lean, agile, flow-oriented, but also reliable product development organization, as shown in Figure 25.1.

On the upper level you have Critical Chain as your multi-project management, ensuring that the due dates are reliable and the work in process is under control. If you look more deeply, you'll recognize that a product development organization is similar to the actual production of a product, and is steered in the same way. The staggering at the constraint is no different than a production planning system of the third generation—drum-buffer-rope steering.

On the level below multi-project management are the single projects. These are more complex. You have to take care of the dependencies and handle the deviations. Here you can use Critical Chain to get them stable and reliable. This is real project management.

If you look another level lower, you'll see, perhaps, some sub-projects (or even some smaller projects) that have very few external dependencies that can be broken down into small tasks. For these parts of projects, full-fledged project management is far too much overhead. It looks more like a production again. Yes, all the agile methods are in the core production steering methods. That's not bad, that's good, because production steering is much easier and more lightweight than projects. You can use drum-buffer-rope (Reliable and TameFlow-Scrum).

That's the blueprint of an optimal development organization. Based on the level and complexity, you have the appropriate steering method at your disposal, and consequently, you'll get the optimal throughput, minimum lead time, and most motivated employees.

PEOPLE BUSINESS

That was just the beginning. Now that you have optimized the development process and some of the supporting processes, you will have even more free capacity. But, what will

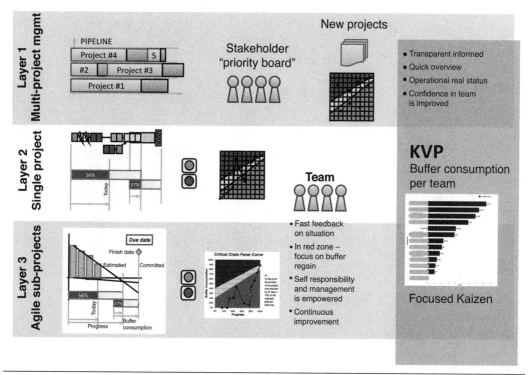

Figure 25.1   Critical Chain and Advanced Agile integrated into one framework

you do with this free capacity? You can use the newly gained capacity and ability to invest in people, in your vision, and in all the other necessary ideas to finally gain hyper-productivity.

APPENDIX A

Note: This Appendix A is reproduced on the basis of the GNU General Public License, as published by the Free Software Foundation, and is considered as source code. In respect to the entirety of this book, the GNU GPL covers exclusively the text of this Appendix A, while the remainder of the book, which is not source code but ordinary text, is covered by the Copyright of the authors (Steve Tendon and Wolfram Müller) and the publisher (J. Ross Publishing).

The original text of these Core Protocols as of the November 19, 2014, was retrieved online at *http://www.mccarthyshow.com/online/*.

THE CORE PROTOCOLS V.3.03

(The Core is distributed under the terms of the GNU-PL. For exact terms see http://www .gnu.org/licenses/gpl.txt. The Core is considered as source code under that agreement. You are free to use and distribute this work or any derivations you care to make, provided you also distribute this source document in its entirety, including this paragraph.)

The following Core Protocols are made up of both commitments and protocols.

The Core Commitments

1. I commit to engage when present.
    (a) To know and disclose
        i.   what I want,
        ii. what I think, and
        iii. what I feel.
    (b) To always seek effective help.
    (c) To decline to offer and refuse to accept incoherent emotional transmissions.
    (d) When I have or hear a better idea than the currently prevailing idea, I will immediately either
        i. propose it for decisive acceptance or rejection, and/or
        ii. explicitly seek its improvement.
    (e) I will personally support the best idea
        i.   regardless of its source,
        ii. however much I hope an even better idea may later arise, and
        iii. when I have no superior alternative idea.
2. I will seek to perceive more than I seek to be perceived.
3. I will use teams, especially when undertaking difficult tasks.
4. I will speak always and only when I believe it will improve the general results/effort ratio.

5. I will offer and accept only rational, results-oriented behavior and communication.
6. I will disengage from less productive situations
    (a) When I cannot keep these commitments,
    (b) When it is more important that I engage elsewhere.
7. I will do now what must be done eventually and can effectively be done now.
8. I will seek to move forward toward a particular goal, by biasing my behavior toward action.
9. I will use the Core Protocols (or better) when applicable.
    (a) I will offer and accept timely and proper use of the Protocol Check protocol without prejudice.
10. I will neither harm - nor tolerate the harming of - anyone for his or her fidelity to these commitments.
11. I will never do anything dumb on purpose.

The Core Protocols

Pass (Unpass)

The Pass protocol is how you decline to participate in something. Use it anytime you don't want to participate in an activity.

Steps

1. When you've decided not to participate, say "I pass."
2. Unpass any time you desire. Unpass as soon as you know you want to participate again by saying "I unpass."

Commitments

- Hold reasons for passing private.
- Pass on something as soon as you are aware you are going to pass.
- Respect the right of others to pass without explanation.
- Support those who pass by not discussing them or their pass.
- Do not judge, shame, hassle, interrogate or punish anyone who passes.

Notes

- In general, you will not be in good standing with your Core Commitments if you pass most of the time.
- You can pass on any activity; however, if you have adopted the Core Commitments, you cannot
- pass on a Decider vote and you must say "I'm in" when checking in.
- You can pass even though you have already started something.

Check In

Use Check In to begin meetings or anytime an individual or group Check In would add more value to the current team interactions.

Steps

1. Speaker says "I feel [one or more of MAD, SAD, GLAD, AFRAID]." Speaker may provide a brief explanation. Or if others have already checked in, the speaker may say "I pass." (See the Pass protocol.)
2. Speaker says "I'm in." This signifies that Speaker intends to behave according to the Core Commitments.
3. Listeners respond, "Welcome."

Commitments

- State feelings without qualification.
- State feelings only as they pertain to yourself.
- Be silent during another's Check In.
- Do not refer to another's Check In disclosures without explicitly granted permission from him or her.

Notes

- In the context of the Core Protocols, all emotions are expressed through combinations of MAD, SAD, GLAD, or AFRAID. For example, "excited" may be a combination of GLAD and AFRAID.
- Check In as deeply as possible. Checking in with two or more emotions is the norm. The depth of a group's Check In translates directly to the quality of the group's results.
- Do not do anything to diminish your emotional state. Do not describe yourself as a "little" mad, sad, glad, or afraid or say "I'm mad, but I'm still glad."
- Except in large groups, if more than one person checks in, it is recommended that all do so.
- HAPPY may be substituted for GLAD, and SCARED may be substituted for AFRAID.

Check Out

Check Out requires that your physical presence always signifies your engagement. You must Check Out when you are aware that you cannot maintain the Core Commitments or whenever it would be better for you to be elsewhere.

Steps

1. Say "I'm checking out."
2. Physically leave the group until you're ready to Check In once again.
3. Optionally, if it is known and relevant, you can say when you believe you'll return.
4. Those who are present for the Check Out may not follow the person, talk to or about the person checking out or otherwise chase him or her.

Commitments

- Return as soon as you can and are able to keep the Core Commitments.
- Return and Check In without unduly calling attention to your return.
- Do not judge, shame, hassle, interrogate, or punish anyone who checks out.

Notes

- When you Check Out do it as calmly and gracefully as possible so as to cause minimal disruption to others.
- Check Out if your emotional state is hindering your success, if your receptivity to new information is too low, or if you do not know what you want.
- Check Out is an admission that you are unable to contribute at the present time.

Ask For Help

The Ask For Help protocol allows you to efficiently make use of the skills and knowledge of others. Ask For Help is the act that catalyzes connection and shared vision. Use it continuously, before and during the pursuit of any result.

Steps

1. Asker inquires of another, "[Helper's name], will you X?"
2. Asker expresses any specifics or restrictions of the request.
3. Helper responds by saying "Yes" or "No" or by offering an alternative form of help.

Commitments

- Always invoke the Ask For Help Protocol with the phrase "Will you . . .
- Have a clear understanding of what you want from the Helper or if you do not have a clear understanding of what help you want, signal this by saying "I'm not sure what I need help with, but will you help me?"
- Assume that all Helpers are always available and trust that any Helper accepts the responsibility to say "No."
- Say "No" any time you do not want to help.
- Accept the answer "No" without any inquiry or emotional drama.
- Be receptive of the help offered.
- Offer your best help even if it is not what the asker is expecting.
- Postpone the help request if you are unable to fully engage.
- Request more information if you are unclear about the specifics of the help request.
- Do not apologize for asking for help.

Notes

- Asking for help is a low-cost undertaking. The worst possible outcome is a "No," which leaves you no further ahead or behind than when you asked. In the best possible outcome, you reduce the amount of time required to achieve a task and/or learn.
- Helpers should say "No" if they are not sure if they want to help. They should say nothing else after turning down a request for help.
- You cannot "over-ask" a given person for help unless he or she has asked you to respect a particular limit.
- If you don't understand the value of what is offered, or feel that it wouldn't be useful, or believe yourself to have considered and rejected the idea offered previously, assume a curious stance instead of executing a knee-jerk "But . . ." rejection. (See the Investigate protocol.)

- Asking in time of trouble means you waited too long to ask for help. Ask for help when you are doing well.
- Simply connecting with someone, even if he or she knows nothing of the subject you need help on can help you find answers within yourself, especially if you ask that person to Investigate you.

Protocol Check

Use Protocol Check when you believe a protocol is being used incorrectly in any way or when a Core Commitment is being broken.

Steps

1. Say "Protocol Check."
2. If you know the correct use of the protocol, state it. If you don't, ask for help.

Commitments

- Say "Protocol Check" as soon as you become aware of the incorrect use of a protocol, or of a broken Core Commitment. Do this regardless of the current activity.
- Be supportive of anyone using Protocol Check.
- Do not shame or punish anyone using Protocol Check.
- Ask for help as soon as you realize you are unsure of the correct protocol use.

Intention Check

Use Intention Check to clarify the purpose of your own or another's behavior. Use it when you aren't expecting a positive outcome resulting from the current behavior. Intention Check assesses the integrity of your own and another's intention in a given case.

Steps

1. Ask "What is your/my intention with X?" where X equals some type of actual or pending behavior to the person whose intention you want to know.
2. If it would be helpful, ask "What response or behavior did you want from whom as a result of X?"

Commitments

- Be aware of your own intention before checking the intention of another.
- Investigate sufficiently to uncover the intention of the person or his actions.
- Make sure you have the intention to resolve any possible conflict peacefully before intention checking someone else. If you do not have a peaceful intention, Check Out.
- Do not be defensive when someone asks you what your intention is. If you can't do this, Check Out.

Notes

- If conflict arises that seems irresolvable, Check Out and Ask For Help.

Decider

Use Decider anytime you want to move a group immediately and unanimously towards results.

Steps

1. Proposer says "I propose [concise, actionable behavior]."
2. Proposer says "1-2-3."
3. Voters, using either Yes (thumbs up), No (thumbs down), or Support-it (flat hand), vote simultaneously with other voters.
4. Voters who absolutely cannot get in on the proposal declare themselves by saying "I am an absolute no. I won't get in." If this occurs, the proposal is withdrawn.
5. Proposer counts the votes.
6. Proposer withdraws the proposal if a combination of outliers (No votes) and Support-it votes is too great or if proposer expects not to successfully conclude Resolution (below). You can approximate "too great" by using the following heuristics:
   (a) approximately 50% (or greater) of votes are Support-it, OR
   (b) the anticipated gain if the proposal passes is less than the likely cost of Resolution effort
7. Proposer uses the Resolution protocol with each outlier to bring him or her in by asking, "What will it take to get you in?"
8. Proposer declares the proposal carried if all outliers change their votes to Yes or Support-it.
9. The team is now committed to the proposed result.

Commitments

- Propose no more than one item per proposal.
- Remain present until the Decider protocol is complete; always remain aware of how your behavior either moves the group forward or slows it down.
- Give your full attention to a proposal over and above all other activity.
- Speak only when you are the proposer or are directed to speak by the proposer.
- Keep the reasons you voted as you did to yourself during the protocol.
- Reveal immediately when you are an absolute no voter and be ready to propose a better idea.
- Be personally accountable for achieving the results of a Decider commitment even if it was made in your absence.
- Keep informed about Decider commitments made in your absence.
- Do not argue with an absolute no voter. Always ask him or her for a better idea.
- Actively support the decisions reached.
- Use your capacity to "stop the show" by declaring you "won't get in no matter what" with great discretion and as infrequently as possible.
- Insist at all times that the Decider and Resolution protocols be followed exactly as per specification, regardless of how many times you find yourself doing the insisting.
- Do not pass during a Decider.
- Unceasingly work toward forward momentum; have a bias toward action.
- Do not look at how others are voting to choose your own vote.

- Avoid using Decider in large groups. Break up into small subgroups to make decisions, and use the large group to report status.

Notes

- Vote No only when you really believe the contribution to forward momentum you will make to the group after slowing or stopping it in the current vote will greatly outweigh the (usually considerable) costs you are adding by voting No.
- If you are unsure or confused by a proposal, support it and seek clarification offline after the proposal is resolved. If you have an alternate proposal after receiving more information, you can have faith that your team will support the best idea. (See "The Core Commitments")
- Voting No to make minor improvements to an otherwise acceptable proposal slows momentum and should be avoided. Instead, offer an additional proposal after the current one passes or, better yet, involve yourself in the implementation to make sure your idea gets in.
- Withdraw weak proposals. If a proposal receives less than seventy percent (approximately) Yes votes, it is a weak proposal and should be withdrawn by the proposer. This decision is, however, at the discretion of the proposer.
- Think of yourself as a potential solo outlier every time you vote No.
- Vote Absolute No only when you are convinced you have a significant contribution to make to the direction or leadership of the group, or when integrity absolutely requires it of you.

Resolution

When a Decider vote yields a small minority of outliers, the proposer quickly leads the team, in a highly structured fashion, to deal with the outliers. The Resolution protocol promotes forward momentum by focusing on bringing outliers in at least cost.

Steps

1. Proposer asks outlier "What will it take to get you in?"
2. Outlier states in a single, short, declarative sentence the precise modification required to be in.
3. Proposer offers to adopt the outlier's changes or withdraws the proposal.

Notes

- If the outlier's changes are simple, a simple Eye Check is performed to determine if everyone is still in.
- If the outlier's changes are complex, the proposer must withdraw the current proposal and then submit a new proposal that incorporates the outlier's changes.
- If the outlier begins to say why he voted No or to explain anything other than what it will take to get him or her in, the proposer must interrupt the outlier with "What will it take to get you in?"

Perfection Game

The Perfection Game protocol will support you in your desire to aggregate the best ideas. Use it whenever you desire to improve something you've created.

Steps

1. Perfectee performs an act or presents an object for perfection, optionally saying "Begin" and "End" to notify the Perfector of the start and end of the performance.
2. Perfector rates the value of the performance or object on a scale of 1 to 10 based on how much value the Perfector believes he or she can add.
3. Perfector says "What I liked about the performance or object was X," and proceeds to list the qualities of the object the Perfector thought were of high quality or should be amplified.
4. Perfector offers the improvements to the performance or object required for it to be rated a 10 by saying "To make it a ten, you would have to do X."

Commitments

- Accept perfecting without argument.
- Give only positive comments: what you like and what it would take to "give it a 10."
- Abstain from mentioning what you don't like or being negative in other ways.
- Withhold points only if you can think of improvements.
- Use ratings that reflect a scale of improvement rather than a scale of how much you liked the object.
- If you cannot say something you liked about the object or specifically say how to make the object better, you must give it a 10.

Notes

- A rating of 10 means you are unable to add value, and a rating of 5 means you will specifically describe how to make the object at least twice as good.
- The important information to transmit in the Perfection Game protocol improves the performance or object. For example, "The ideal sound of a finger snap for me is one that is crisp, has sufficient volume, and startles me somewhat. To get a 10, you would have to increase your crispness."
- As a perfectee, you may only ask questions to clarify or gather more information for improvement. If you disagree with the ideas given to you, simply don't include them.

Personal Alignment

The Personal Alignment protocol helps you penetrate deeply into your desires and find what's blocking you from getting what you want. Use it to discover, articulate, and achieve what you want. The quality of your alignment will be equal to the quality of your results.

Steps

1. Want: Answer the question: "What specifically do I want?"

2. Block: Ask yourself, "What is blocking me from having what I want?"
3. Virtue: Figure out what would remove this block by asking yourself "What virtue—if I had it—would shatter this block of mine?"
4. Shift: Pretend the virtue you identified is actually what you want.
5. Again: Repeat steps 2 to 4 until this process consistently yields a virtue that is powerful enough to shatter your blocks and get you what you originally thought you wanted.
6. Done: Now write down a personal alignment statement in the form "I want [virtue]." For example, "I want courage."
7. Signal/Response/Assignment: Create a signal to let others know when you are practicing your alignment, and provide a response they can give you to demonstrate support. For example, "When I say/do 'X,' will you say/do 'Y'?" Optionally, turn it into an assignment by saying you will do X a certain number of times per day, where X equals an activity that requires you to practice living your alignment.
8. Evidence: Write, in specific and measurable terms, the long-term evidence of practicing this alignment.
9. Help: Ask each member of your group for help. They help by giving the response you would like when you give your signal that you are practicing your alignment.

Commitments

- Identify an alignment that will result in your personal change and require no change from any other person.
- Identify blocks and wants that are specific and personal.
- Identify blocks that, if solved, would radically increase your effectiveness in life, work, and play.
- Choose a virtue that is about you and preferably one word long. For example: integrity, passion, self-care, peace, fun.
- Ask for help from people who know you and/or know alignments.
- Identify evidence that is measurable by an objective third party.

Notes

- The most popular personal alignments are "I want (Integrity, Courage, Passion, Peace, Self-Awareness or Self-Care)".
- If you are struggling with figuring out what you want, adopt the alignment "I want self-awareness." There is no case where increased self-awareness would not be beneficial.
- A personal block is something you find within yourself. It does not refer to circumstances or other people. Assume that you could have had what you want by now, that your block is a myth that somehow deprives you of your full potential.
- Ideally, identify both immediate and long-term evidence of your alignment. Write down results that start now (or very soon), as well as results you'll see at least five or more years in the future.
- As a default signal, tell your teammates or others who are close to you that you are working on your alignment when you are practicing it. If they don't know the protocol, just tell them what virtue you are working on and ask for their help.

- When members of a team are completing their personal alignments together (asking each other for help), the final step of the process is most powerful if done as a ceremony.

Investigate

Investigate allows you to learn about a phenomenon that occurs in someone else. Use it when an idea or behavior someone is presenting seems poor, confusing, or simply interesting.

Steps

1. Act as if you were a detached but fascinated inquirer, asking questions until your curiosity is satisfied or you no longer want to ask questions.

Commitments

- Ask well-formed questions.
- Ask only questions that will increase your understanding.
- Ask questions only if the subject is engaged and appears ready to answer more.
- Refrain from offering opinions.
- Do not ask leading questions where you think you know how he or she will answer.
- If you cannot remain a detached, curious investigator with no agenda, stop using the protocol until you can come back to it and keep these commitments.

Notes

- Do not theorize about the subject or provide any sort of diagnosis.
- Consider using the following forms for your questions:
  ◊   What about X makes you Y Z?
  ◊   Would you explain a specific example?
  ◊   How does X go when it happens?
  ◊   What is the one thing you want most from solving X?
  ◊   What is the biggest problem you see regarding X now?
  ◊   What is the most important thing you could do right now to help you with X?
- Ineffective queries include the following:
  ◊   Questions that lead or reflect an agenda.
  ◊   Questions that attempt to hide an answer you believe is true.
  ◊   Questions that invite stories.
  ◊   Questions that begin with "Why."
- Stick to your intention of gathering more information.
- If you feel that you will explode if you can't say what's on your mind, you shouldn't speak at all. Consider checking your intention or Check Out

BIBLIOGRAPHY

Achouiantz, Chris (2013): *The Kanban Kick-start Field Guide, v1.1.* (online: http://leanagile projects.blogspot.com/2013/11/the-kanban-kick-start-field-guide-v11.html)

Ackerman, L. and Gonzalez, C. (2010): *Patterns-Based Engineering: Successfully Delivering Solutions via Patterns.* Boston, MA: Addison-Wesley.

Addison, T. and Vallab, S. (2002): "Controlling Software Project Risks: An Empirical Study of Methods Used by Experienced Project Managers. *Proceedings of the 2002 Annual Research Conference of the South African Institute of Computer Scientists and Information Technologists on Enablement Through Technology.* South African Institute for Computer Scientists and Information Technologists (SAICSIT 02).

Albers, A., Deigendesch, T., Turki, T., and Müller, T. (2009): "Design Patterns in Microtechnology." *Proceedings of the International Conference on Engineering Design*, ICED '09. Stanford University.

Alderfer, C. P. (2011): *The Practice of Organizational Diagnosis, Theory, and Methods.* New York: Oxford University Press.

Alexander, C. (1999): *Notes on the Synthesis of Form.* Reprint. New York: Oxford University Press.

Alexander, C. (April, 1965): "A City Is Not a Tree." *Architectural Forum* V122N1: 58-61 (Part 1) and (2): 58-62.

Alexander, C. (1977): *A Pattern Language: Towns, Buildings, Construction.* New York: Oxford University Press.

Alexander, C. (1979): *The Timeless Way of Building.* New York: Oxford University Press.

Alexander, C., et al. (1985). *The Production of Houses.* New York: Oxford University Press.

Alexander, C. (September/October, 1999). *The Origins of Pattern Theory, the Future of the Theory, and the Generation of a Living World.* IEEE Software. Transcript of Keynote Speech at OOPSLA '96.

Anderson, B. (April, 1993): "Workshop Report: Towards an Architecture Handbook." *OOPSLA Messenger* 4(2): 109-114.

Anderson, B., Coad, P., and Mayfield, M. (1994): Addendum to the Proceedings of OOPSLA '93. "Workshop Report: Patterns: Building Blocks for Object Oriented Architectures." *OOPSLA Messenger* 5(2): 107-109.

Anderson, D. J. (2003): *Agile Management for Software Engineering: Applying the Theory of Constraints for Business Results.* Upper Saddle River, NJ: Prentice Hall.

Anderson, D. J. (2008): "Why We Lost Focus on Development Practices" (Blog: http://www.djaa.com/why-we-lost-focus-development-practices).

Anderson, D. J. (2010): *Kanban: Successful Evolutionary Change for Your Technology Business.* Sequim, WA: Blue Hole Press.

Anderson, D. J. (2012): *Lessons in Agile Management: On the Road to Kanban.* Sequim, WA: Blue Hole Press.

Argyris, Chris. (1952): *The Impact of Budgets on People.* School of Business and Public Administration. Cornell University.

Argyris, Chris. (Sept., 1977): "Double Loop Learning in Organizations," *Harvard Business Review,* 115-124.

Argyris, Chris and Schön, Donald A. (1978): *Organizational Learning: A Theory of Action Perspective.* Addison-Wesley Series on Organization Development. Boston: Addison-Wesley.

Argyris, Chris. (May-June, 1991): "Teaching Smart People How to Learn," *Harvard Business Review,* 99-109.

Argyris, Chris. (1999): *On Organizational Learning.* 2nd ed. Oxford (UK): Wiley-Blackwell.

Austin, R. and Devin, L. (2003): *Artful Making: What Managers Need to Know About How Artists Work.* Upper Saddle River, NJ: FT Prentice Hall.

Babatunde, A. O. and Harmon, R. (1994): *Process Dynamics, Modeling, and Control.* New York: Oxford University Press.

Baetjer, H. (1998): *Software as Capital: An Economic Perspective on Software Engineering.* IEEE Computer Society Press.

Bartram, P. (August, 2006): "Forecasting the End of Budgets." *Director* 60(1): 30.

Beck, K. and Cunningham, W. (1987): "Using Pattern Languages for Object-Oriented Programs." *Proceedings of OOPSLA '87.* Orlando, Florida.

Beck, K. (Sept., 1991): "Think Like an Object." *Unix Review* V9N10:39-43.

Beck, K. and Johnson, R. (1994): *Patterns Generate Architectures.* Proceedings ECOOP 1994: 139-149. Berlin (DE): Springer-Verlag.

Beck, K., et al. (2001): *Manifesto for Agile Software Development.* (Online: http://agilemanifesto.org/)

Becker, S., Messner, M., and Schäffer, U. (2010): "The Evolution of a Management Accounting Idea: The Case of Beyond Budgeting." Institute of Management Accounting and Control (IMC) WHU, Otto Beisheim School of Management, Vallendar, Germany.

Beedle, M., et al. (2000): "SCRUM: An Extension Pattern Language for Hyperproductive Software Development" *Pattern Languages of Program Design 4,* N. Harrison, B. Foote, and H. Rohnert, eds., Addison-Wesley, 2000, pp. 637-651.

Benedict, R. (1934): *Patterns of Culture.* Boston: Houghton Mifflin Company.

Benkler, Y. (2006): *The Wealth of Networks: How Social Production Transforms Markets and Freedom.* Yale University Press.

Benkler, Y. (2011): *The Penguin and the Leviathan: How Cooperation Triumphs over Self-Interest.* New York: Crown Business.

Bennett, M., et al. (2007): "An Architectural Pattern for Goal-Based Control." *Proceedings of the IEEE Aerospace Conference,* Big Sky, MT.

Bergin, J. (2000): "Fourteen Pedagogical Patterns." *Proceedings of the 5th European Conference on Pattern Languages of Programs.* EuroPLoP, Irsee.

Boehm, B. W. (1981): *Software Engineering Economics.* Upper Saddle River, NJ: Prentice Hall.

Boehm, B. W. (1991): "Software Risk Management: Principles and Practices." *IEEE Software,* 8(1): 32-41.

Borchers, J. (2000): "A Pattern Approach to Interaction Design." In *Proceedings of the ACM DIS 2000 International Conference on Designing Interactive Systems.*

Borchers, J. (2001): *A Pattern Approach to Interaction Design*. Chichester, West Sussex (UK): John Wiley & Sons Ltd.

Boroditsky, L. (Feb., 2011): "How Language Shapes Thought: The Languages We Speak Affect Our Perceptions of the World." *Scientific American*, V304N2:43-45.

Brabham, D. C. (2008): "Crowdsourcing as a Model for Problem Solving Convergence." *The International Journal of Research into New Media Technologies*, 14:75-90.

Bragg, S. M. (2007): *Throughput Accounting: A Guide to Constraint Management*. Hoboken, NJ: John Wiley & Sons, Inc.

Buschmann, F., et al. (1996): *Pattern-Oriented Software Architecture, Volume 1—A System of Patterns*. Chichester, West Sussex (UK): John Wiley & Sons Ltd.

Buschmann, F., Henney, K. and Schmidt, D. C. (2007): *Pattern-Oriented Software Architecture, Volume 4—A Pattern Language for Distributed Computing*. Chichester, West Sussex (UK): John Wiley & Sons Ltd.

Cain, B. C., and Coplien, J. O. (1996a): "A Role-Based Empirical Process Modeling Environment." AT&T Bell Laboratories. *Proceedings of the Second International Conference on the Software Process*. IEEE Computer Press, pp. 125-133.

Cain, B. C., Coplien, J. O., and Harrison, N. B. (1996b): "Social patterns in productive software development organizations."

Camillus, J. C. (May, 2008): "Strategy as a Wicked Problem," *Harvard Business Review*, pp. 98-106.

Caspari, J. A., and Caspari, P. (2004): *Management Dynamics: Merging Constraints Accounting to Drive Improvement*. Hoboken, NJ: John Wiley & Sons, Inc.

Castells, M. (2010): *The Rise of the Network Society: The Information Age: Economy, Society and Culture, Volume I*. 2nd ed. Oxford (UK): Blackwell Publishers Ltd.

Charette, R. N. (1989): *Software Engineering Risk Analysis and Management*. McGraw-Hill Software Engineering Series. New York: McGraw-Hill.

Charlton, I. (2011): *Theory of Constraints in Software Development*. (Blog: http://www.codeforlife.org/2011/05/theory-of-constraints-in-software.html).

Cloutier, R. J. (2006): "Applicability of Patterns to Architecting Complex Systems." Doctoral Dissertation. Hoboken, NJ: Stevens Institute of Technology.

Coad, P. (1992): "Object-Oriented Patterns." *Communications of the ACM* 35(9): 152-159.

Coad, P., and Mayfield, M. (1993): Addendum to the Proceedings of OOPSLA '92. Workshop Report: Patterns. *OOPS Messenger* 4(2): 93-95.

Cockburn, A. (2001): *Agile Software Development*. Upper Saddle River, NJ: Addison-Wesley Professional.

Cockburn, A., et al. (2005): "The Declaration of Interdependence for Modern Management or DOI." (Online: http://alistair.cockburn.us/The+declaration+of+interdependence+for+modern+management+or+DOI)

Cohn, M. (2005): *Agile Estimating and Planning*. Upper Saddle River, NJ: Prentice-Hall.

Conklin, J. (2005): *Dialogue Mapping: Building Shared Understanding of Wicked Problems*. Chichester, West Sussex (UK): John Wiley & Sons Ltd.

Constantine, L. (1995): *Constantine on Peopleware*. Upper Saddle River NJ: Yourdon Press Computing Series. Prentice-Hall.

Coplien, J. O. (1994): "Borland Software Craftsmanship: A New Look at Process, Quality, and Productivity." *Proceedings of the 5th Annual Borland International Conference*, Orlando, Florida, 5 June 1994.

Coplien, J. O. (1994a): "A Generative Development-Process Pattern Language." AT&T Bell Laboratories. *Proceedings of PLoP/94.* Republished in Coplien, J. O., and D. Schmidt (eds.). (1995) *Pattern Languages of Program Design.* Volume 1 of the Software Patterns Series. Boston NJ: Addison-Wesley Professional.

Coplien, J. O. and Harrison, N. B. (Summer, 1996): "Patterns of Productive Software Organizations." Lucent Technologies Inc. *Bell Labs Technical Journal*: pp. 138-145

Coplien, J. O. (1996): "The Human Side of Patterns." AT&T Bell Laboratories/C++ Report 8(1): 81-85.

Coplien, J. O. (Jan., 1997): "Idioms and Patterns as Architectural Literature." *IEEE Software* 14(1): 36-42.

Coplien, J. O. and Harrison, N. B. (2004): *Organizational Patterns of Agile Software Development.* Englewood Cliff, NJ: Prentice Hall.

Coplien, J. O. (2004b): "The Culture of Patterns." *ComSIS Journal* 1(2): 1-26.

Coplien, J. O. (May 28, 2007): "Organizational Patterns: A Key for Agile Software Development." Presentation at the International Council on Systems Engineering (INCOSE), conference 2007.

Coplien, J. O. (2008): "Scrum Patterns Summary: The Patterns Without Which Scrum Is Unlikely to Work." (Online: https://sites.google.com/a/scrumorgpatterns.com/www/scrumpatternssummary).

Corbett, T. (1998): *Throughput Accounting.* Great Barrington, MA: North River Press.

Costagliola, G., et al. (2006): "Effort Estimation Modeling Techniques: A Case Study for Web Applications." *Proceedings of the Sixth International Conference on Web Engineering,* Palo Alto, CA.

Cox, J. and Schleier, J. (2010): *Theory of Constraints Handbook.* New York: McGraw-Hill Professional.

Csikszentmihali, M. and Nakamura, J. (2001): "Flow Theory and Research," in C. R. Snyder, Erik Wright, and Shane J. Lopez (eds.) *Handbook of Positive Psychology.* Oxford (UK): Oxford University Press.

Csikszentmihali, M. (2008): *Flow: The Psychology of Optimal Experience.* New York: Harper-Collins.

Daum, J. (Feb. 24, 2003): "Interview with Lennart Francke: Managing without budgets at Svenska Handelsbanken." *The New New Economy Analyst Report.* (Online: http://www.juergendaum.com/news/02_24_2003.htm).

Dearden, A., Finlay, J., Allgar, L. and McManus, B. (2002): *Using Pattern Languages in Participatory Design.* Sheffield University.

DeGrace, P. and Hulet Stahl, L. (1990): *Wicked Problems, Righteous Solutions: A Catalog of Modern Software Engineering Paradigms.* Englewood Cliffs, NJ: Prentice Hall.

Dekkers, C. and Gunter, I. (Nov., 2000): "Using 'Backfiring' to Accurately Size Software: More Wishful Thinking Than Science?" Cutter Consortium. *IT Metrics Strategies* V1 (11): 1-8.

DeMarco, T. and Lister, T. (1999): *Peopleware, Productive Projects, and Teams.* New York: Dorset House Publishing.

DeMarco, T. (2002): *Slack, Getting Past Burnout, Busywork, and the Myth of Total Efficiency.* New York: Broadway Books.

DeMarco, T. and Lister, T. (2003): *Waltzing with Bears: Managing Risk on Software Projects.* New York: Dorset House.

Deming, W. E. (1982): *Out of the Crisis.* Cambridge: MIT Press.

Deming, W. E. (1993): *The New Economics for Industry, Government, Education.* Center for Advanced Engineering. Cambridge, MA: MIT Press.

Denning, P. J., Gunderson, C. and Hayes-Roth, R. (Dec., 2008): "The Profession of IT: Evolutionary System Development." *CACM* 51(12): 29-31.

Denne, M. and Cleland-Huang, J. (2004a): *Software by Numbers: Low-Risk, High-Return Development.* Upper Saddle River, NJ: Prentice Hall.

Denne, M. and Cleland-Huang, J. (2004b): The Incremental Funding Method: Data-Driven Software Development. *IEEE Software* 21(3): 39-47.

Derby, E. and Larsen, D. (2006): *Agile Retrospectives: Making Good Teams Great.* Raleigh, NC: Pragmatic Bookshelf.

Dettmer, H. W. (2007): *The Logical Thinking Process: A Systems Approach to Complex Problem Solving.* Milwaukee, WI: ASQ Quality Press.

Diamond, M. A. and Allcorn, S. (2009): *Private Selves in Public Organizations: The Psychodynamics of Organizational Diagnosis and Change.* New York: Palgrave Macmillan.

DiBona, C. and Ockman, S., eds. (1999): *Open Sources: Voices from the Open Source Revolution.* Sebastopol CA: O'Reilly Media, Inc.

Dovey, K. (1990): "The Pattern Language and Its Enemies." *Design Studies* 11(1): 3-9.

Dubakov, M. (September 27, 2011): "The Future of Agile Software Development." (Online: http://www.targetprocess.com/rightthing.html).

Dubner, S. J. and Levitt, S. D. (May 7, 2006): "A Star Is Made." *The New York Times.* (Online: http://www.nytimes.com/2006/05/07/magazine/07wwln_freak.html?_r=0& pagewanted=print).

Eckstein, J. and Voelter, M. (2001): "Learning to Teach, Learning to Learn: Patterns and Pedagogy, a Winning Team." Net Object Days 2001 Conference, 10-13 September 2001, Erfurt (DE).

Erickson, T. (2000): "Pattern Languages as Languages." CHI 2000 Workshop at the ACM SIGCHI conference on Human Factors in Computing Systems, 2-3 April 2000, The Hague (NL).

Fallah, M., Ashtiani B., and Aryanezhad, Mir. B. (June, 2010): "Critical Chain Project Scheduling: Utilizing Uncertainty for Buffer Sizing." *International Journal of Research and Review in Applied Sciences,* 280-289.

Fedurko, J. (2012): "What Is the Current Reality Tree—Two Practical Approaches to Building a CRT. Second International TOCPA Conference, 19-20 May 2012, Moscow.

Fisher, L. M. (1992): "The Borland Barbarian's New Weapon." *The New York Times.* (Online: http://www.nytimes.com/1992/07/26/business/the-borland-barbarian-s-new-weapon. html?pagewanted=print&src=pm).

Fogel, K. (2005): *Producing Open Source Software: How to Run a Successful Free Software Project.* Sebastopol, CA: O'Reilly Media.

Futrell, R. T., Shafer, D. F., and Shafer, L. (2002): *Quality Software Project Management.* Upper Saddle River, NJ: Prentice Hall.

Gabriel, R. P. (1996): *Patterns of Software: Tales from the Software Community.* New York: Oxford University Press.

Galbraith, J., Downey D., and Kates A. (2001): *Designing Dynamic Organizations: A Hands-on Guide for Leaders at All Levels.* New York: AMACOM.

Gamma, E., et al. (1994): *Design Patterns: Elements of Reusable Object-Oriented Software.* Reading MA: Addison-Wesley Professional.

Geekie, A. (2006): "Buffer Sizing for the Critical Chain Project Management Method." Master's Thesis, Department of Engineering and Technology Management, Faculty of Engineering, University of Pretoria.

Gilb, T. (1988): *Principles of Software Engineering Management.* Reading, MA: Addison-Wesley.

Goldin, D., Scott, A. S., and Wegner, P., eds. (2006): *Interactive Computation: The New Paradigm.* Berlin (DE): Springer.

Goldman, R. and Gabriel, R. P. (2005): *Innovation Happens Elsewhere: Open Source as Business Strategy.* Amsterdam (NL): Morgan Kaufmann Publishers.

Goldratt, E. (1990a): *The Haystack Syndrome: Sifting Information Out of the Data Ocean.* New York: North River Press.

Goldratt, E. (1990b): *What Is This Thing Called Theory of Constraints.* New York: North River Press.

Goldratt, E. (1994): *It's Not Luck.* New York: North River Press.

Goldratt, E. (1992): *The Goal: A Process of Ongoing Improvement.* New York: North River Press.

Goldratt, E. (1997): *Critical Chain.* New York: North River Press.

Goold, M. and Campbell, A. (2002): *Designing Effective Organizations: How to Create Structured Networks.* San Francisco: Wiley.

Govindaraj, S. (2011): "Using Class of Service to Manage Product Risk." Silver Stripe Software. (Online: http://www.slideshare.net/Siddhi/using-class-of-service-to-manage-risk-in-new-product-development).

Graham, P. (June, 2006): "The Power of the Marginal." (Online: http://www.paulgraham.com/marginal.html).

Griffiths, M. (2007): "Developments in Agile Project Management." *PMI Global Conference Proceedings,* Atlanta, GA.

Hammarberg, M. and Sunden, J. (2013): *Kanban in Action.* Shelter Island NY: Manning Publications.

Hanmer R. and Kocan, K. (2004): "Documenting Architectures with Patterns." Wiley Periodicals. *Bell Labs Technical Journal* 9(1): 143-163.

Harrison, N. B. and Coplien, J. O. (1996): "Patterns of Productive Software Organizations." *Bell Labs Technical Journal.*1(1): 138-145.

Harrison, N., Foote, B., and Rohnert, H. eds. (1999): *Pattern Languages of Program Design 4.* Volume 4 of the Software Patterns Series. Reading, MA: Addison-Wesley.

Hay, D. C. (1995): *Data Model Patterns, Conventions of Thought.* New York: Dorset House Publishing.

Hein, A. M., Tziolas, A. C., and Osborne, R. (2011): "Project Icarus: Stakeholder Scenarios for an Interstellar Exploration Program." Technische Universität München, Institute of Astronautics, Journal of the British Interplanetary Society (JBIS) Vol 64: 224-233.

Hein, A. M. (2012): "Adopting Patterns for Space Mission and Space Systems Architecting." Fifth International Workshop on Systems and Concurrent Engineering for Space Applications.

Hibbs, C., Jewett, S., and Sullivan, M. (2009): *The Art of Lean Software Development.* Sebastopol CA: O'Reilly Media.

Hope, J. and Fraser, R. (Feb., 2003): "Who Needs Budgets?", *Harvard Business Review*, 108-115.

Howe, J. (2009): *Crowdsourcing: Why the Power of the Crowd Is Driving the Future of Business*. New York: Crown Business.

Humphrey, W. S. (1995): *A Discipline for Software Engineering*. SEI Series in Software Engineering. Reading, MA: Addison-Wesley.

Ilkonen, M., et al. (2011): "On the Impact of Kanban on Software Project Work: An Empirical Case Study Investigation." Department of Computer Science, University of Helsinki, Finland.

Ishikawa, K. (1990): *Introduction to Quality Control*. Tokyo: Productivity Press.

Jacob, D., Bergland, S., and Cox, J. (2009): *Velocity: Combining Lean, Six Sigma, and the Theory of Constraints to Achieve Breakthrough Performance—A Business Novel*. New York: Free Press.

Johnson, E. (pseudonym). (2004): "Function Points: Numerology for Software Developers," in Hacknot, in *Essays on Software Development*. (Online: http://www.scribd.com/doc/98019298/Hacknot-Essays-on-Software-Development).

Jones, C. (Nov., 1995): Backfiring: Converting Lines-of-Code to Function Points. *IEEE Software* 28(11): 87-88.

Jones, C. (1996): *Applied Software Measurement: Assuring Productivity and Quality*. New York: McGraw-Hill.

Jones, C. (2007): *Software Assessments, Benchmarks, and Best Practices*. Boston: Addison-Wesley Professional.

Jones, C. (2007): *Estimating Software Costs: Bringing Realism to Estimating*. New York: McGraw-Hill Osborne Media.

Jones, D., Stewart, S., and Power, L. (1999): *Patterns: Using Proven Experience to Develop Online Learning*. Interactive Multimedia, Queensland University. (Online: *http://www.ascilite.org.au/conferences/brisbane99/papers/jonesstewart.pdf*).

Katz, D. and Kahn, R. L. (1978): *The Social Psychology of Organizations*. New York: Wiley.

Keidel, R. W. (1995): *Seeing Organizational Patterns: A New Theory and Language of Organizational Design*. San Francisco: Berrett-Koehler.

Kerth, N. L. (2001): *Project Retrospectives: A Handbook for Team Reviews*. New York: Dorset House.

Kircher, M. and Jain P., (2004): *Pattern-Oriented Software Architecture, Volume 3 – Patterns for Resource Management*. Hoboken, NJ: John Wiley & Sons.

Kitchenham, B. (March, 1997): "Counterpoint: The Problem with Function Points." *IEEE Software*, 14(2): 29-31.

Kniberg, H. and Skarin, M. (2010): *Kanban and Scrum: Making the Most of Both*. C4Media, Inc.

Koenig, A. (1995): "Patterns and Antipatterns." *Journal of Object-Oriented Programming*, 8(1): 46-48.

Kotler, S. (2014): *The Rise of Superman: Decoding the Science of Ultimate Human Performance*. Boston MA: New Harvest.

Kroeber, A. L. (1909): "Classificatory Systems of Relationships." *Journal of the Royal Anthropological Institute of Great Britain and Ireland*, XXXIX, 77-84.

Kroeber, A. L. (July-December, 1938): "Basic and Secondary Patterns of Social Organiza-tion." *Journal of the Royal Anthropological Institute of Great Britain and Ireland*, LXVIII, 299-309.

Kroeber, A. L. (1944): *Configurations of Culture Growth*. Berkley CA: University of Cali-fornia Press.

Kroeber, A. L. (1963, 1948): *Anthropology: Culture, Patterns and Process*. New York: Har-court, Brace & World.

Kroeber, A. L. (1952): *The Nature of Culture*. Chicago: University of Chicago Press.

Ladas, C. (2008): *Scrumban: Essays on Kanban Systems for Lean Software Development*. Se-attle WA: Modus Cooperandi Press.

Laird L. M. and Brennan, M. C. (2006): *Software Measurement and Estimation: A Practical Approach*. Quantitative Software Engineering Series.-IEEE Computer Society. Hobo-ken, NJ: John Wiley & Sons.

Landy, F. J. and Conte, J. M. (2010): *Work in the 21st Century: An Introduction to Industrial and Organizational Psychology*. 3rd ed. Malden, MA: Wiley-Blackwell.

Lavazza, L. A., del Bianco, V., and Garavaglia, C. (2008): "Model-based Functional Size Measurement." *Proceedings of the Second ACM-IEEE International Symposium on Empir-ical Software Engineering and Measurement*, Kaiserslautern (DE), October 9-10, 2008.

Leach, L. P. (2004): *Critical Chain Project Management*. 2nd ed. Boston: Artech House.

Levesque, G., Bevo, V., and Tran Caho, D. (2008): "Estimating Software Size with UML Models." *Proceedings of the 2008 C3S2E Conference*, 81-87, Montreal, Quebec, Canada.

Lowe, J. D. (2006): *A Design Pattern Language for Space Stations and Long-Term Residence Human Spacecraft*. San Jose CA: American Institute of Aeronautics and Astronautics 2006-7317.

Maltese Culture Movement. (2014): The Great Siege of Malta. (Online: http://www.maltese culturemovement.com/?p=2).

Manns, M. L. and Rising, L. (2004): *Fearless Change: Patterns for Introducing New Ideas*. Boston MA: Addison-Wesley.

Martin, R. C., Riehle, D., and Buschmann, F., eds. (1998): *Pattern Languages of Program De-sign 3*. Volume 3 of the Software Patterns Series. Reading, MA: Addison-Wesley.

Martin, R. (October, 2012): "Why I Decided to Rethink Hiring Smart People." (blog). *Har-vard Business Review*. (Online: http://blogs.hbr.org/2012/10/why-i-decided-to-rethink -hiring-smart-people/).

Mediratta, B. (October 21, 2007): "The Google Way: Give Engineers Room." *The New York Times*. (Online: http://www.nytimes.com/2007/10/21/jobs/21pre.html?pagewanted =print).

Meszaros, G. and Doble, J. (1997): "A Pattern Language for Pattern Writing," in *Pattern Languages of Program Design 3*, Martin, R., et al. (eds.): Reading, MA: Addison-Wesley.

McCarthy, J. and McCarthy, M. (2002): *Software for Your Head, Core Protocols for Creating and Maintaining Shared Vision*. Boston: Addison-Wesley.

McCarthy, J. and McCarthy, M. (2012): "Elements of the Core." *The McCarthy Show*. (On-line: http://www.mccarthyshow.com/core-elements/).

McGrath, R. G. and MacMilan, I. C. (July, 1995): "Discovery-Driven Planning," *Harvard Business Review* 73(4): 44-54.

McGrath, R. G. (2010): *Business Models: A Discovery Driven Approach*. Long Range Plan-ning Series. (43): 247-261. Amsterdam (NL): Elsevier.

McGregor, J. T., *Annals of Software Engineering*: 259-286. Amsterdam (NL): Baltzer Science Publisher.

Mills, Harlan D. (1972): "Mathematical Foundations of Structured Programming." IBM Corporation Technical Report No. FSC 72-6012, IBM Federal Systems Division, Gaithersburg, MD.

Mintzberg, H. (1992): *Structure in Five: Designing Effective Organizations*. Englewood Cliffs NJ: Prentice Hall.

Moreno, J. L. (1931): *Group Method and Group Psychotherapy*. New York: Beacon House.

Moreno, J. L. (1934): *Who Shall Survive?: Foundations of Sociometry, Group Psychotherapy, and Sociodrama*. Washington, DC: Nervous and Mental Disease Publishing Company.

Moreno, J. L. (1951): *Sociometry, Experimental Method, and the Science of Society*. New York: Beacon House.

Moreno, J. L. (1977, 1953): *Who Shall Survive? Foundations of Sociometry, Group Psychotherapy and Sociodrama*. New York: Beacon House.

Morowski, P. (August, 2008): "The Borland Agile Journey: An Executive Perspective on Enterprise Transformation." *Agile Journal*. (Online: http://www.agileconnection.com/article/borland-agile-journey).

Mullins, L. J. (2006): *Essentials of Organisational Behaviour*. New York: Financial Times Prentice Hall.

Murray, A. R. (2000): "Discourse Structure of Software Explanation: Snapshot Theory, Cognitive Patterns, and Grounded Theory Methods." Doctoral Thesis, University of Ottawa.

Nerur, S. and Balijepally, V. (March, 2007): "Theoretical Reflections on Agile Development Methodologies: The Traditional Goal of Optimization and Control Is Making Way for Learning and Optimization. *CACM* 50(30): 79-83.

Nobel, J. and Johnson, R. E., eds. (2010): *Transactions on Pattern Languages of Programming I*. Berlin (DE): Springer.

Nobel, J., et al., eds. (2011): *Transactions on Pattern Languages of Programming II*. Berlin (DE): Springer.

Nolan, T. W. and Provost, L. P. (1990): "Understanding Variation." Quality Progress (May 1990): 70-78.

Noreen, E. W., Smith, D., and Mackey, J. T. *Theory of Constraints and Its Implications for Management Accounting*. Great Barrington, MA: North River Press.

Oestergren, K. and Stensaker, I. (2008): "Management Control Without Budgets: A Field Study of Beyond Budgeting in Practice." Published in European Accounting Review (2011) V10N1 149-181.

Ohno, T. (1988): *Toyota Production System: Beyond Large-Scale Production*. Cambridge MA: Productivity Press.

Patton, J. (2000): "Kanban Development Oversimplified." (Online: http://www.agileproductdesign.com/blog/2009/kanban_over_simplified.html).

Perzel, K. and Kane, D. (1999): "Usability Patterns for Applications on the World Wide Web." PLoP 1999 Conference. Monticello, IL.

Poppendieck, M. and Poppendieck, T. (2003): *Lean Software Development: An Agile Toolkit*. Boston: Addison-Wesley Professional.

Poppendieck, M. and Poppendieck, T. (2007): *Implementing Lean Software Development: From Concept to Cash*. Upper Saddle River, NJ: Addison-Wesley.

Reifer, D. (Nov./December, 2000): "Web Development: Estimating Quick-to-Market Software." *IEEE Software*, 17(6): 57-64.

Reinertsen, D. J. (2009): *The Principles of Product Development Flow: Second Generation Lean Product Development*. Redondo Beach, CA: Celeritas Publishing.

Reis, E. (2011): *The Lean Startup: How Today's Entrepreneurs Use Continuous Innovation to Create Radically Successful Businesses*. New York: Crown Business.

Ricketts, J. A. (2007): *Reaching the Goal: How Managers Improve a Service Business Using Goldratt's Theory of Constraints*. Upper Saddle River, NJ: IBM Press.

Rising, L. (April, 1999): "Patterns: A Way to Reuse Expertise." *IEEE Communications Magazine*. 37(4): 34-36.

Rising, L., ed. (1998): *The Patterns Handbook: Techniques, Strategies, and Applications*. New York: Cambridge University Press.

Rittle, H. W. and Webber, M. M. (1973): "Dilemmas in a General Theory of Planning." Elsevier Scientific Publishing Company. *Policy Sciences* (4): 155-169.

Roll-Hansen, N. (2009): "Why the Distinction Between Basic (Theoretical) and Applied (Practical) Research Is Important in the Politics of Science." Center for the Philosophy of Natural and Social Science, Contingency and Dissent in Science Project, Technical Report 04/09, London School of Economics.

Salingaros, N. A. (2000): "The Structure of Pattern Languages." Cambridge University Press. *Architectural Research Quarterly* 4, 149-161.

Salustri, F. A. (2005): "Using Pattern Languages in Design Engineering." *Proceedings of the International Conference on Engineering Design*, ICED'05, August 15-18, 2005, Melbourne.

Scheinkopf, L. (1990): *Thinking for a Change: Putting the TOC Thinking Processes to Use*. Boca Raton, FL: St. Lucie Press.

Schmidt, D., et al. (2007): *Pattern-Oriented Software Architecture, Volume 2—Patterns for Concurrent and Networked Objects*. New York: John Wiley & Sons.

Schragenheim, E. (1999): *Management Dilemmas: The Theory of Constraints Approach to Problem Identification and Solutions*. Boca Raton, FL: St. Lucie Press.

Schuler, D. (2008): *Liberating Voices: A Pattern Language for Communication Revolution*. Cambridge, MA: MIT Press.

Schwaber, K. (2001): *Agile Software Development with Scrum*. Upper Saddle River, NJ: Prentice Hall.

Schwaber, K. (2011): "Scrum Fails?" on *Ken Schwaber's Blog: Telling It Like It Is*. (Online: http://kenschwaber.wordpress.com/2011/04/07/scrum-fails/).

Senge, P. (2006): *The Fifth Discipline: The Art and Practice of the Learning Organization*. New York: Doubleday.

Shewart, W. A. and Deming, W. E. (2011, 1986, 1939): *Statistical Method from the Viewpoint of Quality Control*. Dover Books on Mathematics. Mineola, NY: Dover Publications. Reprint. Originally published: Washington D.C.: Graduate School of the Department of Agriculture, 1939.

Shustek, L. (2008): "Donald Knuth: A Life's Work Interrupted." *Communications of the ACM* 51(8): 31-35.

Smith, D. (2000): *The Measurement Nightmare: How the Theory of Constraints Can Resolve Conflicting Strategies, Policies, and Measures*. Boca Raton, FL: St. Lucie Press.

Smith, F. J. (2003): *Organizational Surveys: The Diagnosis and Betterment of Organizations Through Their Members*. Mahwah NJ: Lawrence Erlbaum Associates.

Smith, J. M. (2012): *Elemental Design Patterns.* Upper Saddle River, NJ: Addison-Wesley.

Song, J.-M. (2008): "Extending Performance-Based Design Methods by Applying Structural Engineering Design Patterns." Dissertation, University of California, Berkeley.

Spolsky J. (2007): "Evidence Based Scheduling" (Online: http://www.joelonsoftware.com/items/2007/10/26.html).

Stanford, N. (2007): *Guide to Organisations Design: Creating High-performing and Adaptable Enterprises.* London (UK): The Economist/Profile Books Ltd.

Stokes, D. E. (1997): *Pasteur's Quadrant: Basic Science and Technological Innovation.* Washington, D. C.: Brookings Institution Press.

Sullivan, T. T., et al. (2012): *The TOCICO Dictionary,* 2nd ed., New York, McGraw-Hill.

Surowiecki, J. (2005): *The Wisdom of Crowds.* New York: Doubleday.

Sutherland, J. (2001): "Inventing and Reinventing SCRUM in Five Companies." Patient-Keeper, Inc. (Online: *http://faculty.salisbury.edu/~xswang/research/papers/serelated/scrum/inventingscrum.pdf*)

Sutherland, J. (2003): *"Scrum: Another way to think about scaling a project."* (Online: http://www.scruminc.com/scrum-another-way-to-think-about/).

Sutherland, J. (2005): "Future of Scrum: Parallel Pipelining of Sprints in Complex Projects." Agile 2005, July 24-29, 2005, Mariott Denver City Center.

Sutherland, J., A. Viktorov and J. Blout (2006): "Adaptive Engineering of Large Software Projects with Distributed/Outsourced Teams." Sixth International Conference on Complex Systems (ICCS), June 25-30, 2006, Boston, MA.

Sutherland, J., et al. (2007): "Distributed Scrum: Agile Project Management with Outsourced Development Teams." Fortieth Annual Hawaii International Conference on System Sciences (HICSS'07).

Sutherland, J. (2007): "Origins of Scrum" (Online http://jeffsutherland.com/2007/07/origins-of-scrum.html).

Sutherland, J. (2008): "Pretty Good Scrum: Secret Sauce for Distributed Teams." Scrum Gathering, October 2008, Stockholm (SE).

Sutherland, J., et al. (2008): "Fully Distributed Scrum: The Secret Sauce for Hyperproductive Offshored Development Teams." Sixth International Conference on Complex Systems (ICCS), June 25-30, 2006, Boston, MA.

Sutherland, J. (2009a): "Shock Therapy Self Organization in Scrum." (Online: *http://jeffsutherland.com/SelfOrganizationShockTherapyBT2Apr2009.pdf*).

Sutherland, J. (2009b): "Agile Architecture: Red Pill or Blue Pill." Netherlands Scrum Meeting, June 2009, Hilversum (NL). (Online: *http://jeffsutherland.com/scrum/agile architectureredpillbluepillv3.pdf*).

Sutherland J. (2010a): "Agile Contracts: Money for Nothing and Your Change for Free." First presented at Agile Toronto, 2008. Updated 2010, and 2013. (Online: *http://jeffsutherland.com/Agile2008MoneyforNothing.pdf*).

Sutherland, J. (2010b): "The Roots of Scrum, How the Japanese Lean Experience Changed Global Software Development." ACCU Conference, April 12-17, 2010, Oxford (UK).

Sutherland, J. and Schwaber, K. (2011): "The Scrum Papers: Nut, Bolt, and Origins of an Agile Framework." Draft, January 29, 2011, Scrum, Inc.

Sutherland, J. and Schwaber, K. (2012): "The Scrum Papers: Nut, Bolt, and Origins of an Agile Framework." Version 1.1, April 2, 2012, Scrum, Inc. (Online: *http://jeffsutherland.com/ScrumPapers.pdf*).

Sutherland, J., Harrison, N., and Riddle, J. (2013): "Teams That Finish Early Accelerate Faster: A Pattern Language for High Performing Scrum Teams." Hawaii International Conference on System Sciences (HICSS), 6-9 January 2014, Hawaii."

Swieringa, J. and Wierdsma, A. (1992): *Becoming a Learning Organization: Beyond the Learning Curve.* Reading, MA: Addison-Wesley.

Takeuchi, I. and Nonaka, I. (1986): "The New New Product Development Game." *Harvard Business Review*, January-February 1986: 137-146.

Tendon, S. (2002): "Mobile Marketing Patterns." Research with Prof. Douglas Lamont, Northwestern University, Chicago. (Unpublished).

Tendon, S. (2010): "Tailoring Agility: Promiscuous Pair Story Authoring and Value Calculation." in Smite, D., et al. editors: (2010): *Agility Across Time and Space: Implementing Agile Methods in Global Software Projects.* Berlin (DE): Springer.

Thomas, J. C. (2005): "Patterns to Promote Individual and Collective Creativity." New York: IBM Research. (Online: http://www.slideshare.net/John_C_Thomas/hcii-2005-paper).

Tidwell, J. (1998): "Interaction Design Patterns." PloP'98 Conference on Pattern Languages of Programming, 11-14 August, 1998. Monticello, IL.

Tidwell, J. (2010): *Designing Interfaces, Patterns for Effective Interaction Design.* 2nd ed. Sebastopol, CA: O'Reilly.

Tuckman, B. W. (June, 1965): "Developmental Sequences in Small Groups." *Psychological Bulletin* 63(6), 384-399.

Van Welie, M. and Troettenberg, H. (2000): "Interaction Patterns in User Interfaces." PLoP 2000 Conference on Pattern Languages of Programming, August 13-16, 2000. Monticello, IL.

Vlissides, J. M., Coplien, J. O., and Kerth, N. L., eds. (1996): *Pattern Languages of Program Design 2.* Volume 2 of the Software Patterns Series. Reading, MA: Addison-Wesley.

Weber, J. (February 23, 1992): "Kahn the Barbarian." *Los Angeles Times.* (Online: http://articles.latimes.com/print/1992-02-23/business/fi-5118_1_borland-international-chairman-philippe-kahn).

Wegner, P. (1997): "Why Interaction Is More Powerful Than Algorithms." CACM 40(5): 80-91.

Wegner, P. and Goldin, D. (1999): "Interaction, Computability, and Church's Thesis." Draft, Brown University. (Online: *http://cs.brown.edu/~pw/papers/bcj1.pdf*)

Wegner, P. and Goldin, D. (July, 2006): "Principles of Problem Solving." CACM 49(7): 27-29.

Weinberg, G. M. (1998): *The Psychology of Computer Programming, Silver Anniversary Edition.* New York: Dorset House Publishing.

Wilkinson, N. M. (1998): *Using CRC Cards.* New York: SIGS Books.

Woeppel, M. (2005): *Projects in Less Time: A Synopsis of Critical Chain.* Plano TX: Pinnacle Strategies.

Womack, J. P. and Jones, D. T. (2003): *Lean Thinking: Banish Waste and Create Wealth in Your Corporation, Revised and Updated.* 2nd ed. New York: Free Press/Simon & Schuster, Inc.

Wong, J. M. (2008): *Extending Performance-based Design Methods by Applying Structural Engineering Design Patterns.* University of California, Berkeley.

Ziv, H. and Richardson, D. J. (1996): "The Uncertainty Principle in Software Engineering." ICSE '97 19th International Conference on Software Engineering, May 17-23, 1997. Boston.

INDEX